Grimm Realities

Grimm Realities

Essays on Identity and Justice in the Television Series

Edited by Daniel Farr *and* Melanie D. Holm

McFarland & Company, Inc., Publishers
Jefferson, North Carolina

This book has undergone peer review.

ISBN (print) 978-1-4766-8266-2
ISBN (ebook) 978-1-4766-4650-3

LIBRARY OF CONGRESS AND BRITISH LIBRARY
CATALOGUING DATA ARE AVAILABLE

Library of Congress Control Number 2022059602

© 2023 Daniel Farr and Melanie D. Holm. All rights reserved

No part of this book may be reproduced or transmitted in any form or by any means, electronic or mechanical, including photocopying or recording, or by any information storage and retrieval system, without permission in writing from the publisher.

Front cover: image of path in dark forest
(Shutterstock/ Mimadeo)

Printed in the United States of America

McFarland & Company, Inc., Publishers
Box 611, Jefferson, North Carolina 28640
www.mcfarlandpub.com

Acknowledgments

Dan and Melanie thank their husbands, family, and friends for their support and encouragement of this project. We also thank the contributors, reviewers, and editors for their patience and kindness in the completion of this project during difficult times.

Table of Contents

Acknowledgments	v
Introduction Melanie D. Holm	1

Part One: Identity and Identification

All About Eve: Juliette's Original Sin Melanie D. Holm	19
Liminal Spaces and Identity in *Grimm* Andrea Yingling	36
Opening the Trailer Door to Queer Possibilities Daniel Farr	52
Grimm: Fantasy, Procedurals, and Rape Culture Anastasia Rose Hyden	69

Part Two: Justice and Social Spaces

Grimm: Disillusioning Privilege and Developing a Practice of Listening Matthew Grinder	87
The Wesen Next Door: The Racial Dynamics of *Grimm* Melanie D. Holm	104
Folk Creatures: What Can Justice Do with These People? Fernando Gabriel Pagnoni Berns and Emiliano Aguilar	123
Witches, Stepmothers, and Princesses: Rethinking Gender and Money in *Grimm* Sarah Revilla-Sanchez	140

Pro-Animal Ideology and the Philosophy of Coexistence:
   An Ecocritical Perspective on *Grimm*
      Tatiana Konrad   155

Part Three: Media and Genre

Who's Still Afraid of the Wolf? Fairy-Tale Characters
   as a Medium of Cultural Change
      Sara Casoli   171

It Is Up to the "One" ... Or Is It? The Significance
   of Others in 21st-Century TV Hero Tales
      Kathleen McDonald   188

Grimm Afterlives: The Show Lives On in the Media
   Tie-In Novels
      Rachel Noorda   202

About the Contributors   217

Index   219

Introduction

Melanie D. Holm

> "There once was a man who lived a life
> so strange, it had to be true."[1]

So begins the iconic epigraph to season two of *Grimm*. Created by showrunners Jim Kouf and David Greenwalt and produced by Universal Television, the series *Grimm* aired on NBC from 2011 to 2016, spanning one-hundred and twenty-three episodes across its six seasons. It follows the adventures of Detective Nick Burkhardt in a fantasy variation of contemporary Portland, Oregon, as he discovers an underworld of monstrous creatures that he, as a Grimm, is bound to destroy. While the line is brief, it encapsulates what long-time fans know well and what those new to the series quickly discover: the world of *Grimm* is both strange and true. It is strange in its magical and fantastical departure from the everyday: it transports viewers to an enchanted world of mysterious beings and magic spells, where the unknown lies around every corner. However, the series is true insofar as it captures and reconstructs those aspects of contemporary life that anchor a modern understanding of being human. Sometimes these representations reflect what is best prized in humanity: ingenuity, cooperation, courage, strong friendships, parent-child devotion, and love that transcends race and ethnicity. Other times, *Grimm* draws attention to the less palatable truths of humanity, its grim realities, especially as realized in current, western ideas of living happily ever after.

Fully expressed, the epigram of season two depicts a dangerous world thinly disguised, alerting audiences to its occult malignancies with an eye toward their eradication.

> There once was a man who lived a life so strange, it had to be true. Only he could see what no one else can ... the darkness inside, the real monster within. And he's the one who must stop them. This is his calling. This is his duty. This is the life of a Grimm.

2 Introduction

Here the nature and promise of the Grimm are carved out alongside the fairy-tale context of the Brothers Grimm's *Kinder- und Hausmärchen* (*Children's and Household Tales*). However, whether or not the context is a fairy tale, heroes are only required when something has gone wrong (or, perhaps, has always been wrong) and someone is required to set things right. Here, the obscure source of those wrongs has been relegated to the shadows or dismissed as fantasy. Except for the hero, practically no one recognizes that everyday life is shared with the monsters and malevolence thought only to exist in fairy and folk tales.

The fictional world of *Grimm* (or Grimmverse) comprises a divided reality. On one side, there is an illusory world of 21st-century human beings taken for reality, where fairy and folk tales are mere stories or superstitions of the past. On the other side is a mirror image of that illusion that makes darkness visible—the real world in which fairy tales are the truth though hidden from human sight. Thus, *Grimm* crafts an ironic depiction of people telling fairy and folk tales dismissed as fiction to support a fairy-tale reality that denies the truth of a dark and hidden fairy-tale world rooted in discounted or neglected histories. In so doing, *Grimm* holds up a mirror that reflects the current world of its audiences in which the inner darkness of the present and hidden monstrosities of the past are brought to light, embodied in the fantastical forms of familiar fairy and folk tales.

What audiences see in this mirror is both themselves and not themselves. It is the world of the original audience, 21st-century Americans (though this audience has rapidly expanded with international demand),[2] however, it is that world mediated through metaphors and allegorical representations from fairy tales and folklore that communicate unutterable fears and suppressed desires. Fairy tales, argued Sigmund Freud, like dreams, express symbolically the anxieties, desires, and conflicts which waking consciousness cannot directly confront.[3] Similarly, folklorist Bengt Holbert explains, fairy tales may be read as expressions of the thoughts, feelings, and norms of traditional storytellers and their audiences revolving around a series of trans-historical conflicts, where "the 'marvelous' elements … may be read as expressions of emotional impressions associated with experiences in their own lives," though the nature of these conflicts is variable, particularly in terms of economic change.[4]

As a fantasy series based on fairy tales and folklore, *Grimm* offers an uncanny representation of 21st-century Portland that plays out complex social conflicts and all too human desires from a critical distance. In this way, it functions very much like a modern-day version of the 18th-century folk tales of western Europe, which would be incorporated into 19th-century fairy tales. In their traditional source communities:

[such] tales were escapist fantasies in so far as they offered temporary relief from the intrusive awareness of poverty and oppression that was the storyteller's usual lot. However, at the same time, they depicted a world in which wrongs were righted and the poor and powerless were justly recognized for their true worth. They thus kept alive a keen sense of justice and rightness; they depicted a true world, that is, a world in which the audience's norms were validated.[5]

The folk tale thus reflects the outlook of the storyteller and its intended audience in two directions: distraction or diversion from difficult conditions and a visualization of the potential for altering these conditions or one's place within them. This is particularly the case in terms of economics, status, and class. The *Kinder und Hausmärchen* of the Brothers Grimm features protagonists at either extreme of the wealth spectrum, from princesses with golden balls to hungry children lost in the woods, reflecting the divisive social inequities of their moment.[6] It is a world of peasants and nobility, starvation and splendor.

As Jack Zipes has argued, folk tales are the oral tales of the poor and feature radical visions of possibility. They offer escapes with marvelous corrective solutions of status ascension from the peasantry to the nobility or the symbolic destruction of a wealth-hoarding nobility.[7] He argues that their fantastic utopianism recedes as folk tales become fairy tales for an emergent 19th-century bourgeoisie. The projective and critical faculty of the folk is thereby translated into a world of explicit fantasy that serves (primarily juvenile) didactic ends. No longer tales of what could be or what is, they are stories of discipline and consequence for the young, centered on fears of non-conformity or moral decay. Nevertheless, as a palimpsest, the repressed, early folk-tale desire to rewrite reality still lies within them, although the world to be rewritten has irrevocably changed.

Taken as a modern fairy tale reflective of its historical place and moment, *Grimm* enchants 21st-century Portland for a middle-class American viewership. However, it is distinct from its fairy- and folk-tale sources in two dramatic ways. First, unlike 19th-century fairy tales and the *Kinder* population of the *Kinder- und Hausmärchen*, *Grimm* focuses on adults. Second, these are adults of the middle class who lead more or less comfortable lives: police detectives, artisans, veterinarians, and small business owners. They are homeowners who shop at farmers markets and buy the latest Apple products. Thus, the features of life from which the audience seeks to escape, the wrongs they need righted, and their normative beliefs (which are not necessarily those of the culture at large) are necessarily different. So, too, are the means of escapism and vindication.[8]

The medium and mediation of *Grimm*'s modern fairy tales are as different from the orality and literacies of their antecedents as are the audiences. The story is technologically mediated rather than personal. No one is present, telling a gathered audience of the same physical community a story, nor is the experience limited to a lone reader with his or her print book. Instead, audiences engage in an intermedial experience, looking at a television, or increasingly, their laptops and tablets with all of video's richness of sound and image. Episodes of the series are often enjoyed in isolation or by the family unit alone. The place of story reception is not a common-dwelling, but often that most intimate, vulnerable, and relaxed of locations: the home.[9] However, the experience is not shared physically in one gathering; it is shared across a wide viewership who reach out to one another via social media to share feelings, interpretations, questions, theories, and personal connections.[10] As the "About" section of one venue, *Bring Back* Grimm on Facebook, describes, "*Grimm* fans, crew, and cast are one big family."[11]

The crises that animate individual episodes of *Grimm* also reflect the differences in audience, reception, and representation. The darknesses, for example, do not include peasant poverty, a very present concern for 18th- and 19th-century audiences of folk tales. Instead, they combine explicit, everyday challenges of modernity with those existing at the edge of the (predominately white) American middle-class. On the one hand, the show depicts highly visible and socially sanctioned conflicts of love, family, and identity through its main characters. On the other, it looks at those uncomfortable, taboo issues that are less common and less visible, lurking in the shadows of middle-class American life. *Grimm* illuminates darknesses that are seen but ignored as well as those that many choose not to see because they do not openly intrude into their normative world such as drug addiction, sexual and domestic violence, child-homelessness, criminalized mental illness, and the legacies of sexism, racism, and historical privilege. *Grimm* invites its audience to enjoy losing themselves in the alluring enchantments of its fairy tale reality with its marvelous creatures, gorgeous cast, and vivid color saturation. At the same time, it shows them their own reality from a different and often challenging angle that brings contemporary conflict to the surface. It is a central thesis of this collection that *Grimm*, while a product of the culture industry, nevertheless reverses the trajectories of modern fairy tales to revive its original spirit of possibility and cultural critique.

However, if *Grimm* uses fairy tales to consider contemporary culture critically, it also uses the landscape of our modern world to re-examine traditional fairy tales and draw out their continuing influence upon our ability to imagine how our lives could or should look. From their origins in orality to their modern literary incarnations, fairy tales have "enunciated, articulated, and communicated feelings in efficient metaphorical terms that enabled listeners and readers to envision possible solutions to their problems so that they could survive and adapt to their environments."[12] *Grimm* thereby brings together two worlds: the modern world we experience and the fairy-tale versions we create, both tacitly and explicitly. The essays in this collection explore and illuminate the relationships between the two so that viewers may further engage with *Grimm*'s strange and true world and its often amusing, frequently touching, sometimes disturbing, and always provocative dialogue with the world around us.

"Grim" Fairy Tales

As the name suggests, *Grimm* constructs its world through a well-known fairy-tale canon, primarily those popularized by the Brothers Grimm, emplaced in the familiarity of current western culture, specifically of the 2010s. For those brought up in the western cultural tradition, hearing "There once was a man" echoes the "once upon a time" of innumerable fairy-tale beginnings. As with those words, "we immediately and naturally think that we are about to hear a fairy tale. We are disposed to listening and reading in a particular way and register metaphors in our brain so that they make sense and so we can replicate them in our own way and in our own time."[13] *Grimm*'s titular allusion to the Brothers Grimm articulates a direct connection between the series, the tales of *Kinder- und Hausmärchen,* and, more broadly, the fairy-tale genre. However, unlike the ABC network's evocative and inviting, *Once Upon a Time,* a fairy-tale-themed series that premiered four days before *Grimm,* there is "a symbolic appeal of the word 'Grimm' that harbors notions of rage, terror, forbidding gloom, and recognized authority."[14] The mere mention of Grimms' fairy tales summons images of dark forests, dangerous animals, wicked stepmothers, and grisly, retaliatory violence. Grimms' fairy tales are indeed grim and so too, as the series demonstrates, is the work of being a Grimm and the world Grimms inhabit.

When Nick's Aunt Marie insists from the outset, "This is no fairy tale," "fairy tale" signals less the folklore recorded by the Grimm brothers or the fairy tales of Perrault than the modern, somewhat derogatory usage associated with "Disneylore."[15] From the close of the 19th-century forward, fairy tales experienced a softening as they became embedded in the canon of children's literature. In this form, they have become part of our cultural vocabulary: sanitary versions of the originals adapted to reflect early 20th-century conservative values in which virtue is rewarded with domestic fulfillment.[16] Emphasis is more often than not placed on what the princess wears, while bodily, retributive violence is excised from the tale.

Evil stepmothers accidentally slip off cliffs rather than dance to death in blazing hot shoes, while mean stepsisters are shamed for their foot sizes instead of publicly pecked blind.[17]

However, bloodshed, beheadings, and disembowelment are all relatively common events in *Grimm*, reflecting a different kind of relationship to their source material than its more anodyne peers. With the visual spectacle of violence, *Grimm* distances itself from children's tales and other, more broadly pitched fairy-tale adaptations that have tended to focus on cultural remediation of one kind or another. Eschewing the sort of gleeful violence common in *Grimm*, many contemporary adaptations work to amend or rebuke portions of those earlier tales now considered offensive through the lenses of race, gender, and colonialism, with many churning out increasingly didactic and, at times, facile representations of modern values. The grim violence of *Grimm*, however, indicates a more unsettling and unsettled adaptation is at hand.

Grimm employs fairy-tale structures and motifs to disrupt and trouble the fairy tales of modern American life rather than correct stories of the past to imitate an ideal present. In most respects, the protagonist, Nick Burkhardt, begins the series having already achieved or just on the edge of attaining the happily-ever-after of the modern American cultural fairy tale: he has a fulfilling job that gains him recognition and respect; he has strong friendships with his male colleagues; he is a homeowner; and, perhaps most importantly, he has a successful romantic relationship. Audiences meet Nick in the "Pilot" when he is getting ready to propose to his long-term girlfriend Juliette Silverton and thereby achieve an abiding fairy-tale ending. He is already living his happy-ever-after in terms of the heteronormative American dream, short of two children and a dog.

His first Wesen encounter with Hulda, a *Hässlich* or monstrous Grim Reaper, interrupts and ultimately derails his attainment of the domestic American dream, signaling disruption in one of the most deeply inscribed social narratives of the present. It also shares narrative space with another disruption of the happily-ever-after fantasy—the revelation that Nick's Aunt (his only known living relative at the time) is dying of terminal cancer, and her ever-after will soon come to an end. Thus, his idyllic world begins to unravel quickly. When the Grimms' "stories" become true, when Nick becomes a Grimm, the terms of the life he had led and intended to lead are unmasked in all of their fallacious, illusory simplicity. His life is a fairy tale no longer. At least it is not *that* fairy tale. Instead, traditional fairy tales rupture his reality, tearing out spaces where he can and must reconceive who he is outside of the "American dream" framework. Bruno Bettleheim observed that "Fairy tales, unlike any other form of literature, direct the child to discover his identity and calling, and they also suggest what experiences are needed to develop his character further."[18] Nick, of course, is no longer a child; however, through encounters with fairy tales (ontological rather than literary), he finds his calling, develops his character, and realizes his "true" identity. He, in turn, abandons the illusory conceits of a typically successful life as though they were nothing more than a childhood fairy tale he had outgrown.

Grimm's demystification of contemporary American and Western ideals as fairy tales extend the threads of what Cristina Bacchilega terms the "fairy-tale web" from past fairy tales to the tacit fairy tales of contemporary culture. Bacchilega describes the fairy-tale web as a metaphorical approach that considers fairy tales within a network of intertextual and historical connections and adaptations. The web is thus both the world wide web of interconnections and possibilities and the spider web which reproduces itself radially as it links new threads with the old. She proposes this approach

> for two reasons: first "to further the conduction of a history and remapping of the genres that are not insulated from the power structures and struggles of capitalism, colonialism, coloniality, and disciplinarity" and second, "to envision current fairy-tale cultural practices in an intertextual dialogue with one another that is informed not only by the interests of the entertainment or culture industry and the dynamics of globalization in a 'postfeminist' climate but also by more multivocal and unpredictable uses of the genre."[19]

Grimm exists as one of these unpredictable uses of the fairy-tale genre and self-consciously traces through the network of colonialism, violence, race, and privilege surrounding western fairy tales such as those of the Brothers Grimm or Charles Perrault. At the same time, it demonstrates how the tacit forms of cultural belonging in the Western present are linked in that same network. In this way, *Grimm* is a part of a fairy-tale web whose threads reveal interconnected webs of the fairy tales of the past and their legacies alongside sticky and dangerous cultural fairy tales of the past and present.

While *Grimm* dismantles tacit narratives of contemporary American culture, it nevertheless retains fairy-tale structures and characters whose familiarity provides aesthetic reassurance and the pleasures of recognition. Making connections between characters in the series to those of traditional folk- and fairy-tale plots and identifying the show's opening quotations gives satisfaction to those "knowing" audiences who immediately recognize the broader folk- or fairy-tale tradition engaged or the specific text cited in the epigram of each episode.[20] Alongside these pleasures, audiences also partake in the novelty of the adaptation's creativity of familiar fairy-tale tropes. Beyond characters and content, *Grimm* reproduces a familiar dominant "male" fairy-tale trajectory throughout its series arc: a man is given a magical gift that he did not seek and must use to overcome evil and protect the innocent from the hidden terrors of the unknown.[21] The ability to see the monstrous and the magical, enhanced perceptual skills, and superior strength and speed are the unique gifts that designate Nick as the male fairy-tale hero. Yet, at the same time, the elasticity of adaptation relocates his heroics from the realm of the fantasy kingdom to the unlikely destination of the Portland Police Department. In so doing, the adaptive novelty doubles as the series simultaneously adapts another well-known genre—the police procedural.

Grimm's combination of fantastic elements with the familiar police procedural drama produces a very different show than the preceding series of this type, particularly the dominant *Law & Order* franchise. The drama of such programs hinges on the possibility that the story will end badly—someone will get shot, someone will be wrongly convicted, the villain will escape, justice will not be served. *Grimm* is notably not a drama in this respect. With every episode, however violent and whatever the risks Nick and his friends take, audiences are secure in the fairy-tale promise that they will survive and triumph. There are, of course, ambiguities embedded in the narrative—what is right? who is good?—but there is never any doubt that a tentative, local happy ending lies ahead. Nevertheless, those ambiguities do serve an essential function for the series. They repeatedly raise the questions, what does a happy ending look like and who is entitled to it when "the darkness inside" and "the real monster within" have come out into the light?

The Grimm *World*

When Marie Kessler says that "the stories are real," she gestures toward the stories of the Brothers Grimm, treating them more as cryptozoology than philological data or didactic exemplars. The stories are real, but not as a mere history of something that once happened. As David Greenwalt joked in one interview, "the original Brothers Grimm were, in fact, criminal profilers."[22] Unlike the historical episodes recounted in the Grimm casebooks (or Grimmlore), the Grimms' fairy tales indicate a strange and true fairy-tale past and a current, mystical population hidden in plain sight. The population includes royal families, powerful and mysterious witches and warlocks (*Hexenbiests* and *Zauberbiests*), and shape-shifting creatures of ambiguous human-animal status known as Wesen that live secretly among regular humans. They pass as ordinary people, possibly as co-workers, friends, even spouses.

Wesen are the primary source of the fantastical and marvelous in the series. Their different species draw from anthropomorphized and non-anthropomorphized animal characters of fairy and folk tales—from a family of the three bear-like creatures wary of goldilocks-style home invasions to something big, bad, and wolfish stalking a young woman in red. The word "Wesen" indicates in its Germanic form, *"ein Wesen,"* a "being" or "creature," which can be used alternately to denote a living thing such as a human "being" or something quite unusual, like a supernatural being. It can be both mundane and exotic. The terminology is similar in the Scandinavian languages, with the Swedish *"Vaesen"* indicating a spectrum of acquaintanceship from the familiar to esoteric that inclines toward the occult and fantastical. As Johan Egerkrans summarizes, "These beings—whether we call them fae, nature spirits, the invisible folk, the little people, or vaesen as they are known in Scandinavia—live in our world but also in a separate reality of their own."[23]

> All over the world and throughout the ages, people have been convinced that we are not alone on this earth. That other creatures exist in our world, alongside humans and animals, and that even though they may resemble us, they are entirely different beings, neither human nor divine but representing something else.... Normally we can't see them unless they choose to reveal themselves, but they make their presence known all the time ..., personif[ying] nature in all its capriciousness, and some beings are literally at one with nature. In days gone by, they were an accepted part of life and a constant reminder to respect mother nature.[24]

These descriptions extend, at least in part, to the Wesen of *Grimm*. Wesen live both in the human world and within their own secretive, complex social ecosystem. The Grimm's special powers notwithstanding, they only appear to most humans when they want to be seen. Similarly, their behaviors and appearance tend to reflect the animal or natural world from which human beings have traditionally dissociated themselves.

Nevertheless, *Grimm*'s Wesen also trouble this very separation, demonstrating in a symbolic form how intimately and vitally linked humanity or "human nature" is with the same thing it declares that it is not. Fairy tales have traditionally "spoke[n] to the conflicts and predicaments that arose out of attempt by social orders to curb and 'civilize' our instinctual drives."[25] Wesen demonstrate drives, desires, and primal instincts so often repressed and euphemized in human civility that they would seem not to exist. They animate these drives, demonstrating how precariously close to the surface they lurk, as well as the intense pressure to release them. In *Grimm*'s fairy-tale space, Wesen let the people of Portland and audiences at home watch and interact with what, in some respects, we already are but cannot, will not, or have been conditioned not to see.

Building on these revelations, *Grimm* portrays the struggle between a being's appearance and its true nature, as well as the inherent in being human. It does so by creating complex characters whose interrelationships force reconsiderations of values, practices, and ideas that have previously defined them. Their personalities expand and grow with each new revelation and challenge—secular or supernatural—resisting any easy reduction to static symbolism. Some characters may be "good" but do bad things; others may be generally inclined to evil but have moments when they surprise us with a heroic gesture. Characters have layers that are successively uncovered in each new episode, like a matryoshka, revealing something uncanny within. Just as the disintegration of Nick's America-dream fairy tale leads him to discover the layered history of his reality, so too do he and audiences increasingly discover more about the beings who live within it. As a result, there is no moral that the fairy-tale world of *Grimm* enforces or ideology it perpetuates. Instead, it is a series that continues to push beneath the surface to uncover the new and the strange.

Grimm *Realities*

Through its ambiguities and uncertainties, *Grimm* raises questions about the current historical moment and interrogates how both magical and modern fairy tales affect the ability to conceptualize the self and the world. This volume presents a collection of essays that consider these questions and their interrelationships, exploring how *Grimm*'s unique interpenetration of reality and fantasy, fairy tales and the real world enables audiences to think critically about their world while enjoying their immersion in the fantastical life of a Grimm. The essays are arranged in three thematic sections. The first section, "Identity and Identification," examines how *Grimm* asks questions about constructing identities, both personal and social. The inaugural essay, "All About Eve: Juliette's Original Sin," asks readers to consider what the series looks like from Juliette's point of view, proposing that if seen as her story instead of Nick's, *Grimm* offers a powerful critique of male-heroic culture, and opens up provocative possibilities for a heroine narrative. "Liminal Spaces and Identity in *Grimm*" examines the boundaries of social categories and existential spaces, exploring the dissonance of characters who are unable to fit into the structures conceived for social existence. "Opening the Trailer Door to Queer Possibilities" investigates the queerness of characters in *Grimm* and the destabilization of traditional social identities. "*Grimm*: Fantasy, Procedurals, and Rape Culture" explores how *Grimm* identifies and challenges socially embedded mythologies of sexual violence in contemporary life, disenchanting enduring mythologies of rape culture through complex adaptations and liberalizations of fairy-tale tropes.

In the second section, "Justice and Social Spaces," essays center on questions of society's legitimate use of power in current state systems and in histories that mark the present. "*Grimm:* Disillusioning Privilege and Developing a Practice of Listening" argues that *Grimm* models a practice by which dominant cultures can initiate and sustain meaningful dialogues with marginalized and minority cultures. "The Wesen Next Door: The Racial Dynamics of *Grimm*" examines the many angles through which *Grimm* probes race relations and a necessary, contemporary reckoning with imperial and racist histories. "Folk Creatures: What Can Justice Do with These People?" inquires into *Grimm*'s portrayal of the modern American justice system as anything but blind by using the ambiguous status of Wesen to unmask the biases and limitations of criminal guilt. "Witches, Stepmothers, and Princesses: Rethinking Gender and Money in *Grimm*" examines gender scapegoating, illustrating how female villains are always doubly guilty—guilty of acting like villains and guilty of not acting like gender-normative women. Finally, "Pro-Animal Ideology and the Philosophy of Coexistence: An Ecocritical Perspective on *Grimm*" asks readers to consider *Grimm*'s Wesen as more animal than human, demonstrating how the Wesen narrative troubles traditional distinctions between human and animal.

The third and final section, "Media and Genre," focuses on *Grimm* as a cultural artifact that raises questions about and experiments with genre boundaries and adaptive processes. "Who's Still Afraid of the Wolf? Fairy-Tale Characters as a Medium of Cultural Change" argues that *Grimm* exemplifies a critical parodic methodology by which fairy tales can be redeployed to alter the value and meaning of the fairy tale in our contemporary social vocabulary. "It Is Up to the 'One' … Or Is It? The Significance of Others in 21st-Century TV Hero Tales," distinguishes *Grimm* from other hero-driven television franchises and traditions, spotlighting its metafictional critique of the individual hero and identifying a group-heroic dynamic or "camaraderie heroism" in the series. The final essay, "*Grimm* Afterlives: The Show Lives On in the Media Tie-In Novels," addresses questions of what is, is not, and could be considered part of *Grimm* or a Grimm canon by interrogating the role of *Grimm* novels that complement and postdate the series' official television conclusion.

While the creation and circulation of folk and fairy tales is a universal and transhistorical phenomenon, the folk are local and specific.[26] Today's stories and story adaptations reflect the texture and trials of their location and moment, present-day people with present-day problems. However, they nevertheless feature ancestral ties that bind them with folk and fairy tales of the past. Arthur W. Frank has written that stories "work to *emplot* lives: they offer a plot that makes some particular future not only plausible but also compelling." But stories are not static: "We humans spend our lives ... adapting stories we were once told" and "not least among human freedoms is the ability to tell the story differently and to begin living according to that different story."[27] The stories we inherit or which surround us are therefore not destiny. Building upon Frank's observation, Bacchilega has considered that

> The dynamics of emplotment seem ... particularly relevant to reflecting on fairy tales in social practice because this genre is so basically tied up in plot, has been hegemonically utilized to emplot or frame our lives within a heteronormative capitalist economy, and yet has such a history of and potential for adaptability as well as subversion because it operates in the optative mode.[28]

It is the nature of folk and fairy tales to endure as well as adapt. *Grimm* is such an adaptation. However, *Grimm* is also a means and invitation to adapt, reflect upon, expand, and subvert the stories surrounding its audiences in the real world. This collection intends to extend that invitation: to spark further conversation and creative engagement with the series so that, like the work of its fairy-tale forefathers the Brothers Grimm, *Grimm* too will flourish and live on.

A Note on the Text

This collection has made deliberate choices of presentation regarding terms to reflect the values and critical spirit of its essays. While Wesen is conventionally written in lower case, in the context of the collection, "Wesen" is capitalized as a proper noun, drawing attention to its affinity to the status of a racial or ethnic group in the series. Capitalization emphasizes their position. Doing so is significant mainly because of the questions posed in the series regarding the value of Wesen lives compared to humans and their historical persecution as Other. These features structurally and metaphorically resonate with (though do not reproduce or approximate) the experiences of racial and ethnic minorities resulting from colonialism, imperialism, and enslavement. The choice has also been made to represent types of Wesen in italics. Throughout the series, words for Wesen types have been linked with non–Anglophone sources. These names are primarily, at least initially, Germanic. However, as the series progresses, *Grimm* becomes more inclusive of other cultures and their languages and creates Wesen whose names bear a resemblance to the language of their origin-culture. Therefore, Wesen types are italicized like foreign language words to respect and retain their mark of cultural difference without appropriation.

Just as "Wesen" is capitalized, so too are Wesen types; however, this choice responds to the Germanic tradition, from which most types arise, of capitalizing nouns. Capitalization is a serious and sensitive issue. By being transparent in the logic applied, the hope is to clarify that the choices result from a specific and intentional framework. There will undoubtedly be disagreement, but it is taken as given that any other scholarly approaches will be employed with similar good faith.

References to episodes are given by season number, episode number, and name:

S1, E5: "Danse Macabre."

The names of the main cast and their roles are presented below in the order of cumulative episode appearances to avoid redundancy across essays. However, individual authors present their own descriptions about the nature of Grimm, Wesen, and other common features of the series to allow for a multiplicity of interpretations and intellectual contributions. For references to specific minor characters, the name of the performer is provided in endnotes of the individual essays.

Central Cast

Actor	*Character*
David Giuntoli	Nick Burkhardt
Russell Hornsby	Hank Griffith
Silas Weir Mitchell	Monroe
Sasha Roiz	Captain Sean Renard
Reggie Lee	Sergeant Drew Wu
Elizabeth Tulloch	Juliette Silverton/ Eve
Bree Turner	Rosalee Calvert
Claire Coffee	Adalind Shade
Jacqueline Toboni	"Trubel" (Teresa) Rubel
Mary Elizabeth Mastrantonio	Kelly Burkhardt
Kate Burton	(Aunt) Marie Kessler

14 Introduction

Notes

1. The narration was introduced in the episode "Bad Teeth" (S2, E1), which first aired on August 13, 2012, on NBC. It was repeated for the following two episodes, "The Kiss" (S2, E2) and "Bad Moon Rising" (S2, E3), before being altogether dropped from the opening credits.

2. *Grimm* is available in seventeen international broadcasts: Argentina, Australia, Belgium, Canada, Cuba, Finland, France, Germany, Hungary, Malaysia, Mexico, New Zealand, the Philippines, Poland, Spain, Sweden, and the United Kingdom. For an example of international demand, there is the case of France. According to Parrot Analytics, for June 2021, Grimm was in the 95.5th percentile for television drama series in France—meaning that it had a higher viewer demand than 95.5% of drama series and 2.4 times the demand for any television series in that month, putting it in the top 8.6% of shows. See Parrot Analytics.

3. Freud 102–8.

4. Holbek 43.

5. Holbek 42.

6. See "The Frog King or Iron Henry" ("*Der Froschkönig or der eserne Heinrich*") and "Hansel and Gretel" ("*Hänsel und Gretel*") in Zipes *Brothers Grimm* 1–13; 43–9.

7. For example, Jack Zipes reads the witch in "Hansel and Gretel" as symbolic of feudal nobility that has failed in its obligation to care for the peasantry by selfishly amassing resources (like food) and working peasants to death and leaving them to starve. See Zipes *Breaking the Magic Spell* 127–29.

8. The roles of media, intermediality, and intertextuality in fairy-tale adaptations and transmission have been addressed by various impressive scholarly projects in the last two decades. Among these are the following: Walter Rankin, *Grimm Pictures: Fairy Tale Archetypes in Eight Horror and Suspense Films*. McFarland, 2007; Pauline Greenhill and Sidney Eve Matrix, *Fairy Tale Films: Visions of Ambiguity*. Utah State University Press, 2010; Jack Zipes' *The Enchanted Screen*. Routledge, 2011; Cristina Bacchilega, *Fairy Tales Transformed? Twenty-First-Century Adaptations and the Politics of Wonder*. Wayne State University Press, 2013; Kristian Moen, *Film and Fairytales*. Bloomsbury, 2013; Pauline Greenhill and Jill Terry Rudy, editors, *Channeling Wonder*. Wayne State University Press, 2014; Sue Short, *Fairy Tales and Film Old Tales with a New Spin*. Palgrave Macmillan, 2015; Pauline Greenhill and Jill Terry Rudy, editors, *Transcultural and Intermedial Fairy Tales and Television*. Special issue of *Marvels and Tales*, vol. 21, no. 1, 2017; Pauline Greenhill and Jill Terry Rudy, editors, *The Routledge Companion to Media and Fairy-Tale Cultures*. Routledge, 2018; Pauline Greenhill and Jill Terry Rudy, *Fairy-Tale TV*. Routledge, 2021.

9. Pauline Greenhill and Jill Terry Rudy have signaled the television adaptation of fairy tales as medially distinct from fairy-tale film adaptations, arguing that "Film has a formal and professional mode of transmission and reception, and TV a more informal and local one" (*Channeling Wonder* 4).

10. Since its last episode aired on NBC on March 31, 2017, *Grimm* has maintained a loyal, vocal, and large fanbase. For example, the "Grimm Wiki" (grimm.fandom.com), a fan-built *Grimm* encyclopedia with over 1750 pages, maintains an active series of discussion threads with a high degree of internet traffic (over 400,000 visits per month in 2021 (simiarweb.com). Similarly, the subreddit "Grimm: Discussion of the NBC Series," continues to expand with over 10,600 members, while the Facebook group "Bring Back Grimm" (created September 13, 2016), boasts over 27,000 members and features active daily engagement.

11. "About."

12. Zipes, *Why Fairy Tales Stick* xii.

13. Zipes, *Why Fairy Tales Stick* xi.

14. Zipes. *Grimm Legacies* 155.

15. Poniewozik 394.

16. Hearne and Karasek 396.

17. See for example, the distinctions between Disney's animated film *Snow White and*

the Seven Dwarves and the Grimm's "Little Snow White" (*Schneewittchen* [*Scheeweßen*]) and Disney's animated film *Cinderella* and the Grimm's "Cinderella" (*Aschenputtel*). See Zipes, *Brothers Grimm* 170–77, 69–76. In the latter case, Disney Studios chooses the softer *Cendrillon, ou la petite pantoufle de verre* as its source text, despite the likely historical priority of *Aschenputtel* and its variants, the Brothers Grimm also soften their *Achenputtel* in the 1857 edition of the *Kinder und Hausmärchen* to resemble Perrault's fairy tale more closely, signaling the kind of deradicalization of the folk discussed above.
    18. Bettleheim 24.
    19. Bacchilega 18.
    20. Linda Hutcheon has discussed how an adaptation allows for different pleasures of engagement for those audiences she calls "knowing," those who know and recognize the adaptation source, and the "unknowing," those who are unaware of a source and for whom the adaptation exists as an original and independent work. In the case of *Grimm*, because of the saturation of fairy tales and the name "Grimm" in the western cultural imagination, most viewers of the first episodes are necessarily "knowing." The situation becomes more complex as the series expands into various cultural traditions and historical figures. It establishes a context in which while they may not be "knowing," the experienced viewer of *Grimm* knows that they should or could know, taking delight in discovering unfamiliar lore through the familiarity of the series. See Hutcheon 2–15, 113–28.
    21. The term "male" draws on Holbek's distinction between the male fairy tale trajectory, in which the protagonist goes out into the world for adventure, and the "female," in which the female protagonist remains centered in the home. See Holbek 48–9.
    22. Sherrow.
    23. Egerkrans 9.
    24. Egerkrans 8.
    25. Zipes, *Why Fairy Tales Stick* xii.
    26. Hearne and Karasek 389.
    27. Frank 10.
    28. Bacchilega 6.

WORKS CITED

"About." *Bring Back Grimm*, facebook.com/groups/BringBackGrimm/about, Accessed 17 July 2021.
Bacchilega, Cristina. *Fairy Tales Transformed? Twenty-First-Century Adaptations and the Politics of Wonder*. Wayne State UP, 2013.
Bettelheim, Bruno. *The Uses of Enchantment: The Meaning and Importance of Fairy Tales*. 1975, Vintage Books, 2010.
Cinderella. Directed by Clyde Geronimi, Wilfred Jackson, and Hamilton Luske. Disney, 1950.
Egerkrans, Johan. *Vaesen*. B. Walstroms Bokforlag, 2017.
Frank, Arthur K. *Letting Stories Breath: A Socio-Narratology*. U Chicago P, 2010.
Freud, Sigmund. *Writings on Art and Literature*. Edited by Neil Hertz, Stanford, 1997.
Greenhill, Pauline, and Jill Terry Rudy, editors. *Channeling Wonder*. Wayne State UP, 2014.
Hearne, Betsy, and Barbara Karasek. "Disney Revisited, Or, Jiminy Cricket, It's Musty Down Here!" *Fairy and Folk Tales*, 4th ed., edited by Martin Hallet, Broadview Press, 2009, pp. 386–394.
Holbek, Bengt. "The Language of Fairy Tales." *Nordic Folklore: Recent Studies*, edited by Reimund Kvideland and Henning K. Sehmsdorf, Indiana UP, 1990, pp. 40– 62.
Hutcheon, Linda. *A Theory of Adaptation*. Routledge, 2006.
Parrot Analytics. "France TV Audience Demand for *Grimm*." tv.parrotanalytics.com/FR/grimm-nbc, Accessed 17 July 2021.
Perrault, Charles. "Cendrillon, ou la petite pantoufle de verre." *Histoires ou contes du temps passé, avec des moralités: Contes de ma mère l'Oye*, Paris, 1697.

Poniewozik, James. "The End of Fairy Tales? How Shrek and Friends Have Changed Children's Stories," *Fairy and Folk Tales*, 4th ed., edited by Martin Hallet, Broadview, 2009, pp. 384–396.

Sherrow, Rita. "New NBC drama 'Grimm' Melds Fairy Tales With Police Work." *Tulsa World*, 23 Oct. 2011, updated 20 Feb. 2019, tulsaworld.com/entertainment/television/new-nbc-drama-grimm-melds-fairy-tales-with-police-work/article_37f5ebc5-59ae-5521-a169-4f12057f2434.html, Accessed 21 July 2021.

Snow White and the Seven Dwarves. Directed by Clyde Geronimi, Wilfred Jackson, and Hamilton Luske. Disney, 1937.

Zipes, Jack. "Breaking the Magic Spell: Politics and the Fairy Tale." *New German Critique*, vol. 6, 1975, pp. 116–135.

———. *Grimm Legacies: The Magic Spell of the Grimms' Folk and Fairy Tales*. Princeton, 2015.

———. *The Original Folk and Fairy Tales of the Brothers Grimm*. Princeton, 2014.

———. *"Why Fairy Tales Stick" The Evolution and Relevance of a Genre*. Taylor and Francis, 2013.

PART ONE

Identity and Identification

All About Eve

Juliette's Original Sin

Melanie D. Holm

Midway through the NBC series *Grimm*, the character Juliette Silverton turns into a *Hexenbiest*, a "Witch-like creature that somewhat resembles a demon/goblin" (S1, E3: "Beeware"). The change comes as quite a surprise to Juliette and every other principal character in *Grimm's* fictional world, to say nothing of the audience watching the show. The transformation shifts her position in the series' social network from show-lead Nick Burkhardt's girlfriend and co-tenant to his hostile antagonist and powerful enemy. She embarks on rage-fueled sprees of destruction others are helpless to stop that culminate in her near and symbolic death. After that, her status changes yet again as she emerges as the self-fashioned independent agent and sometimes superhero, "Eve." Many of the characters in the show understand these developments as a type of existential deformation or fall. In this light, the identification with Eve offers a rich irony by recalling Eve's fall from grace by eating the forbidden fruit. Here, Eve is disobedient and wicked, the source of sin. But this is a somewhat limited and biased accounting: Eve is also the first woman, the first witch,[1] the first to choose to defy what a hero desired, and the first to seize power for herself. By becoming something other than what she was supposed to be, she disrupts and proposes alternative narratives. There is more, much more, to the story of *Grimm's* Eve than a fall from the grace of heroic romance in modern, domestic, middle-class guise.

Understood in a more extensive network of meanings, those characters who view her progression from Juliette to Eve as tragedy or loss misunderstand who she becomes and who she has been. Monroe labels her a "split personality," suggesting an undesirable breaking off or breaking away from the friend he and others so valued (S5, E10: "Map of the Seven Knights"). Similarly, during an unprecedented display of her destructive force, the three main supporting heroes of the show, Monroe, Hank, and, as he is referred to in the show by the other central characters, Wu,[2] voice a collective denial that the remorseless fury before them is the Juliette they once knew: Monroe, "This is not Juliette. This is—"; Hank, "This is Vengeance"; Wu, "I just can't believe it. Even if she is a *Hexenbiest*" (S4, E20: "You Don't Know Jack"). That Hank suggests, she is "Vengeance," should give pause: what reason would Juliette have for seeking revenge? Revenge for what?

The assessment their denial engenders, that this is not "Juliette," is quite accurate in a sense: the uncontrollable figure of adverse emotion hardly resembles the helpful, patient, pasta-making Juliette that everyone liked so much.[3] By stepping away from her original position in the narrative's social network, she is no longer recognizable as the character they understood as Juliette. She has shed the outward "likeability" that endeared her to the Grimm gang, especially to the hero Nick. As Roxanne Gay has introduced the term, likeability is "a performance, a code of conduct dictating the proper way to be."[4] Chimamanda Ngozi Adichie elaborates that:

> our society teaches young girls ... that likability is an essential part of you, of the space you occupy in the world, that you're supposed to twist yourself into shapes to make yourself likable, that you're supposed to hold back sometimes, pull back, don't quite say, don't be too pushy, because you have to be likable.[5]

Alissa Burger and Stephanie Mix have explored the complexity of female likeability in media in relationship to the narratives of witches in modern television. They argue that female characters "negotiate the dual, intertwined debates of women's power and likeability, highlighting the cultural discomfort with the former and a steadfast demand for the latter."[6] They "refus[e] to pretend to be someone or something they are not, eschewing the lie to instead embody the truth of themselves, their identities, and their unapologetic strength."[7] Applying this paradigm to modern fantasy narrative suggests "witches … eschew the demand to be sympathetic or 'likeable' to instead pursue their own desires and claim their power."[8] In her transition into Eve, the character herself does not essentially change. Instead, her progression unmasks what was always apparent in Juliette's character: her "self-determined strength and purpose." Her inclination to be the hero (or to be whatever a hero might be, disentangled from its gendered mooring—but obscured by all the trappings of being "Juliette") remains: the change lies in explicitness (S6, E11: "Where the Wild Things Were"). Attaining power by the accident of becoming a *Hexenbiest* empowers her to become what she already is.

From the beginning of the series, even in its fictional pre-history,

Juliette exhibits traits that mirror Nick's heroics as a police detective and Grimm. Sometimes they are openly demonstrated, while at other times, they are expressed in altered contexts or forms (such as compassion, counseling, and outreach) or overshadowed by Nick's amplified power and the prominence of his heroism in the show's gender-asymmetrical power network. As Michael Hale writes in his review of the series pilot, "In *Grimm* our world needs protection from mostly frightening supernatural forces; the stars are men."[9] The world of *Grimm* develops along an intersection of social and fairy-tale conventions in which the hero saves the day and usually the girl. The tension lurking in the background of this romantic idyll is that this particular girl neither wants nor needs to be saved. Juliette's journey of becoming "Eve" explores what possibilities there are and what possibilities there can be for women whose power has been made equal to the hero and who, therefore, no longer need to be liked.

The reality within the series is characterized by Grimm versus Wesen (and sometimes the Royals) and constituted on the premise of a male hero with supernatural powers and a transcendental destiny to protect, rescue, avenge, and decapitate. There is little space left for a successful female, Anthropologie-clad veterinarian who bikes to work, speaks fluent Spanish, and is financially and psychologically independent. Juliette exhibits autonomy and competence in her sphere of work while demonstrating an increasing facility in those roles and with those skills that are central to Nick's identity—be it detective work, firing a gun, or risking her life for a perceived greater good. However, if there is little room for a woman in close proximity to the hero's role, there is even less when she gains superior powers. A new space, identity, or role must be created. So it will be, and painfully so, for all of its resistance to absorption in the status quo.

Considering Juliette as the focus of *Grimm*'s six-season narrative suggests a radical counter-history to the story of Nick's "hero's journey."[10] As conceived by Michel Foucault, a counter-history is "centered around those experiences and memories that have not been heard and integrated in official histories."[11] The story of Juliette does not fit into the dominant discourse of Grimm's fictional world. In that view, becoming Eve is a singular transformative event either transacted in the basement of Hadrian's Wall (the government organization and headquarters with which she works near the end of the series). Alternatively, it is seen as the collateral damage of becoming a *Hexenbiest* from Nick's Grimm reinvigoration. However, outside of the heroic framework, it is not an event, rupture, or change at all. Instead, it is a progressive intensification of existing characteristics, impulses, and desires that her *Hexenbiest* power intensifies: "Eve" was there all along, trapped inside "Juliette."

"Juliette": The Girl of Nick's Two Dreams

Perhaps it is more appropriate to say that it was Nick's socially authorized understanding of Juliette's identity as supplemental to his own that made the "Juliette trap." Simone de Beauvoir describes such a trap as a gendered distinction between being for oneself, a condition of freedom and transcendence from a given reality, and being in itself, the opposite position of immanence, understood as a function or characteristic rather than an independent subject: "She is defined and differentiated with reference to man and not he with reference to her; she is the incidental, the inessential as opposed to the essential. He is the Subject, he is the Absolute—she is the other."[12]

From the beginning of the series, audiences are presented with two competing Juliettes. One is quite literally the girl of Nick's dreams. The other is Eve in early form, realized in her excess from Nick's "dream girl." In the Pilot, Nick has a dream that establishes a role for Juliette in his formative heroic story: it emphasizes sexualized victimhood and physical dependence. In season two, he has a second dream that complements and advances the first, emphasizing and idealizing docility and devotion (S2, E7: "Bottle Imp"). Both dreams illustrate absolute reliance on him. The first dream depicts Juliette running through the woods barefoot in a clingy red silk nightgown. She is presumably chased by Hulda,[13] a *Hässlich* Wesen that Nick shot to death the day before while rescuing his aunt, Marie Kessler.[14] In this tableau, Juliette structurally fulfills the role of "Little Red Riding Hood," in the eponymous fairy-tale which anchors the episode. The tale focuses on predation on women by metaphorical wolves, mirrored here by a *blutbad* (wolf Wesen) and Wesen more generally.

Earlier in the episode, another woman is attacked without Nick's intervening heroism (because he had not yet become a Grimm). In this case, Sylvie,[15] a female college student, runs through the daylit woods wearing a red hoodie to the pulsating beats of the Eurythmics' "Sweet Dreams (Are Made of This)." The song repeats throughout the episode as a leitmotif, connecting women and victimization by Wesen. More crucially, a complex relationship arises between the song and Nick's emerging heroic identity, one that suggests that the dream of an endangered Juliette's helplessness. The dream represents a larger heroic fantasy that Juliette is a potential victim who needs him to protect and rescue her.

In the Pilot and throughout the series, human women are mainly divided into those who are already victims (e.g., Sophie, the murdered jogger) and those who need Nick's protection (e.g., Robin,[16] the young girl abducted). Despite her Grimm bona fides, Aunt Marie falls into the second category. When Nick rescues her for the first time, shooting her assailant, he acts as a policeman in the line of duty: he does not yet know about Grimms. However, in rescuing her a second time, like with Robin, Nick's nascent Grimm identity has begun to take hold, linked with the song "Sweet Dreams." The postman hums it, alerting them to his status as the murderer and kidnapper, enabling Nick to rescue the girl (damsel in distress). It plays again as the episode's closing music as Nick rescues his now comatose Aunt from the *Hexenbiest* Adalind. This time, it is a cover of the song by Marilyn Mason. As it plays, attention turns to Captain Sean Renard saying to Adalind Schade, "We'll just have to try [to kill her] again. Let's hope she doesn't wake up first." In her sleep, Marie is a victim as defenseless as a little girl lost in the woods. She needs Nick to protect her. In Nick's sweet dreams, so does Juliette.

The Pilot persuasively thematizes the victimization of women, establishing the need for Nick's protective interventions. However, this gendered victim-hero binary gives rise to a persistent question: is Juliette necessarily a victim but for the protection of (and partially because of) him as a Grimm, or does Nick only begin to see her as a victim as a necessary part of becoming a Grimm? Marie certainly primes him and viewers for the former with her advice: "I'm so sorry. I know you love Juliette, but you have to end it and never see her again. It's just too dangerous" (S1, E1: "Pilot"). Nevertheless, from the outset, we see Juliette not as a passive victim but as her self-sufficient agent, one who protects herself, others and, in many cases, saves Nick himself.

The first Juliette, the dream girl, is sanctified by overlapping social norms and expectations of traditional gender roles and well-known Western European fairy tales. As Karen E. Rowe writes, folktales and fairy tales

> have always been one of culture's primary mechanisms for inculcating roles and behaviors. The ostensibly innocuous fantasies symbolically portray basic human problems and appropriate socials prescriptions. These tales which glorify passivity, dependency, and self-sacrifice as a heroine's cardinal virtues suggest that culture's very survival depends upon a women's acceptance of roles which relate her to motherhood and domesticity.... They transfer from fairy tales into real-life those fantasies which exalt acquiesce to male power.[17]

Nick's two dreams exemplify the glorification of such female passivity. While the first emphasizes her physical dependence, the second portrays a psychological or ontological dependence upon Nick for an infallible version of reality.

Nick's second dream is set within an episode that narrates the story of a Wesen father trying (and frequently failing) to protect society from the pubescent violence of his daughter's powers. It opens with Juliette watching fireworks from the window, recalling a girlhood memory of her father taking her to see fireworks (S2, E7). The scene establishes an equivalence, recasting Nick as the paternal authority while she remains every bit the little girl. This Juliette is docile and unquestioning; she is apologetic for ever having been so silly as to have doubted Nick in any way: "I'm so sorry. Everything I put you through.... All the terrible stuff that happened, it totally makes sense. Of course, I believe you." They kiss, with her in the position of a supplicant, and the relationship reboots from an apparent premise of Nick's infallible purchase on reality, his authority to determine it for her, and her childishness in having ever doubted him.

Juliette's presumptive structural place is a feminized position that intersects two subordinate groups: first, people unaware of Wesen and thus potentially their prey, and second, women, who are generalized to a subjugated status. Nick, however, mistakes Juliette's position for her essence, her status for her capacity, and her access to power for her identity. His emergent, coalescing identity as a Grimm takes these power structures for granted (not least because of his position within it). His early encounters with Wesen, which are vital for the show's fictional world, articulate a reality in which (1) Wesen dominate humans apart from Grimms, who have superhuman capabilities, and (2) men dominate women, including *Hexenbiests*. This is a world of sexualized violence, discipline, and predation.

The Other Juliette

While Nick's dreams construct a Juliette who is highly dependent on him for physical and psychological security, the story arcs of the first, second, and third season propose an alternative that demystifies this fantasy: a Juliette that rescues rather than needs rescuing. Juliette's character continually resists and transcends the categories of vulnerable and victim, so much so that season one could be read as establishing Juliette as being more than her role allows as she duplicates many of Nick's heroic traits and actions. For example, when a *Siegbarste*—a giant troll-like creature desensitized to most forms of pain—is beating Nick nearly to death, Juliette arrives onto the scene to rescue him, scaring the creature off by throwing a pot of boiling water in its face (S1, E8: "Game Ogre"). The encounter's domestic element is revealing. When the superhuman violence of Grimm's power fails, Juliette's quick thinking repurposes an icon of female domesticity—a pot of pasta water boiling on the stove—to rescues him, scaring off the monster and demonstrating that every tool is a weapon if you hold it right.[18] Such proves to be the case in the second season Juliette risks her life to rescue Nick for the second time: she steps in front of Nick's loaded gun, breaking his involuntary infatuation with a *Musai* while preventing him from murdering a romantic rival in cold blood, by wielding true love's kiss—as though she, not he were prince charming (S2, E20: "Kiss of the Muse").

While these examples have a playful relationship with gender inversions, her heroic impulses frequently emerge in contentious, dissonant displays. In one simple example, when a scuffle outside the house alerts Nick and Juliette to a possible intruder, he tells her to stay put while he investigates (S1, E11: "Tarantella"). He reasons that she should stay behind because he has the gun—a symbol of phallic power and a menacing demonstration of it as he waves it in front of her. She nevertheless moves from rejection to ridicule of his logic and presumed authority when the potential perpetrator is revealed to be merely (Wesen) children throwing eggs. Her confidence and curiosity work together to portray his power claim as hyperbolic bullying. Her instincts outshine his official capacity when they take homeless siblings out to dinner as part of an investigation: Juliette, not Nick, coaxes the necessary information from the sister (S1, E10: "Organ Grinder"). Nick recognizes her success, acknowledging, "You know, you're pretty good at this," and then joking, "You should've been a cop," easing his anxiety of the claim's legitimacy through comic deflation.

Nevertheless, in a subsequent encounter, she identifies a case of domestic violence in a house neighboring their romantic vacation rental (S1, E16: "The Thing with Feathers"). Her quick assessment forces an unenthusiastic Nick to act, though he acts no further than calling local police (who are later shown to be involved). On the other hand, she makes direct contact with the victim, offering outreach for her escape. It is only when it is revealed she is Wesen, and thus the province of Grimms, that Nick becomes interested, and while he is in pursuit, Juliette takes on the role of her own protector.

The similarities intensify when she is the first to come to a crime scene as a vet treating an attacked horse and begins investigating the nature of the mysterious assailant, who turns out to have also murdered two people (S1, E21: "Big Feet"). She sends a hair sample for DNA testing, discovering the sample's genetic duality. She proposes to Nick the possibility of a human-hybrid creature, echoing Marie's earlier words: "Maybe the stories are true." However, rather than affirm her conjecture, he remains silent, exercising one of the few remaining powers he holds over Juliette. As Marilyn Frye explains, "the creation and manipulation of power is constituted of the manipulation and control of access."[19] His is the power to withhold knowledge, keeping her an ignorant, potential victim. Denying Juliette access to knowledge of the Wesen world mirrors her rationale for delaying their engagement—she feels that he is hiding something, denying her information. However, his withholding has legitimacy only within a power structure that codes Juliette as necessarily too weak to put that knowledge to use.

The second season explores the concept of power in terms of access and lack of access to information via Juliette's memories. When Adalind's spell erases her memories, she inhabits a new, independent identity. On the other hand, Nick is denied access to Juliette as a girlfriend—the punishment Adalind cunningly cooked up. While Juliette eventually regains these memories, she does so with a difference. While they are her memories, the "she" who participates and is invested in the memories is not the one who is remembering them. This distance allows Juliette to consider him and their relationship dispassionately and construct her own narrative. Thus, the resolution is not a simple one where she slides into a subjugated role. Instead, she becomes increasingly autonomous, immediately working to rescue and protect Nick during his Zombie-interlude from the royals and the police.

If Nick's two dreams suggest wish-fulfillment for their relationship at different stages of his self-conception as a Grimm, then Juliette's "waking up" from her sleep marks the disruption of that first dream and the grounds for the second. When Juliette awakes at the kiss of police Captain Sean Renard (a half-royal, and thus prince for the spell's purposes), Nick's claim as the hero is doubly undermined. Another man rescues her, and he is a man who, by many measures, exceeds his status. The status of Juliette as a victim or in need of rescue is also troubled. As the season unfolds to show Juliette as an active participant in her own rescuing—not just in breaking the attraction to Renard (a team effort) but also in reclaiming and reconciling her memories. Juliette wakes up from her unnatural sleep. Understood metaphorically, she "wakes up" to a clean slate of possibilities for Nick and their relationship. Seeing Nick from an outsider's perspective recreates their relationship not as a continuum from before the spell but with objectivity and hindsight.

It is perhaps no surprise that the relationship is renewed on the grounds of full disclosure. Whatever Nick had withheld in season one must be declared. It is also unsurprising, given her demonstrated characteristics, that knowledge of Wesen and Grimms does not drive her crazy. Nor does she run away. Instead, she responds with intellectual curiosity, integrating this new information into her world picture and striving to learn more.

Further, early in season three, when Nick needs to be rescued first from Eric Renard and the *Cracher-Mortel*, and then, later, from his zombified tour of aggression and rage, Juliette is on the frontline and ultimately saves him (S3, E2: "PTZD"). As Nick is about to charge on Hank, who has a gun pointed at him, ready to shoot, Juliette gets behind him, distracts him by calling his name, and then delivers the antidote via the *piqure-giantesque*. She is alone risks coming into direct contact with Nick in his aggravated state, and she pays a hero's price: a walloping punch in the face. Juliette risks her life to save Nick for the third time—ultimately rescuing him from his own superpowers.

Juliette takes a prominent position of near equality with Nick in season three. She solves cases he cannot, provides critical information from her areas of expertise that is usually crucial to resolving the episode's crisis, and protects the vulnerable from hostile Wesen. For example, in "A Dish Best Served Cold" (S3, E3), Juliette discovers a key piece of evidence in unexplained deaths by drawing on her knowledge as a veterinarian "an extreme form of gastric dilatation volvulus," a breed-specific bloating phenomenon for dogs and cattle. Her connection allows for the dramatic resolution of the episode's conflict between *Blutbads* and *Bauerschweins*. In "El Cucuy" (S3, E5), she draws from her Spanish background to provide the story of *El Cucuy*, leading to its identification as a Wesen-like creature. Further, in "Stories We Tell Our Young" (S3, E6), she is the one who recognizes that the *Grausen* condition is not supernatural but the result of a parasite.

While Juliette has access to specialized knowledge, which she readily shares, she also acts in situations where Nick is unwilling. For example, after the email revelation that Nick's mother, Kelly, is alive, Juliette discovers her location via internet sleuthing and then takes the chance of emailing her directly, establishing a back-channel for communication (S3, E5; S3, E12: "The Wild Hunt"). Somewhat perversely, her accomplishments are met not with gratitude. Instead, Nick scolds her, "I hope you know how dangerous this is." Her actions also unfold in empathic outreach to her friend Alicia[20] to dismantle any shame surrounding her experience as a victim of domestic violence and as a Wesen (S3, E10: "Eyes of the Beholder"). It is a particularly significant moment because Juliette decides not to keep information secret, choosing instead to get all information out in the open. She further puts herself in physical danger by fighting against Alicia's abusive husband, keeping him from harming her or worse. Commenting on this episode and season three as a whole, Elizabeth Tulloch argues of Juliette: "You know's she's kind of a badass, and there is scene I'm shooting for episode 10 that's really fun. She's just kind of coming into her own, and something is empowering her."[21]

Juliette also performs more abstract versions of rescuing people. For example, she advises Rosalie in the Christmas decoration debacle that threatens her relationship with Monroe. More dramatically, she breaks a wall of silence to give Wu a perspective on his *Aswang* experience in "Mommy Dearest" (S3, E14), allowing him to move forward and out of the mental hospital. (S3, E8: "Twelve Days of Krampus"; S3, E15: "Once We Were Gods"). Examples can be found throughout the season of agency and efficacy. She does not need to be rescued: she is a rescuer.

A Woman Divided

Juliette tenuously grasps two roles—rescuer and girlfriend—only to lose hold of both to a female duo who draws focus in season three. The reappearance of Adalind into the narrative and introduction of Trubel displace Juliette from her emergent status as equal and enduring status as Nick's love interest by each assuming one of those roles individually. Trubel enters the show's narrative as a female Grimm who is a powerful fighter but, as the name implies, is troubled, mainly because of her ignorance of the Wesen world. Taken under Nick's wing, Trubel becomes a version of Juliette from Nick's second dream, wide-eyed and adoring, credulous, and devoted. In Trubel's initial episodes, Juliette is pushed to the margins because there is nothing much for her to do or say with a female Grimm occupying her prior position as Nick's *de facto* partner.

Nevertheless, if her rescuer status is threatened, her status as Nick's domestic partner becomes uninhabitable, wrenched away by Adalind's illusory scheme. In the first of many *Verfluchte Zwillingsschwester* body transformations, Adalind assumes Juliette's physical form to have sex with Nick and steal his Grimm powers (per the request of Royalty). Thus, "Juliette" is reduced to a sexualized body, not unlike the "Juliette" running through the woods in Nick's first dream. Tellingly, this scene and the dream are the only times Juliette dresses in silk lingerie in the entire series. That Adalind will soon assume victim status, relying on Nick for protection, and then take on the roles of mother and lover completes the circuit of his dream women.

The paradigm of Nick's heroism that structures the show accepts Trubel as a female Grimm and a "rescuer" because she rejects any form of femininity and supports Nick's authority unquestioningly.[22] At the same time, the narrative accepts women as sexualized and vulnerable female bodies. These role duplicates negate Juliette's rise in status through earlier seasons. In the heroic narrative economy, she no longer has positive value—there is nothing left for her to do. However, if there is no room for her in the heroic order, it should come as no surprise that she will take the antagonistic position of the monstrous woman. It is the only place for her to go before smashing the narrative itself to pieces.

The Break

Juliette becomes a *Hexenbiest* when she discovers that she has not become a mother: her domestic confidence toward marrying Nick is shaken, and her heroic aspirations are dashed. Motherhood and marriage are decidedly emphasized among the feminized characters: Rosalee is married to Monroe, Adalind announces she will do anything she can to get her baby back, Kelly Burkhard, Nick's mother, is off, reprising a maternal role with Adalind's and Sean's daughter, Diana,[23] and Elizabeth Lascelles[24] dedicates herself to finding her grandchild rivaling Kelly in her newfound commitment to the maternal role, after risking her life to give life to her son. Juliette will do none of these things: she is not a Grimm; she is not a wife; and she is not, as is now known for certain, a mother. Instead, she stands in the bathroom and looks at herself in the mirror: the face of the *Hexenbiest* returns her gaze (S4, E8: "Chupacabra"). Juliette screams in shock and alarm, leaving the bathroom, going for her phone to call Nick. But as she dials, she catches a glimpse of herself in the mirror and hangs up the phone (S4, E9: "Wesenrein"). Whatever Juliette may feel about becoming a *Hexenbiest*, there is one certain thing: she does not want Nick to rescue her, or for that matter, for him to even be involved. Whatever this is, it is hers.

Initially, Juliette uses her *Hexenbiest* powers to enhance her evolving protector role: she protects Rosalee from the *Wesenrein*, later killing one member who tries to attack her, telekinetically blowing off the back of his skull (S4, E10: "Tribunal"). Among the collection of remaining warrior-heroes in the show—Wu, Sean, Monroe, and Nick—she has become by far the most powerful. However, she is initially ambivalent about her power: what it means and its consequences. This ambivalence surfaces in two of her own dreams. In the first, Rosalee persistently harries her to call Nick and force him to look for Monroe, ignoring her pleas to stop because she has a terrible headache (S4, E9). When Rosalee mocks her, Juliette erupts, freeing the *Hexenbiest*, and rips out Rosalee's windpipe. In a second dream, she sees Nick in the trailer surveying weapons and selecting an ax (S4, E11: "Death Do Us Part"). He carries it into their bedroom and wakes her, saying, "I know what you are," before chopping off her head. The first dream demonstrates the eradication of her likeability, communicating a desire to put a violent end to the demand that she subjugates herself to the interests of others. On the other hand, the second recognizes the lethal illegitimacy of being a woman with power will not be told what to do or be.

There is a double-tension that arises in this early stage of *Hexenbiest*-becoming. On the one hand, Juliette is ambivalent about her powers. She enjoys being able to defend herself against Wesen and deliver poetic justice to mere humans. However, she is also angry that this is not a power she asked for, but something that has been done to her which she cannot change. She resents her pre–Grimm life being taken from her and all that had since ensued. Her anger is less about being a *Hexenbiest* than it is at having been *made* a *Hexenbiest*. It is not about having new powers, but it is about power acting upon her, about being repeatedly pushed toward the role of victim that is demanded by Nick being a Grimm.

A different tension emerges in Nick's intolerance of what Juliette has become and his commitment to rescuing her from it. Juliette characterizes the *Hexenbiest* transformation as hers to manage, resenting Nick's rescue narrative. That narrative is dramatically disrupted when a Wesen hitman, a *Manticore* known as the *Maréchaussée,* attacks Juliette in her home (S4, E12: "Maréchausée"). Home, however, was a site of saving Nick from a *Siegbarste* and her friend from a *Klaustreich* by her wits alone. As a *Hexenbiest*, dispatching the *Manticore* barely ruffles her hair.

Grimm rarely repeats the monster-of-the-week species. That the Wesen she kills is a *Manticore* is therefore notable because, in a previous season, Nick and his team were unable to defeat one, believing only another *Manticore* could kill it (S3, E11: "The Good Soldier"). Juliette proves them wrong. She kills it with ironic flair, impaling this Lion-Scorpion Wesen with its own poisoned tail. Later, Nick comes rushing in, ostensibly to save her. Seeing blood instead on her clothes and a body on the floor, he asks in exasperation: "What the hell happened?" With a dry, flat delivery, Juliette replies: "He missed." Nick apologizes for the situation and his absence: "I am so sorry. Look, this never should have happened. And I swear to God, it's never going to happen again." The two seem to be playing parts in different genres; Nick is the hero who controls and protects the innocent girl. A dissonant Juliette is calmly aware of her superior potential and flatly rebuffs his necessary heroism: "You can't protect me, Nick. That's something I'm gonna have to do for myself." The "me" in her statement is different from the object of Nick's fantasy, as is evident when she unmasks herself as a *Hexenbiest*: he responds not with heroics but disgust.

Nick's light-hearted fantasy of killing Adalind—"Well, one less Hexenbiest wouldn't be a bad thing, would it?"—sets the terms for Juliette's self-unmasking at the end of the episode after she, not Nick, defeats (though does not kill) Adalind (S4, E12). Not understanding how she could have defended herself against Adalind, Nick asks Juliette if she shot her. Prefacing that he knows how much she loves him, she woges shocking and repulsing Nick. Nick's words echo those of his cohorts: "You're not Juliette." Only with her proof of her self-continuity does he accept this new reality, though he is angry, seeing himself as a victim. He is angry that she did not tell him about it immediately: bewildering hypocrisy given the time passed between discovering his Grimm identity and sharing it with Juliette unless there is not a feeling of mutuality. His anger and frustration grow upon finding out that Renard knows more about her change than he does, recalling his displacement in the prince charming affair of the past.

Further, Renard can and has done something for Juliette by sending her to another *Hexenbiest*, Henrietta, for answers. The answer, which he rejects, is that he cannot "fix this." Juliette cannot be rescued.

The assertion that she is not Juliette echoes when she moves out, leaving behind both Nick and the "Juliette" who had lived there with him (S5, E14: "Lycanthropia"). Nick explains that he will not give up trying to save her, but Juliette deflects his rhetoric: "You can't change it." It, of course, refers to her transformation into a *Hexenbiest*, with all of the powers that characterize it. Nick attempts a kind of sympathetic reciprocity, telling her, "You learned to understand me, now I have to learn how to understand you." However, this modified repetition of Henrietta's advice—to accept Juliette in the same way that she accepted him being a Grimm (or kill her)—has a hollow ring for Juliette. This is not because the equivalence is false but because she knows that he will only ever accept her as "Juliette" (S4, E14: "Bad Luck").

In becoming a Grimm, Nick extends his purchase on traditional masculinity, while in becoming a *Hexenbiest*, Juliette is abjected from traditional female structures of the heroic narrative. Reflecting on historical representations in England, Sara F. Williams has explained that the witch is "a mirror reversal of all that the patriarchy deemed good in a woman."[25] In the case of this *Hexenbiest*, the reversal is not limited to kinetic power. It extends to visual sexuality. Woged Juliette is the antithesis of desirability for the masculine gaze: a dominant, desexualized hag. Juliette models this inversion when she walks up to Nick, woges, and asks: "Is this what you want to spend the rest of your life with? Is it?" Nick responds from a place of victimization, "Why are you doing this?" What is implied is, "Why are you doing this to me?" which parallels "Why are you not being who you used to be?" or "Why aren't you the Juliette that I liked?" That Juliette intuits this is clear in her response, "If I'm the girl of your dreams, the least you could do is kiss me. Kiss me. You can't even look at me. This is what's forever." Juliette leaves with Nick and any pretension to the good girlfriend, and the only place that remains in the constellation of female roles is the bad girl. Being the bad girl provides an outlet for her rage, or a Wu phrased it, "vengeance," severing her ties to Nick and gendered subjugation. Feminist philosopher Catharine MacKinnon argues that gender "difference is the velvet glove of the iron first of dominations. The problem is not that differences are not valued; the problem is that they are defined by power."[26] It may then be said that when Juliette becomes a *Hexenbiest*, the gloves come off.

Once her frequent demonstrations of power exhaust her rage, she re-examines which of the values she abandoned in her total negation of "Juliette" are authentically her own. Her protector instinct can thus be expressed in her last vignette as mere *Hexenbiest*: she protects Diana, an unsupervised toddler, during the melee of violence that kills Kelly (S4, E22: "Cry Havoc"). Her heroic instinct remains, but it is cloaked in futility because the identity does not exist in female form, particularly for a woman whose past is no longer clean. Hopeless, she wants Nick to kill her, but he cannot, so strong is his fantasy of reclaiming his Juliette, inflaming her rage. Trubel shoots her to defend Nick and is met with the same please for death. "Bad girl" was a bad fit for Juliette, but there is nothing left for her to be.

The Birth of Eve

The opening quote for the episode debuting Eve, "I have been bent and broken, but, I hope, into a better shape," provides a model for understanding the continuity of self in Juliette's progression to Eve (S5, E7: "Eve of Destruction").

When the male heroic ensemble—Nick Burkhardt, Monroe, Hank Griffin, Drew Wu, and Sean Renard—first encounter Eve, they recognize her as Juliette, yet changed. As Nick says, "Her hair was different, the way she moved was different, but it was her; I know it was her." While Nick is focused on her appearance and her dissonance with the form of his Juliette, Hank makes a significant, complementary observation: "Well, whoever it was, she just saved our lives." Here a change of hair is a synecdoche for her change of identity. Eve is no longer tethered by Juliette's long, romantic red hair—a red inextricably linked with the status of the female victim from episode one.

It is never made clear how the transition from Juliette to Eve is materially accomplished: as she lay between life and death, the secret government agency defending the world from a violent wave of Wesen authoritarianism, Hadrian's Wall, collects her. Its leader, Meisner—an enigmatic, minor heroic figure of earlier episodes—is understood to be linked with the process. When Trubel, who has joined the cause, asks him what he did to her, she may be asking, "What did you do to make her not like Juliette?" However, as Meisner replies, "What we had to," the inquiry is revised to mean: what did you do to her to help her become Eve, the heroic force in the fight against Black Claw. In this murky transition, what is clear is, as Eve states to Nick, "I found a reason to live." While this reason is entirely independent of his past Juliette, it also suggests an "I" who had no reason to live. She does not indicate a new self but a self-fashioned anew from the despair of exhausted possibilities in this heroic paradigm.

Eve is outside of the traditional narrative of male heroism. She does not demonstrate the likable traits of a subjugated, feminized position, nor does she demonstrate the slightest concern about being liked. Instead, she focuses on using her power to rescue and defend, achieving a purpose that is her own. In a complex scene where she and Nick prepare to fight the *Zerstörer* (an apocalyptic entity), she clarifies that she does not want to be rescued and is not in the fight because of him or to work off her guilt. Instead, she is there because, as Eve, "I have a strength and a purpose that I never had before," and it transcends both fairy-tale and modern-domestic definitions of happiness (S6, E11). To get to the trans-dimensional battle-ground, Eve made *Hexenbiest* blood-sacrifice that became a sacrifice of her *Hexenbiest* powers upon return. Still, as a non–*Hexenbiest*, her purpose does not waver: she continues to draw upon her intelligence, solving the riddle of the stick, clarifying for all the task that lies ahead. Without her powers, however, she is quickly killed by the male *Zerstörer*, reiterating what the story arc had already told us: there is no place for a woman with an autonomous purpose in this reality without supernatural strength to defend it.

Changing History: Eve's Happy Ending

Returned to life, Juliette gets her powers back again at the end of the series in what seems like an aside quickly passed over in the dominant focus on Nick and his future progeny. However, that she gets her powers back is not insignificant, nor is *how* she gets them. They do not return naturally, nor are they gained through ceremony or granted by a Grimm. Rather, they are the gift of a young girl who sets the world right. Earlier in the series, Kelly explained that Diana "has an extraordinary destiny. In the wrong hands, it could do great evil. But in the right hands, it could do great good." Juliette replies, "So we're talking, like, 'changing the course of history' kind of a person" (S3, E17: "Synchronicity"). Being rescued from the *Zerstörer* by the team effort in the finale is not Diana's history making-act; it is a strike in the plus column of Grimm heroism. Diana instead warps history, taking the benefits of this final battle while returning to an earlier moment before the battle begins, and everyone is still alive and none the wiser. Apposite this act, she quietly returns Eve's powers as a gift of grace. Perhaps that is how the course of history changes. She allows Juliette's counter-history to continue: for now, Eve has the power to follow her purpose beyond the male heroes and female victims who have framed her and beyond the confinements of narrow domestic happiness. That is Eve's happy ending: and it is happier still for not being an ending at all, but a new beginning for different kind of narrative.

34   Part One: Identity and Identification

Notes

1. The arguments that identify Eve as the first witch are foundational to the conceits of European witchcraft. The Genesis interpretation portrays Eve conspiring (often wantonly) with the Devil to steal the fruit and tempt Adam, framing this as diabolic fraternization representing witches' alliances with the Devil for unnatural power. See, Clark 54–65, esp. 57; Krause 61–65.

2. While the show makes great strides with racial representation and equity, it cannot pass without comment that Drew Wu is repeatedly referred to by his last name, which indicates his racial difference from the rest of the cast. While Captain Renard is often referred to as "Renard," "Sean," "Captain," and "The Captain" are also used frequently. The few times Sergeant Drew Wu is addressed by his first name are in the S3, E14: "Mommy Dearest" and spoken by fellow Filipino characters.

3. The frequency with which pasta is made in this show, usually by Juliette, has not escaped the notice of the active and exuberant *Grimm*-fan base. As one poster urges in the title of a post in the popular "r/Grimm" subreddit: "I swear to god if they eat spaghetti one more time...: Please Juliette, learn to cook something else" (@SirNarcotics). This recognition is followed by the witty, insightful connection that Adalind later boasts, "I actually make a pretty good Bolognese" (S5, E2: "Clear and Wesen Danger"). That she makes this claim at the beginning of their cohabitating, parental romance is deeply suggestive, however silly, that pasta signifies something more than a quick dinner in the gender dynamics of the show.

4. Gay 85.
5. See Adichie.
6. Burger and Mix 15.
7. Burger and Mix 21.
8. Burger and Mix 31.
9. Hale C1.
10. Joseph Campbell defines the hero's journey as a monomyth: a progressive sequence of events common to all mythological journeys. The hero is gender male (either a man or a male figure), who travels through the following stages: the call to adventure, refusal of the quest, accepting the call, entering the unknown, tests & the supreme ordeal, reward, and the journey home, master of two worlds or restoring the world. The monomyth also shares features of supernatural aid and help from allies. Women or female characters feature in these stories as allies who help the hero throughout the quest or temptresses who threaten or endanger the hero. In this constellation, a figure such as Rosalee operates as an ally. At the same time, Juliette and Adalind serve alternately as either allies or temptresses, with Nick in the role of the hero.
11. Medina 12.
12. Beauvoir xxii.
13. Actor, Danny Hernandez.
14. Actor, Kate Burton.
15. Actor, Joy Flatz.
16. Actor, Sophia Mitri Schloss.
17. Rowe 210–11.
18. See note 10 above for the ironic and substation implications.
19. Faye 103.
20. Actor Alicia Lagano.
21. See Sherrow.
22. Trubel is visually portrayed in opposition to the typically-gendered women: she has a short, traditionally "male" haircut and wears a white t-shirt, loose jeans, a hoody (not red), and rugged boots. Marking her distinction through the rejection of female clothing repeats in season three to establish her character. For example, in the episode "My Fair Wesen" (S3, E20), Trubel's inability to walk in heels serves a comic purpose and operates as a signifier of her alienation from this female role. When she needs shoes, she steals practical, gender-neutral boots (S3, E19: "Nobody Knows the Trubel I've Seen"). Later, she

refuses Juliette's offer to take her shopping for new clothes (S3, E21). In the most reductive and stereotypical of tropes, it is made clear to the audience that Trubel does not act like a "girl."
    23. Actor, Hannah R. Loyd (child); various actors in role as baby/infant.
    24. Sean's mother. Actor, Louise Lombard.
    25. Williams 3–4.
    26. MacKinnon 219.

Works Cited

Adichie, Chimamanda Ngozi. "Chimamanda Ngozi Adichie 2015 Girls Write Now Awards Speech." *Youtube,* Uploaded by GirlsWriteNow, 20 May 2015, https://www.youtube.com/watch?v= 3uNcvtjT8Pk.
Beauvoir, Simone de. *The Second Sex.* Vintage, 1974.
Burger, Alissa, and Stephanie Mix, "Something Wicked This Way Comes? Power, Anger and Negotiating the Witch in *American Horror Story, Grimm,* and *Once Upon a Time.*" *Buffy to Batgirl: Essays on Female Power, Evolving Femininity and Gender Roles in Science Fiction and Fantasy,* edited by Julie M. Still and Zara T. Wilkinson, McFarland, 2019, pp. 9–32.
Campbell, Joseph. *The Hero with a Thousand Faces.* New World Library, 2008.
Clark, Stuart. "The Gendering of Witchcraft in French Demonology." *New Perspectives on Witchcraft, Magic, and Demonology: Witchcraft, Healing, and Popular Diseases,* edited by Brian P. Levack, Vol. 5, Routledge, 2001, pp. 54–65.
Frye, Marilyn. *The Politics of Reality: Essays in Feminist Theory.* Crossing Press, 1983.
Hale, Michael. "The Enchanted Forest, in Sunshine and Shadow." *The New York Times,* 21 Oct. 2011, p. C1.
Gay, Roxanne. *Bad Feminist.* Harper Perennial, 2014.
Krause, Victoria. *Witchcraft, Demonology, and Confession in Early Modern France.* Cambridge, 2016.
MacKinnon, Catharine A. *Toward a Feminist Theory of the State.* Harvard UP, 1989.
Medina, José. "Toward a Foucaultian Epistemology of Resistance: Counter-Memory, Epistemic Friction, and Guerrilla Pluralism." *Foucault Studies,* Vol. 12, 2011, pp. 9–35.
Rowe, Karen E. "Feminism and Fairy Tales." *Don't Bet on the Prince: Contemporary Feminist Fairy Tales in North America and England,* edited by Jack Zipes, Routledge, 1989, pp. 209–266.
Sherrow, Rita. "Grimm Season 3 Starts with Juliette Finally in the Know." *Tulsa World,* 24 Oct. 2013, Updated 18 Feb. 2019. https://tulsaworld.com/entertainment/television/grimm-season-3-starts-with-juliette-finally-in-the-know/article_654038b4-7e5f-55d0-b056-0c713e7ad876.html. Accessed 1 Jul. 2021.
SirNacotics, "I swear to god if they eat spaghetti one more time…" *Reddit,* 7 Oct. 2018, https://www.reddit.com/r/grimm/comments/9m7i36/i_swear_to_god_if_they_eat_spaghetti_one_more_time/. Accessed 1 Jul. 2021.
Williams, Sarah F. *Damnable Practises: Witches, Dangerous Women, and Music in Seventeenth-Century English Broadside Ballads.* Routledge, 2020.

Liminal Spaces and Identity in *Grimm*

Andrea Yingling

"Let me put it this way," Monroe says as he is surrounded by twinkling Christmas lights and the whirr of an antique toy train, "the first time you feel the surge and you fang-out, it is pretty weird. I bit through my lip, I ripped my pants. It scared the crap out of me" (S1, E7: "Let your Hair Down"). He is describing the experience of his first woge: the transition Wesen go through to change between humanlike appearance and their animalistic counterpart. In Monroe's case, he transitioned into a *Blutbad*, a creature that resembles a werewolf. That Wesen must learn to balance these two identities—human and creature—results in their embodying a position of liminality. Their continuous potential for transition is demonstrated throughout the *Grimm* series by the liminal spaces that the characters inhabit. Such spaces are part of any transition—they are in-between, the interstice, where a person is *somewhere* yet not *anywhere* in particular. These spaces can be physical or mental: a parking garage, an abandoned building, or a state of transition between, for example, a human and a *Blutbad*.

Ethnographer and folklorist Arnold van Gennep first introduces the concept of liminality in *The Rites of Passage,* where he outlines the three stages of social transitions: separation, transition/liminal, and reincorporation.[1] Expanding on these works, anthropologist Mary Douglas has explored the nature of the middle phase, or the *marge* (the margin or edge), as van Gennep sometimes terms it. The liminal condition, according to Douglas, is perilous. In discussing the liminal state's implications, she emphasizes that people who are inhabiting the second phase of a transition, wherein they have exited one place in society, are fully engulfed in their transition. They become exiles as they "have been in the margins," and to be so is "to have been in contact with danger, to have been at a source of power."[2] Theorists like Douglas recognize that the in-between state of a transition has the potential to alienate a person from their community, especially if there is a lack of ritualized reintegration at completion. Gennep argues that a person is included in society when in a pretransitional state but removed or excluded while in transition. This exclusion is the time of liminality that Victor Turner dubs the "betwixt and between."[3]

This "betwixt and between" state often coincides with physical spaces where transitions occur. According to cultural anthropologist David I. Kertzer, "the land between two territories is often accorded a kind of sacrality, a sacrality that van Gennep identifies with the *marge*,"[4] and it is these sacred, betwixt and between places that *Grimm* (2011–17) portrays in the spaces that Wesen, *Kehrseite-Schlich-Kennen,ennen,*[5] and Grimms occupy. Wesen occupy a particularly complex state of liminality within the series' fictional world. Modernity has upset the hierarchy of a world where humans were traditionally Wesen prey, relegating Wesen and their "monstrous biology" into a subjugated status. At the same time, Grimms operate in secrecy and *Kehrseite-Schlich-Kennen* are increasingly rare. This essay explores liminality in physical space, time, and community structure within *Grimm* and how various characters demonstrate different aspects of the *marge*—the loss of identity brought about by a failure to reintegrate into society.

Throughout the series, Nick Burkhardt, the protagonist who discovers he is a Grimm, acts as a catalyst for the rising forces challenging the hierarchal order of the Wesen community. He troubles the status quo that has shaped the modern experience of Wesen. His refusal to affirm the established Wesen hierarchy places Nick on the outside of an already marginalized community, destabilizing his identity and that of any Wesen with whom he interacts. However, his liminality is not just related to the Wesen community. Throughout the series, Nick experiences significant personal transformation, which also facilitates the total collapse of his first romantic partner in the show, Juliette Silverton's, identity. She ultimately creates a new persona as the first of her kind: Eve. Nick's next romantic partner, Adalind Schade, is also driven deeply into the *marge* after coming into contact with Nick, eventually turning to motherhood to pursue a post-transitional equilibrium. Captain Sean Renard, with whom she shares her first child and who is Nick's boss, demonstrates an amplified version of Wesen liminality in his half–*Zauberbiest* status and historical liminality as a representation of the Royal families as they struggle against modernity. Monroe, a Wesen who becomes an indispensable friend to Nick, exhibits another kind of liminality concerning the crises of historical change. Monroe is the betwixt and between the old ways and the new:

he is the timekeeper of the *Grimm* world, helping usher in a new way of life for the Wesen, accepting their dual identities live within society. Each of these characters strives for equilibrium and integration, a final state where they can fully reincorporate into the latest structure of an ever-changing world.

Nick Burkhardt: A Grimm Identity

Throughout the series, Nick's transition manifests mentally and physically. Although he was born a Grimm, he was unaware of his powers until adulthood. Before they emerged, Nick led a fulfilling life as a successful police detective in a stable relationship with his live-in girlfriend, Juliette. Therefore, as he transitions into his new role as a Grimm, it is difficult to reconcile his new identity as a person in the *marge*. During his transitional period, where he is learning how to accept his role as a Grimm, Nick begins to lose his position in society—not just established mental and bodily places, but also societal places.

In becoming a Grimm, he must transition from his identities as a dutiful policing professional, best friend and police partner to Hank, and devoted boyfriend to Juliette to an unfamiliar and uncertain space. Denoting this transition, Nick is portrayed with various liminal spaces such as bridges, woods, and his Aunt Marie's trailer. One particularly emphatic example is the house where he lives with Juliette at the beginning of the series. At first, this space appears stable and static, occupied by a stable couple about to r affirm that stability ritualistically through an engagement. However, Nick later proclaims that this was never meant to be a permanent home; despite appearances, this seemingly permanent space is actively constructed as liminal (S2, E2: "The Kiss"). Its uncanny tentativeness is reinforced visually within the house by a portrait of St. John's Bridge hung in the stairwell. The symbolic representation of liminality doubles by depicting a transitional space between one place to another placed (the portrait of the bridge) within a transitional space (the staircase).

The impermanent house and its features are only one set of signifiers of Nick's liminality. His transitional period is also represented by another significant space, his Aunt Marie's Trailer. The trailer is important to him for what it contains, journals, records, and weapons that help his Grimm pursuits. It also links him with his family and heritage.[6] This trailer is set on wheels: it is a place of potential motion and instability and is unto itself a place of potential transience and liminality. Rather than keeping the trailer near home, Nick parks it at the Forest Hills Storage facility, a place of impermanence where people store the marginalia of their lives (S4, E5: "Cry Luison"). Nick's choice to place the trailer in a storage facility reflects the furtive and liminal status of being a Grimm: it is hidden in plain sight. Similarly, the trailer is a physical representation of Wesen transformation—it is a modern piece of equipment. Yet, upon entering, one is taken to a place outside of time where artifacts and books recount hundreds of years of Grimm and Wesen conflict. The history contained in the trailer is on the marge, separated and hidden from society at large. In his mental state of *marge*, Nick frequently seeks the sanctuary of this twofold liminal space during the first three seasons. In this space, Nick can contemplate his transition to a Grimm without having to perform an identity. This trailer is a place where Nick does not have to act but considers how to act.

After the transitional period of the first three seasons, Nick's identity as a Grimm begins to stabilize. Beginning with season four, the spaces he occupies demonstrate a greater stability as he begins the reintegration process. As he begins training with ancestral weapons, his Grimm identity coalesces, and he is better able to rejoin society. During this process, Nick moves the trailer to a more permanent patch of land in the woods (S3, E22: "Blond Ambition"). While still symbolic of impermanence, Nick demonstrates a greater sense of stability through this translocation. Although the forest remains outside of society, indicating an identity in the margins, it is also a place where he has chosen to set roots.

The newfound "permanence" of his ancestral possessions speaks to Nick's choice to embrace the identity of a Grimm. When first discovered, this seemed a fated, inevitable identity. He was born into his abilities and was unable to deny his family's responsibility. However, in the same episode in which he relocated the trailer, his arch-rival Adalind, a *Hexenbiest* or witch-like creature, takes his powers: this gives him the opportunity of living as a Grimm or returning to life as a human (albeit a *Kehrseite*, one who knows of Wesen existence). In this way, he can take control of his transition. Thus, Nick has a choice: he can deny his Grimm identity and return to a peaceful life with Juliette or go through a process to reinstate his powers.

When the opportunity to regain his powers presents itself, Nick's decision is not easy because the implications extend beyond fixing his identity. Learning of the risks Juliette must take for him to regain his powers, Nick seems firm in his decision to remain a *Kehrseite*, yet his dialogue indicates that he mourns the loss of his powers. In the most meaningful conversation Nick has about his lost powers, he tells Monroe that it would be very appealing to "pack up" the idea of being a Grimm, move someplace new and "start a family" with Juliette. However, Nick says, "the problem is, I like being a Grimm, Monroe. [...] and I'm pissed that it was taken away from me" (S4, E5). It turns out that Nick was indeed fated to be a Grimm because the only element of resistance disappears. Later in the episode, Juliette turns to him and says, "you need to be a Grimm again." With the decision made, Nick returns to a liminal state of Grimm-ness, now able to fully transition and ultimately reintegrate into society with the realization that this is the life that he and Juliette ultimately want. Ironically, this choice throws Juliette into a state of perpetual liminality and takes away her identity completely, which will be explored shortly.

Throughout the series, Nick is frequently haunted by Aunt Marie's words, where she advised Nick to leave Juliette (S1, E1: "Pilot"). She urged him to leave his old life behind and completely embrace his new position as a Grimm, stating that he would be putting Juliette in danger if he stays. Nick has to choose between the two fixed points concerning Juliette: stay or go. Ultimately, Nick followed the advice of his mother, later given by his long-absent mother, not to abandon someone he loves because he would live to regret it (S2, E2). The push and pull place him in a liminal mental state regarding Juliette, where he carried guilt and fear because of her ever-increasing danger.

Juliette's perpetual liminality in relationship to Nick, mainly manifested by restoring Nick's powers, enhances his increasing stability when she destroys his trailer (S4, E19: "Iron Hans"). This destruction has a two-fold effect upon his Grimm liminality. It symbolically forces Nick to fully integrate his new identity and leave his last space of impermanence. This effectively ends the guilt he felt about Juliette. She destroys the symbolic representation of his Grimm identity, forcing him to recognize that his abilities and identity are within. Many of the weapons and some books were salvaged, and Nick can take these to a place of equilibrium, the Spice and Tea Shop. Its physical permanence is reinforced by the marital permanence of the owner, his friend Rosalee, a *Fuchsbau*, to Monroe. Even the destroyed ancient Wesen books are later replaced in this space. Nick's identity as a Grimm is no longer confined to a perpetually liminal space; instead, it resides in a brick-and-mortar safe house owned by his dearest friends.

Although Nick faces mental distress and anxiety about his choices in relation to Juliette for the remainder of the show, comfort in his identity as a Grimm increasingly intensifies. His physical, relational, and reintegrated social spaces in the show grow increasingly stable. After he and Adalind become parents and subsequently partners, he abandons the transitional home shared with Juliette and chose a fortress/home or "fome," as Adalind dubs it (S5, E3: "Lost Boys"). The new dwelling is post-liminal, a space that was intended as a warehouse, a place associated with storage and waiting for permanence, now converted into a home, fitting the protagonist's status. This loft will be the scene of much bloodshed during the last two seasons of the show. However, it is where they create a family unit, completing the final stage of Nick's transition. Placed in a permanent home with a role in a family as father and partner, Nick completes the cycle and reintegrates into society.

Nick's new, solidified identity is further displayed when his bodily space is challenged. When transformed into Renard using Adalind's infamous spell, Nick is at first unable to pass behaviorally. His friends coach him to be "a little more Renard-y," and help him recreate appropriate mannerisms (S6, E3: "Oh Captain, My Captain"). This moment contrasts with other transformations, such as when Adalind becomes Juliette or when Eve becomes Renard (S3, E22; S5, E16: "The Believer"). In these transformations, characters were able to impersonate and embody a new identity without coaching or hesitation; these body doubles were so convincing that they could engage sexually without their partners noting the difference. Nick, however, maintained his identity even when first occupying Renard's body with little understanding of how to be Renard and not Nick. This demonstrates Nick's solidified character: his identity is so strong that it can occupy a separate bodily space yet remain psychically intact.

Juliette / Eve: Rebirth and Liminality

Juliette's identity is the most fractured of all characters in *Grimm*, as indicated by her name change to Eve and the increasingly liminal spaces she occupies. In fact, as Eve, she is eventually homeless, couch-surfing among Nick's loft, Renard's house, The Spice and Tea Shop, Monroe and Rosalee's house, the headquarters of Hadrian Wall, and abandoned underground tunnels. Her character has no space of her own as her transformation unfolds over the course of several rebirths.

Juliette's first rebirth happens when she wakes from the coma brought about by Adalind's potion, which had been meant to erase Juliette's memories of Nick (S2, E2). After waking, her mental state becomes increasingly fractured and is symbolized by the black holes that appear in her living space. These black holes seem infinitely deep, denoting the gaps left in her mind by erased memories of Nick. Juliette is a professional woman at this point in the series. She has a substantial and fulfilling career as a veterinarian, but the mental black holes that infiltrate her living space create havoc and begin to destroy her hitherto stable life. Juliette attempts to keep living within her former societal roles. She tries to maintain the same psychological and physical state she had always embodied, but the outside world continuously thrusts change upon her. The changes from the outside world force change on Juliette, both physical and psychological. The next rebirth marks the end of Juliette's identity: she becomes a *Hexenbiest* as a direct result of the spell used to bring back Nick's Grimm abilities. His complete acceptance of his identity denies Juliette her identity as a human, relationships, and career.

The first time Juliette encounters herself as a *Hexenbiest* reflected in a mirror, she screams: This non-recognition and horror at her reflection symbolize the lapse in her identity (S4, E8: "Chupacabra"). Her new reality as a *Hexenbiest* is terrifying on a physical level, but at this point, Juliette is unaware of how terrified she should be; this transformation causes the final and unequivocal rupture from Nick as a romantic partner, ultimately leading to Juliette's complete identity collapse. Recognizing Nick's disgust for her as a *Hexenbiest*, she grows increasingly resentful and engages in risky behaviors. These behaviors eventually lead her to try and kill Nick in what used to be their home. During this scene, as they fight, the portrait of Portland's St. John's Bridge that has always hung in their stairwell is visible. Likewise, after Trubel, another young Grimm shoots Juliette, another larger image of Portland and the St. John's Bridge is visible behind Trubel (S4, E22: "Cry Havoc"). These two portraits of the bridge represent the transition that Juliette faces. She has been in a state of increasing liminality throughout season four, and now she must cross the bridge to her new identity as Eve in an attempt to reincorporate into society.

The labyrinthian nature of Portland allows for maze-like structures while also providing spaces of respite for Juliette. According to Stefan L. Brandt, cityscapes often lend themselves to liminality because of their maze-like structure.[7] The postmodern cityscape, such as *Grimm's* Portland, creates labyrinthian features that mimic a character's whirling mental state.[8] Nevertheless, sometimes these labyrinths offer a respite, a place for a character to gain a semblance of control. The underground labyrinthian headquarters of Hadrian's Wall (HW), a secret society of Wesen who later employ Eve and Trubel includes separate rooms for the people who are working for HW. When Juliette is taken to HW, she is kept in a separate room while she heals. Juliette's room at HW is one of these womb-like respites: a space where Juliette's character can be reborn as Eve.

Unfortunately, Eve has the same curse as Juliette: she can never find equilibrium and a nonliminal space for herself. The first destabilization of Eve is when her birthplace and home, HW headquarters, is destroyed (S5, E21: "The Beginning of the End"). She then undergoes yet another death and rebirth during season six, when she is killed and revived by a magical stick, an ancient artifact with incredible healing powers.[9] Once revived, she has a severe seizure and finds herself unable to woge, a dangerous position for her character. The inability makes her non-transitional, which in this case is not the same thing as stable. She has the urge to transition, and the *Hexenbiest* remains within, but she cannot access this side of her identity. This places Eve deep in the *marge* socially: she homeless and apparently useless to HW, no longer called to fight. Eventually, Eve spends an unspecified amount of time in the tunnels beneath Nick's fome (S6, E5: "The Seven Year Itch"). She carves symbols on the walls, all the while becoming physically weaker. Her body is not her own. She later says that she tried to leave the tunnels several times, but her body would not let her. At this point, her liminality is at its deepest; she is in the literal transitional labyrinth of the underground tunnels, unable to control her body, and she is between two bodily states, neither Wesen nor human.

Eve inhabits liminality that poses dangers to the entire *Grimm* world. After Adalind finds and brings her back to the surface from the tunnels, her identity crisis nearly destroys the human world.[10] Eve tries to regain some sort of autonomy after this rebirth, telling Adalind that she could not continue to stay at their loft. Further, when trying to understand her identity, Eve's gazing into a mirror accidentally opens a portal into another time and place. When she gazes again into a mirror, she asks her image, "Who were you? Who are you now?" (S6, E8: "The Son Also Rises"). Seeking an identity causes a skeleton man to reach through the portal to grab her neck, causing Eve to regain her ability to woge. When she throws the mirror, it shatters, just like her identity has from the time of Juliette; however, the pieces realign, and the mirror becomes covered in her blood. This blood-covered mirror, fractured and then realigned, reflects Eve's identity through the series while registering as a liminal space. It is a transition between Portland and the world of the Skeleton Man, a Wesen with the potential to destroy Eve's world.

Eve's reintegration into society begins with her acceptance of perpetual liminality. Although her character never again establishes a space of her own, she can assert herself as a liminal figure, explaining to Nick that they are not who they used to be and never would be again. She explains that they only knew a fraction of themselves (S6, E13: "The End"). Thus, she begins to rebuild an identity, although viewers never see her reach a real point of equilibrium, and she is absent from the flash-forward at the end of the final episode, indicating that she may very well live in a state of perpetual liminality after the show ends.

Adalind Schade: Motherhood and Liminality

Nick's reattainment of his Grimm identity has a similarly destabilizing effect upon Adalind Schade, the *Hexenbiest* who begins the series as Nick's nemesis and eventually becomes his romantic partner and the mother of his son. *Hexenbiests* are uniquely accepting of their status. They are portrayed as living in the mainstream of society rather than marginalized, as many Wesen seem to be. Many hold powerful positions, as do their male counterparts, *Zauberbiests*. What makes Adalind's liminality especially striking is that she is the first indication of Nick's ability to see as a Grimm. When first introduced to Adalind, she is a high-powered lawyer with a full social life, a beautiful apartment, and a close relationship with her mother. Later, Nick dismantles her life by taking away her powers (S1, E17: "Love Sick"). With the loss of her powers, Adalind is separated from her matriarch and heritage. She explains, "you killed me [...] I'm nothing now. I don't have any powers. You've taken everything. I'm just like everybody else. I'm nothing."[11] Adalind's identity is fractured by the loss of her powers and further dismantled by her mother's death. In the language of liminal objects, this is rendered in the shattering of two mirrors during the fight culminating in her mother's death. These broken mirrors denote Adalind's destroyed identity; moreover, unlike Eve's one broken mirror, Adalind's two broken mirrors signify two identities fracturing, both *Hexenbiest* and independent-career woman. The fracturing of her identities throws her unwillingly into the second stage of transition that places her out of her social location, making her very dangerous.

Pregnancy and motherhood eventually create a new identity and equilibrium for Adalind. Nevertheless, her first pregnancy deepens her status of marge, rather than concretizing her identity or reincorporating her society. While pregnant, she is in constant transition. Geographically, she travels to Vienna, living in a state of fear and uncertainty. She stays as a guest in a not resident of a castle and hotel—all the while performing the last rituals of a spell that will help her regain her powers. Often Wesen learn to see themselves as occupying a constant state of physical liminality, neither human nor other at the same time. For Adalind, this liminal state is compounded during her pregnancy with Diana[12] because, at this point, Adalind is not fully human yet is also no longer a *Hexenbiest*.

Adalind loses her autonomy once she becomes a mother. From that moment forward in the series, she occupies a series of liminal spaces. Her dependency is first demonstrated by the stark change of setting for Adalind after becoming pregnant for the first time. While she is pregnant with Diana, she stayed in a hotel. Then, she is whisked away to a shabby cabin in the woods, where she gives birth to Diana (S3, E14: "Mommy Dearest"). Over the next two episodes, Adalind and her baby move from one liminal space to another. She thereby inhabits two identities at once: she is the person Adalind, but she is also the physical means of transportation to safety for her daughter, which is also Adalind's safety. Adalind's experience in the transitional state of individual/not individual is shown by her changing clothing and demeanor. Rather than the high-powered suits, sexy dresses, and high heels of pre-pregnancy Adalind, this new mother often wears soft jeans, baggy sweaters, and flat-heeled boots. In addition, her hair is styled in softer waves rather than the flat-iron straight of her previous, professional self, her gaze is wider-eyed, suggesting a kind of innocence, and she even speaks more softly (at least in non-urgent contexts).

At first, being coded as a mother is problematic for Adalind's former identification as the intelligent, crafty, educated woman who killed without regret: Now, her purpose is to provide and protect life while she is herself in need of protection. When she has Diana with her, she does not act. Instead, she is led by other characters, following obediently though in ignorance. When she finally asks of Nick's mother, Kelly, during her flight from the Royals, "where are you taking me?" Kelly refuses to tell her anything specific. She only acknowledges that "we're going to get in that plane. That's all you need to know." Adalind again demands where they are going but is rebuffed and resigns herself to powerlessness (S3, E17: "Synchronicity"). Adalind occupies a mental and physical liminality so extensive at this point that she is not allowed to see where her transition might lead: once on the plane, she has no idea where she is going, literally and figuratively, nor what agency she can have in that decision.

When pregnant with Nick's son Kelly,[13] Adalind is again placed in a state of bodily liminality, but with more volitional agency. She drinks a potion that suppresses her powers as a *Hexenbiest* to gain Nick's trust. Her need for Nick's help and confidence demonstrates her lack of autonomy while pregnant (S4, E20: "You Don't Know Jack"). She is quite literally powerless during both pregnancies, placing her in a vulnerable state of perpetual mid-transition. In this instance, she is still a *Hexenbiest* but has no access to her power. This is a uniquely mid-transitional state because she knows she will regain these powers. However, during her pregnancy, when a woman is extremely vulnerable, she cannot defend herself.

Within increasing momentum toward a new, maternal and domestic identity, she turns to Nick to regain equilibrium and falls in love with him. Once her *Hexenbiest* powers return, Nick can accept and continue to love her in line with his own transition and integration. With this second return of powers, she is also able to maintain her unthreatening identity because her powers we unsought. Mirrors again emerge as a signifier of identity: this time as an integration rather than loss. Her identity becomes entwined with Nick's, as she affirms, "I won't be looking into any mirrors without you," indicating that she is unwilling to see herself without Nick. Her children also foster her equilibrium, and wherever they are, she can make a home. The brick-and-mortar structures no longer matter to Adalind so long as Diana, Kelly, and Nick are there.

Monroe: Time, Heritage, and Liminality

Monroe's character exemplifies the transitional phase that Wesen experience throughout this series. Monroe is first introduced as a curious mixture of the old world and new. As a *Blutbad*, he marks or spreads his scent around his home, but he is also vegan and does Pilates to curb his more carnivorous appetites. In addition to being a horologist by trade, Monroe is also highly knowledgeable about ancient Wesen history (S1, E1). Monroe's occupation, fixing stopped clocks, indicates his state as a Wesen: he feels perpetually liminal, yet he wishes to continue accepting modernity within the Wesen community. His fascination with all things antique while living in modernity is the perfect example of the dual poles of the transitional state that Wesen experience. As Nick says, Monroe has "too much time on [his] hands," offering multiple readings of liminality and transformation (S1, E7).

Monroe often expresses the difficulty of suppressing his *Blutbad* instincts during the series. His struggle is a central theme for his character. The first season focuses on his mental journey, revealing his efforts with support groups and therapy to help accept his liminal state as Wesen (S1, E21: "Big Feet"). Some Wesen seek support from a Wesen psychologist, Dr. Konstantin Brinkerhoff,[14] who specializes in this transitional state: he publishes books. He holds conferences about the idea that Wesen are constantly fighting a battle between their humanity and their inner Wesen selves. Brinkerhoff speaks of the Wesen identity as a separate entity that needs compassion, suggesting Wesen think of their inner self as a "stray dog" that should not be feared because it is "base and primitive."[15]

The Wesen of the Portland region seem to concur with Brinkerhoff's analysis of their liminality and subsequent identity confusion: his book talk is packed with those seeking advice. Unfortunately, his experimental herbal drug meant to keep Wesen in their human form backfires. When the *Wildermann*, a type of Wesen who resemble the mythical Big Foot, try this herbal implant, they become stuck in a woged state and are in mental and physical anguish. Trying to deny a portion of their identity causes nothing but chaos and death. Monroe serves as a contrast to this rejection of the inner self, accepting himself as *Blutbad* and working through his more violent tendencies rather than denying his Wesen side altogether. This allows him to lead a less liminal lifestyle: he can live in a house, hold a job, and later have a fulfilling relationship. On the other hand, these *Wildermanns* who try to deny their liminal state cannot function and eventually die.[16]

Although he has adaptive behaviors, Monroe does not always have the easiest time accepting his transitional identity. He finds his role as the friend of a Grimm to be especially difficult to trust, particularly early in their friendship. Early in the series, Monroe is the most crucial person in Nick's identity transition, as he is the only one to know of Nick's Grimm identity. However, raised in a traditional *Blutbad* household, Monroe was taught to hate and fear Grimms. As a result, his liminality between the old world and new is frequently called into question during his budding friendship with Nick. For example, during Nick's first encounter with a family of *Jägerbar*, a type of Wesen who resemble bears, Monroe is asked to guard Aunt Marie (S1, E2: "Bears Will Be Bears"). While initially refusing the task, he eventually acquiesces. Although in doing so, he recounts a time when a Grimm killed a family member. Monroe explains that his family would be distraught if they knew he was guarding a Grimm, illustrating the mental entanglement in his new role. Adding a new facet to Monroe's already liminal state causes him to become exceptionally violent when he discovers the men who have come for Aunt Marie, even stating afterward that things went "a little too far."[17]

However, because Monroe can accept his dual identities, he can find peace with his liminality and, therefore, always has a distinctly stable space in Portland. His attempts to create balance are reflected by his home, which borders the city and a park. Later, he finds further stability in his relationship with Rosalee. Together, in addition to a home, they share the Exotic Spice & Tea Shop, a place of permanence for the show's main characters.

Captain Renard: Being Comfortable with Being Liminal

Even among Wesen, Captain Renard has a uniquely liminal status. As a half-human, half–*Zauberbiest* born from a royal extra-marital affair, he occupies a liminal space within the community. He is neither an entirely magical being nor human royalty. Socially above Wesen, he is considered beneath his legitimately-born brother and Royals at large. Living in Portland places him in a liminal setting on the coast of the United States surrounded by forests. This, it seems, is among the most marginal locale Renard could have found for himself away from his family in Europe.

Further enforcing liminality, he is often placed in spaces of transition, such as parking garages. Indeed, he commits his first atrocity against his family in a parking garage, killing his cousin and longtime chauffeur to protect Nick (S1, E17: "Love Sick"). This is where Renard takes his first steps toward protecting a Grimm and turning against the Royals. It is an essential transition for his character and the Wesen community, which upsets a centuries-old hierarchy.

Unlike other characters in *Grimm*, Renard seems comfortable with his liminality and seems to relish and embrace his transient nature. He occupies many spaces within Portland, frequently changing his abode from a house, to an apartment, to a hotel room. However, he does not seem attached to any of these homes and appears unbothered by relocating from one to the next. The most permanent place he occupies is his office in the center of the precinct. This is where the transitional nature of his personality can maintain a space of permanence. His office mimics the womb-like room Eve occupied at the center of HW headquarters. As Terrie Waddell in her book *Wild/lives: Trickster, Place and Liminality on Screen* writes, characters in perplexing psychic liminal spaces often have these womb-like retreats where they can gather equilibrium.[18]

Like his *Hexenbiest* counterparts Adalind and Juliette, Renard is often connected to mirrors. The signification is especially prominent when he explores a change of identity and talks to himself in mirrors. For example, when taking a potion to make his heart pure to break Juliette's sleeping spell (the coma brought on by Adalind's potion), he woges while looking in a mirror. He struggles to return to his human form during another transition, telling himself to "get a grip" (S2, E2) disgusted with losing control of his identities. This liminal space is uncomfortable for him because he did not choose this woge, but he quickly regains the control typical of Renard's character.

He has a similar fascination with mirrors during his tenure as Jack the Ripper (S4, E20: "You Don't Know Jack"; S4, E21: "Headache"). When he feels himself losing control and realizes that unwelcome identity possesses him, he leans into the closest mirror, searching his body and face for recognition. This is the closest Renard's character comes to losing control of his multiple identities and the liminal space he occupies. When transitioning into Jack, not only is it physically painful, it is also terrifying because he is powerless in this identity shift. Like Eve's transition into the mirror world, the completion of Renard's transformation into Jack is marked by blood on a mirror. This blood spell is a potential catalyst to end Renard's liminality and reincorporate into Jack forever. In fact, his Jack-self writes, "Welcome back, Jack," signaling the beginning of his final transformation. Renard's subsequent death and rebirth were the only way Renard could return to his primary identity.

Renard's words could be no more revealing than when he told Meisner,[19] the leader of HW, "I never choose sides" (S5, E21). Unlike others in *Grimm*, Renard is comfortable with his multiple identities as a character of perpetual liminality. The strength of his identity is so pervasive that two characters take a potion to transform into him over the course of the series physically. Renard, on the other hand, never changes his body into that of another. He only changes within, and as long as he has control over this change, he is comfortable with it.

Wesen of the Week: Liminal Bodies in Liminal Spaces

The *marge* is not exclusive to the main characters of the show. The Wesen-of-the-week not only occupy liminal mental and bodily spaces but also often live in marginalized settings. Rather than garnering acceptance, modernity's changes have pushed them even farther into the *marge*, creating newer liminal settings and causing difficulties within the Wesen community. This marginalization is often seen in the liminal settings they occupy in their careers and homes. Many, especially those at the extremes of the "food chain," are either extremely rich or extremely poor. Like the Royals, many Wesen are incredibly wealthy, such as the *Jägerbars* and *Murciélago*. (S1, E2; S1, E20: "Happily Ever Aftermath"). These wealthy Wesen tend to choose homes that border forests, bridging the modern and the ancient. By contrast, extremely poor Wesen tend to be placed close to bridges, rivers, and rocky cliffs. For example, a small family of *Reinigen*, a rat-like Wesen, occupies a trailer, a liminal structure because of its potential transient nature, under a bridge (S1, E5: "Danse Macabre"). As illustrated by the son Roddy, a talented musician, who attends a posh private school, they strive for social mobility. However, he cannot overcome his marginalized status and is shunned by the other students and their families because of his discordant poverty and talent. Instead, he chooses to occupy ever more liminal settings, DJing in abandoned warehouses and spending time with his caged pet rats under a bridge.

Bridges serve as a common theme throughout the series among marginalized Wesen, mainly when an episode focuses on modernity encroaching upon tradition. The *Eisbiber*s, beaver-like Wesen, undergo this sort of transformation when liberated from the *Hässlich*, a trollish Wesen, who seek to uphold the old ways of forcing those who wish to build bridges to pay a toll (S1, E19: "Leave it To Beavers"). When Sal, a *Hässlich*, murders a prominent *Eisbiber*, it is under a bridge. Later in the episode, viewers may note pictures of bridges on every wall of Sal's office. The *Hässlich* wish to control the liminal space of bridges by controlling their construction.

The bridges of this episode serve two symbolic purposes in terms of liminal transitions. First, the *Eisbiber* bridge-builders are eventually freed from the *Hässlich,* the trollish Wesen, who hold a mafia-like monopoly on bridge construction in Portland. With Nick's help, they build and cross this figurative bridge into their new identity in modernity, free from control. Secondly, these bridges symbolize Nick's identity shift as he embraces his Grimm identity and begins training with his ancestral weapons. Contrary to his police training to act as a Grimm, Nick kills two Wesen reapers and illegally disposing of their bodies. This episode marks the beginning of his journey or crossing the bridge to accepting his complete Grimm identity.

On the other hand, in the case of the *Inugami*, a ghost-like dog Wesen, bridges are used to perpetuate liminality in order to exact punishment (S5, E17: "Inugami"). The *Inugami* throw the heads of their victims under bridges to prevent them from reaching the afterlife. This ritual is sacred and leaves their victim in endless agony, unable to find a liminal resolution, reinforcing the symbolic importance of liminality among the Wesen.[20]

Many Wesen-of-the-week episodes focus upon those unwilling to integrate into modernity and seek to persist in traditions and rituals, placing these Wesen in various liminal spaces. Exemplifying this, a *Jägerbar* family seeks to continue the ancient tradition of *Roh-hatz*, a murderous coming-of-age ritual (S1, E2). While the father is the picture of modern Wesenhood, wearing suits and providing a comfortable, well-maintained home for his family, he remains unaware of the wife and son's plans. Yet, his family is still living in a liminal space between modernity and wilderness past, in a large house in the forest. The son and his friends all display tribal tattoos denoting their position as *Jägerbar*, and his wife is supportive of the boys completing the *Roh-hatz* ritual. Their identity is changing in the modern world, and although the family's patriarch is trying to settle into modernity, the others yearn for the old ways. Yet, the father demonstrates respect for the old ways and potential internal conflict by keeping relics and displaying tribal symbols in their home. Even though the father is against the bloody *Roh-hatz*, he eventually conveys his internal conflict to Nick when he says, "you don't understand what it means to lose your heritage."

Conclusion

Liminality is not meant to be a place of dwelling, physically or psychologically. Wesen are forced to inhabit an enduring transition state, leading some on a path of destruction and danger. The only resolution is abandoning their transitional state and reintegrating into society, which is impossible for some Wesen communities. Wesen are further subjugated by their inability to carry out traditions and rituals that were historically symbolic of their entrance into Wesenhood and reintegration into Wesen society following their first woge. Because modernity encroaches upon their heritage and place in the *Grimm* world, Wesen are unique in their bodily liminality.

Nevertheless, whether a magical *Hexenbiest* or *Zauberbiest*, Wesen or Grimm, characters' transitional stages in liminal spaces with identity crises experienced throughout the series. Because *Grimm* explores these concepts of liminality, Portland, with its unique location near both forests and water, offers an ideal setting for the *Grimm* world. The city also has various overlapping transit systems, with streets that cross over rivers, light rail, and an underground system that lends itself to secret travel. Thus, it is an ideal representative space for characters to enact their transitions while also offering permanent space for those perpetually in the *marge*.

Notes

1. See van Gennep.
2. Douglas 269.
3. See Turner.
4. See the introduction to Arnold van Gennep *The Rites of Passage*, 2nd ed.
5. Humans who know about Wesen.
6. This relationship is introduced in the episode S1, E2: "Bears Will be Bears."
7. See Brandt.
8. *Ibid.*
9. *Ibid.*
10. *Ibid.*
11. *Ibid.*
12. Full name: Diana Schade-Renard. Actor (child): Hannah R. Loyd.
13. He is named in honor of his grandmother, Kelly Schade-Burkhardt. Character primarily appears as infant or very young child and was played by several actors.
14. Actor: Roger Bart.
15. See Brandt.
16. *Ibid.*
17. *Ibid.*
18. See Waddell's Introduction to *Wild/Lives*.
19. Actor, Damien Puckler.
20. *La Llorona* and the *Naiads* also demonstrate the importance of liminality to Wesen and would constitute an exciting study.

Works Cited

Brandt, Stefan L. "The City as Liminal Space: Urban Visuality and Aesthetic Experience in Postmodern U.S. Literature and Cinema." *Amerikastudien/American Studies*, vol. 54, no. 4, 2009, pp. 553–581.
Carpenter, Stephen, Jim Kouf, and David Greenwalt, creators. *Grimm*. NBC, 2011.
Douglas, Mary. *Purity and Danger: An Analysis of Concept of Pollution and Taboo*. Routledge, 2007.
Gennep, Arnold van. *The Rites of Passage*. 2nd ed., University of Chicago Press, 2019.
Turner, Victor W. *The Ritual Process: Structure and Anti-structure*. Routledge, 1995.
Waddell, Terrie. *Wild/lives: Trickster, Place and Liminality on Screen*. Routledge, 2010.

Opening the Trailer Door to Queer Possibilities

Daniel Farr

Airing from 2011 to 2017, the series *Grimm* builds upon a tradition of genre-blending television. Categories such as "crime, drama, and fantasy"[1] or "fantasy police procedural drama"[2] have been the primary descriptors of this series. However, many of its key elements, such as grotesque and monstrous bodies, mutilation, dismemberment, and storylines of violence, cannibalism, and rituals, align with the horror genre. Indeed, the brief series description accompanying the DVD release of Season 1 denotes "series that critics rave 'offers genuine scares.'"[3] Horror offers opportunities to explore nuanced issues of socially contentious issues, such as racial inequalities, class conflicts, environmental issues, as well as gender and sexuality. Like most horror film and television content,[4] *Grimm* primarily engages queer visibility through symbolic and implicit portrayals. Yet, for a series based upon a heteronormative cast of characters and plot lines, it also offers a rich opportunity for queer readings.

Set in Portland, Oregon, an American city with one of the highest rates of LGBT residence[5] and produced in a period of significant socio-political transformation for lesbian, gay, bisexual, transgender, and queer (LGBTQ) rights,[6] *Grimm* offers little explicit visibility in any component of the show. Among the main characters, none are identified as LGBTQ, and nearly all are linked to a heterosexual romantic relationship. There is very little reference to queer-identified persons throughout the series, and they are never referenced in the policing context of the series (i.e., sexually linked crimes, criminal/perpetrator/inmate identities, or even victims of crimes). This is surprising given the queer population of Portland and the disproportionately high risk of incarceration among LGB persons.[7] Additionally, LGBTQ are nearly four times likely to be victims of violent crime than heterosexuals.[8] One cannot help but question, in a series that centers on policing and violent crimes, albeit supernatural-oriented crimes, where are all the queer folk hiding?

Undertaking a queer analysis of a text, such as a television series, offers a rich opportunity to explore relationships, gender, sexuality, and social dynamics. The multiple identities present among many characters of this show, especially Wesen and Grimm, in part demonstrates the nuance in which we all negotiate and navigate our identities and their social expressions in varying circumstances. Once understood as a primarily derogatory term, the conceptual meaning of queer has transformed to speak to varied interpretative meaning and may be used as noun, adjective, verb, or adverb.[9] Analysis linked to gender and sexuality, especially non-normative sexual and gender identities, have been particularly informative to queer aesthetics and fostered thinking beyond simplistic binary ideologies. Recent decades have demonstrated increased queer presence across many forms of media, with notably increased visibility of gay, lesbian, bisexual, and transgender (LGBT) characters and plots in television[10] and film.[11] Despite cultural shifts and increasing visibility of LGBT characters on television, *Grimm* seems to have surprisingly limited inclusion at first read. Yet, looking below the surface speaks to an exceptional queer aesthetic, demonstrating the varied and fluid manners people experience gender, sexuality, and identity.

Visibility: Problematic and Limited

More than perhaps ever before, today's audience is increasingly familiar with the inclusion of explicitly queer-identified characters. Accompanying a general increased cultural awareness of LGBTQ diversity, a heteronormative audience is increasingly able to draw upon a knowledge base of queer cues and markers that may be implicit in the media. Further, queer consumers are particularly astute at recognizing subtle references and characteristics of potential queerness informed by their cultural knowledge, as well as an ability to identify with storylines and characters that reflect their own identities. Viewing the first episode or pilot of a series often gives the audience a preview of what they might expect. Fans of fantasy and fairy-tale, as well as monsters, horror, and police drama, might all be attracted to this show. Programs are strategically developed to avoid the alienation of a potential fan base. Grimm is particularly conscious of including racial-ethnic diversity and representation but is problematic insofar as its LGBTQ inclusion and visibility.

In *Grimm*'s premiere episode (S1, E1: "Pilot") the central Wesen villain, a *Blutbad* (wolf-like creature) is portrayed in an interpretation of

54 Part One: Identity and Identification

what is understood to be the story of "Little Red Riding Hood." The central plot is the investigation by Detectives Nick Burkhardt and Hank Griffin of a child abduction—a little girl wearing a red hoodie. Simultaneous with this investigative process, Nick learns of his identity as a Grimm—a "special" person with inherited supernatural abilities, who is to hunt and protect the world from Wesen (creatures that are both human and monster). The girl never made it home from school, and her parents are seen being questioned on their front porch by police. On the one hand it may seem odd to have this occur upon the porch, rather than sat in a living room, but this offers an opportunity for the observant to note the house number of "1710," seen both above and beside the front door. Within numerology, the Angel Number 1710 is imbued with meanings briefly described as "you create our own realities,"[12] befitting the emerging journey of our Grimm and the new reality, a world of monsters, unfolding before him.

During the investigation of the missing girl, Nick and Hank are invited into the primary suspect's home. He appears as a soft-mannered man that some audience members may read as queer. This is reinforced within the scene as Hank comments upon a pillow, to which the suspect comments that he "did the needlepoint myself, not that I tell everyone." While sewing and needlecraft in a professional capacity, such as with tailoring, leatherwork, and fashion design, may be socially acceptable occupations for men, there is often an accompanying suspicion that one may be queer, especially within the field of fashion. Knowing our suspect is a postal carrier, this needlework is apparently related to a past-time or hobby, further bolstering audience suspicion that he may be gay. This ponderance is shortly reinforced when he must check on the cooking timer and pulling a pot pie from the oven, he comments, "you know how *delicate* crusts are" (emphasis added). These culturally feminized activities and language use suggest a queer identity, which can be "read" by the audience if so chosen. This reading is further reinforced by the casting of Tim Bagley in this role. He is an out actor and is known for playing gay roles.[13] While not portrayed here, the original tale tells of the wolf donning the grandmother's clothing in disguise—or what could be read as cross-dressing or drag.

While the series, at large, may be read as a queer allegory, the pilot episode's depiction of a likely queer Wesen child-kidnapper particularly feeds upon societal fears around the safety and value of children. Here a gentle-seeming and pleasant postal carrier who kidnaps children offers layers of interpretation. Among the most apparent reads is that one ought never judge a person based upon surface appearance. An impactful consideration in the case of Wesen, but also when one considers the idea that "monsters" may be hidden in plain sight—a kind-seeming, quiet man can be a predator of children, a *monster*. Monsters can be anywhere, even at your door delivering the mail. In this case, being a Wesen is irrelevant—kidnappers and their presumed nefarious intents are monsters unto themselves.

The poignantly stereotypical mythos linked to child abductors is that of inappropriate relations with children. Our perpetrator has a hidden room in his basement, set up as a bedroom for a girl. When hanging up his current victim's red hoodie in the closet, at least four other sweatshirts can be seen, suggesting he is a serial kidnapper. No straight answer is given about what was to happen to this girl or the prior presumed victims. However, given the Red Riding Hood allegory, one can assume that he intends to eat her—leaving the audience to wonder just what was in the pot pie. Many likely affiliate child abuse, especially sexual abuse, with kidnapping. Herein, the queer read of our *Blutbad* becomes especially problematic and frustrating. Having created a villain coded as queer, *Grimm* reifies cultural stereotypes that gay men are pedophiles and abusers of children. This myth of the gay pedophile mainly gained traction in the 1970s but has been repeatedly disproven.[14] While many may no longer believe gay men are pedophiles, this derogatory stereotype impacts cultural belief systems. This episode's imagery does little to counter this potential interpretation.

Moving from this initial queer imagery, consideration must also be given to victims of violence in the series, a mix of both human and Wesen. While it is impossible to know the sexual orientation and identities of all victims and episodic characters of this series, often, the audience is left to presume heterosexuality via markers of marriage and traditional gender portrayals. However, at least one instance is provided in which a couple can be read as lesbian. In its opening sequence, "Blood Magic" (S6, E10) introduces two women leaving a restaurant, "Café Nell," having had dinner. While there are no outward queer markers for the restaurant, the name may be picked up on by some, reminiscent of "nelly" or a stereotypically effeminate gay man. Their conversation and closeness offer multiple readings, open to interpretation: they may be two friends out to dinner, or equally, if not more plausible, they may be a lesbian couple. Their interactions and conversation convey a high level of intimacy and affection, with a notation that they have shared a dessert of crème brûlée. As one has "been in those heels all day," the other tells her to wait at the restaurant as she gets the car. Clearly, they had arrived at the restaurant together and are sharing a vehicle. As a potential nod to lesbian aesthetics, the one walking to the car is seen wearing a black leather jacket before becoming a victim of a Wesen attack. Even without explicit physical interactions of affection, their brief exchange can readily identify them as a couple out to dinner.

While the victimization of women is common in such police series, risks can be exceptionally high for queer women. Ultimately, the series pushes the view that they are friends when Sergeant Wu describes the crime scene as "her friend was waiting for her." Within his phrasing, there appears to be no particular emphasis to suggest a double meaning to "friend," which might imply a romantic relationship. Undoubtedly, had this pair been a woman and a man, the presumption of a heteronormative couple would have prevailed, but as two women there is ample room to frame them as mere friends, erasing a same-sex coupling from the series. Herein, the series can avoid a challenge to heteronormative interpretations but can also include a nod to those seeking queer representation.

As these two episodes highlight, this series tends to relegate queer identities to periphery characters who receive limited screen time. Albeit distinct in their gendering and series' role, with one a male Wesen predator and the other a female human victim, they equally demonstrate the extremely limited implicit visibility of queer characters. The only explicitly gay character ever shown in the series occurs in "Maiden Quest" (S5, E4) in which three Wesen men are competing for a woman's hand in marriage. After the first two have perished in their attempts, it is revealed that the third wanted nothing to do with the quest, when he firmly states "I'm gay." Analysis of the transcripts for the entire series reveal this be the *only* occasion the term gay is used in the entire series. Additionally, other related terms, such as lesbian, queer, or LGBT are also never spoken. The only explicit instance of a queer character is relegated to a periphery role with very few lines or plot activity. It is remarkable how few queer persons and communities are portrayed in a series set in a one of the queerest cities in America: this truly is a land of fairy tale and myth.

Wesen: Queer unto Themselves

Wesen, the supernatural creatures at the center of this series, offer significant appeal as queer allegory. Throughout the series, the audience is introduced to numerous Wesen "species." These are liminal creatures that often exhibit animal-like dual identities within a single-bodied "person." Typically, they can pass physiologically as human but can also woge, or physically transform, into their creature counterpart at will. Even when presenting as human, particularly in moments of stress or high emotion, they may have involuntary brief flashes, or small-woges, revealing their dual identities that are only visible to each other or to Grimm. Wesen can choose to partially reveal their identity or can fully transform for all to see. Wesen range from species characterized as aggressive, violent, or brutal, such as *Coyotl*[15] (Coyote-like), *Köningschlange*[16] (King cobra–like), and

Siegbarste[17] (Ogre-like), to more passive, gentle, and benevolent creatures, such as *Willahara*[18] (Rabbit-like), *Eisbiber*[19] (Beaver-like), and *Glühenvolk*[20] (Alien-like). In total across six seasons, nearly 100 species are portrayed, with additional examples referenced within Grimm written history and folklore. Many of the Wesen species relate to real-world animal counterparts, although some delve into more obtuse mythology and lore traditions such as *Hexenbiest/Zauberbiest*[21] (Witch- and Warlock-like) or *Naiad*[22] (Mermaid-like).

The treatment of Wesen within the series is often constructed upon a dichotomous axis. As is learned from historical records, books, and Wesen reactions to Nick, they have been historically constructed as unilaterally problematic and worthy of execution by Grimms. Within the Grimm tradition, Wesen are not just persecuted or discriminated against; they are treated with a campaign of genocide. Nearly all Wesen, upon encountering Nick and discovering he is a Grimm are fearful or immediately aggressive to protect themselves. Grimms have been socialized to believe all Wesen deserve death and that they are fighting for the good of humanity. Distinct from the historic Grimm/Wesen dynamic of "us" versus "them," Nick embraces a modern ethos, perhaps informed by his police training dividing Wesen into "good" and "bad."

Stereotypes of Wesen persist across the series, particularly among certain species. Many of the canine-like and other large-mammal-like Wesen are portrayed as violent, aggressive, or "bad." They are often seen in antagonistic, deviant, or villainous roles, such as gang members, criminals, inmates, and assassins. These Wesen are societal outlaws, rule-breakers, worthy of Grimm persecution. Yet, this stereotyping is actively problematized throughout the series by the central character of Monroe, a *Blutbad*[23] (wolf-like)—or more specifically, as he self-describes, a *Wider Blutbad*, or reformed *Blutbad*. As a *Wider Blutbad*, Monroe has embraced a lifestyle akin to "born-again spirituality," where he has rejected a post-life of hunting and killing humans and other lesser Wesen, in favor of a vegan lifestyle embracing a calmer, peaceful nature. Introduced in the Pilot, Monroe remains a continuous ally to Nick throughout series, in his orientation to the Wesen world and fighting "bad" Wesen. Interestingly, Monroe's soft demeanor and resistance to violence, and his being of the same species as the queer "Big Bad Wolf" of the Pilot episode leave an opportunity early on to read him as queer. This undetermined identity is resolved later in season one as it is learned that he had a prior relationship with another *Blutbad*, Angelina,[24] and is further enforced with the introduction of Rosalee,[25] a *Fuchsbau* (foxlike Wesen) who becomes his romantic interest and later wife.

Given the potential queer reads established early in the series with the Big Bad Wolf and Monroe, one may ponder if *Blutbads* are being portrayed as sexually-fluid or queer. Building upon this potential interpretation, Monroe's uncle, Felix Dietrich,[26] is introduced in "Map of the Seven Knights" (S5, E10). Felix is an antique books specialist who has come upon a collection of Grimm diaries and is hoping to sell them to Nick. In describing Felix to Rosalee, Monroe shares that he "He never married or had children. He was always more interested in books than anything else." This lifelong bachelor offers the opportunity to read him as queer—perhaps gay, perhaps asexual, who knows? Certainly, phrases like "confirmed bachelor" have been used as a euphemism for a gay man, but this is never explicitly said. Yet, as Monroe suggests to Rosalee, "Honestly, if I hadn't met you, I probably would have ended up the same way, except with clocks." Ultimately, there is no resolution of Felix's identity. He may be queer, but perhaps, as with Monroe, had he met the "right girl," he would be understood as heterosexual. That said, it is helpful to recall that a heterosexual pairing does not preclude a queer identity; it is merely a publicly visible pairing that aligns with heteronormativity, often erasing queer potential.

Most Wesen can hide their creature-like side and pass as humans. The ability to pass as "normal," or in this instance as human, is an important social skill for many who differ in some socially important manner. Allusions can be made to religious, racial, and ethnic identities—the ability to hide or protect such identities was historically important in many societies for one's economic or social success, and indeed at times for simple survival and freedom from persecution or violence. Similarly, those who depart from hegemonic constructs of sex, gender, and sexuality also may need to protect or hide their queer identities. The public sharing of one's identity, especially among stigmatized minority populations, remains a risky venture in many cultural settings today. To be "out," puts not only oneself at risk, but it can also be a threat to the entire community.

The duality of Wesen existence is the most poignant queer aspect of this series. Wesen often live a public life "passing" as human, "closeting" their true nature. Protecting and hiding their nature is not only about protecting themselves, but all Wesen. If one is discovered, they all risk being revealed, persecution, and punishment. For many queer folks, this is an intimately familiar experience. Historically, many LGBTQ persons had to hide, living a closeted lifestyle, for their safety and that of those they loved. The risk of stigma and harm persists, and many continue to selectively be "out," at varying degrees, in variable circumstances. Like Wesen, within one's community, such as a queer enclave or neighborhood, one may be open about their identity or nature. However, in the greater culture, there is more self-awareness of situational safety. Not surprisingly, among Wesen we find enclaves and social clubs persist, as have gay and lesbian clubs and social organizations in many urban centers.

Wesen organizations and governing structure offer allusion to miscegenation, LGBT regulation, and societal norms. In season four, the *Wesenrein*, an organization established in the Middle-ages whose missive is to protect the purity of Wesen species, enters the storyline. Members wear masks and robes, reminiscent of Klan robes,[27] employing a symbol reminiscent of the Nazi swastika. These references of racial purity and hierarchy are unavoidable, but the homophobic and violent treatment of LGBT persons are centerpieces of both organizations as well. For *Wesenrein*, also known as *Secundrum Naturae Ordinem Wesen*, which translates from Latin to "Wesen (who live) according to the natural order,"[28] intermarriage is a crime against man and nature. One may readily read this not only as a racist but also homophobic reference as well, with same-sex sexual activities historically being regarded in the same manner. *Wesenrein* is invested in protecting purity and disavowing activities that cross normative boundaries, such as befriending a Grimm. Among the various social groups, distinction and division remain integral: Wesen species should not intermingle, Wesen should not mingle with Grimm, and interactions with humans are complicated at best and a betrayal if diluting the bloodline. So much regulation speaks to the many intersectional regulations linked to race and sexuality. A singular identity (be it a single race or sexual identity) is the "right" way, and departure (multi-racial, sexual, or gender fluidity) is wrong. Another Wesen organization, Black Claw,[29] offers a poignant allusion to queer rights organizations. Often employing violent and highly visible actions, Black Claw's battle cry "*Occultatum Libera*," which translates to "free the hidden,"[30] makes a direct connection to the notion of visibility and being "out." Here, this organization parallels queer activist groups, albeit through often violent means.

As the series repeatedly portrays, Wesen are all around us, and seemingly everyone knows one, even if they are unaware. What portion of the population is Wesen is never clarified. The nearest the series come to a suggestive percentage is that about half of the prison population is Wesen,[31] which might extrapolate to some suggested minimum estimate. For *Kehrseite*, the humans unaware of Wesen, their lived experience is akin to heteronormative social life in past decades when many were unaware of queer people or their communities. If one is raised to "know" creatures, such as werewolves and mermaids, are mythical beings that "do not" exist, it can be startling to learn of the Grimm reality. Sudden, unexpected encounters with Wesen by *Kehrseite* often elicit significant fear, panic, violence, and insanity. In many ways, such reaction manifests from fear of the unknown and the cultural imagery affiliated with monsters and violence. These reactions parallel many of the homophobic responses experienced still today by contemporary LGBTQ persons.

Learning of and accepting those different from oneself, much like many heterosexuals' social experiences with queer people, is portrayed on several occasions in *Grimm*. While humans typically have a fear response when encountering Wesen, many of the central characters, such as Hank, Juliette, and Wu, demonstrate the ability to not only accept their existence, but also acclimate to seeing them woged. As humans who are aware of Wesen, they become *Kehrseite-Schlich-Kennen*. Often these central human characters are introduced to Wesen co-existence via an established friendly relationship with a presumed human. However, some learn of Wesen in high-stress or frightening scenarios. For example, one of Hanks most impactful early interactions occurs while trying to save the kidnapped daughter of an old friend.[32] Working with Nick to save her, she woges into her *Coyotl* (coyote-like) state accidentally upon encountering a Grimm. Her physical transformation immediately startles and scares Hank, who pulls his gun, prompting Nick to protect her and explain he sees "them" too. Hank is seen rapidly acclimating to and accepting Wesen moving forward. As the episode ends, Hank is writing up a report at the station with his friend and his daughter. Their exchange is uniquely reminiscent of that which may occur when someone comes out.

> FRIEND: I mean it's not easy being this.... Different. I would have told you the truth if I could have.
> HANK: Nothing's changed, okay? I'm just glad you came to me.

Many LGBT persons believe that simply knowing a queer person has a profound impact and leads to growing social acceptance.[33] For many raised in a heteronormative social sphere, there may be little interaction with queer people or communities. In past eras, one might not have even known that such persons existed. For humans, knowing a Wesen as a person prior to learning of their dualistic identity appears to positively impact their acceptance. This use of established relationships before revealing Wesen identity is deployed for both Juliette and Wu as well. Once aware of their existence, all begin to incorporate language, identifications, and ideas from within the Wesen world. Again, this parallels the linguistic and cultural socialization cis- and heteronormative persons may experience when socialized to the queer community.

Trubel'ing Queer: Hidden in Plain Sight

For a series that engages with such strong queer allusions to identity, duality, and public/private personas, its limited inclusion of LGBTQ identities and communities can be read with disappointment by its queer fanbase. However, like the Wesen "hiding" in plain sight throughout this fictional world, the most poignant example of queer visibility may be seen only by those in the know. Introduced in season three, Theresa Rubel, known as Trubel,[34] can undoubtedly be understood at queer or lesbian.

When first introduced to the series, Trubel is seen walking alone down a dark road, surrounded by woods on both sides. She is wearing jeans, a gray t-shirt, a black leather jacket, and a green rucksack upon one shoulder. A short haircut adds to the aesthetic, culminating in an image that can be read as a tomboy. When two men from a truck attack her, it turns out they are Wesen. She was able to see them woged, although it is unclear whether the attackers did so intentionally to frighten her. The next day, Nick and Hank arrive at the scene, where these two men have been found murdered and discover a black knight chess piece that had come from Trubel's bag. The knight piece possesses one of the most distinct and historied movements in this game, suggesting this woman is not only a warrior but has a unique path to play in subsequent battles. Having killed her attackers the night prior, when seen about to shower, she is scarred in a manner that the *Grimm* audience understands to be the result of Wesen claws. Before even interacting with the central cast, she is established as a capable fighter, "one bad-ass woman."[35] Her fashion and aesthetic, despite social transformations, remain stable throughout the series.

As the plot progresses, this "bad-ass woman" is learned also to be a Grimm—the first Nick has met who is not a member of his biological family. During a difficult childhood, Trubel's first encounter with a Wesen was while living in a foster home.[36] Subsequently, her youth and young adulthood were characterized by seeing Wesen, who reacted with repulsion and fear, often exclaiming the word "Grimm," for which she had no understanding or context. Knowing little alternative, she learned to fight off and often kill these monsters. As a Grimm, her preternatural strength and agility helped her survive a solitary hitch-hiking lifestyle.

Ultimately, Nick brings Trubel home to stay with him and Juliette, helping to teach her about Grimmlore and Wesen. Through this process, she gains greater self-assurance and comfort in her identity, providing support to Nick and his friends' Grimm activities. Meeting Nick and learning of Grimms came as a tremendous relief for Trubel, who had thought she was going crazy, seeing things that others did not. This identity transformation and resolution provides an allusion to the shifts that young queer persons often experience as they become acquainted with the queer community and its members. Learning that she is not alone, nor is she crazy, are identity shifts that many of the queer community have historically faced. When others like you are invisible or absent, it can be easy to consider oneself alone and mentally unfit.

Integration into Nick's social network opens Trubel's eyes to the reality of the world around her and the tremendous diversity that remains invisible to many. As she reads Grimm books, the narrative history, and diaries of past Grimm, she is learning of the hidden past of her type—of her community. In learning of these hidden histories of creatures with fluid identities and ways of living and interacting, Trubel's Grimm socialization is akin to queer youth learning of the often-under-discussed queer histories in all societies. Through this education, she also learns to distinguish and define variation within the (queer) Wesen world. She learns the sometimes-subtle distinction between different "species" exist, perhaps akin to a gay youth learning about the varied subcultural identities that may exist in gay men's culture for example. Ironically, gay men's community often makes specific social allusions to animal-like identities as well (i.e., bears, wolves, otters, etc.).[37]

Remaining a regular through the remaining seasons, Trubel maintains a consistent aesthetic of short hair, jeans, t-shirt, black jackets, and black combat boots. Once established and more independent, she is also explicitly linked to riding a motorcycle.[38] Her aesthetic, also accompanied by light makeup and often simply styled hair, is undoubtedly tomboy. Tomboyism is often culturally affiliated with lesbian or same-sex attraction among women,[39] challenging hegemonic notions of femininity and heteronormativity. While she occasionally may be seen with jewelry, such as earrings, when worn they are often small and certainly do not impede the physicality of a Grimm. Indeed, from the moment introduced through the end of the series, her Knightly status remains apparent—she remains ever-ready for battle.

As Trubel synthesizes her identity as a Grimm and becomes more established in the "community," she also grows to recognize her obligation to it. Much as queer elders help to protect and socialize the newest generation, helping them learn the ways of survival and relationship building—particularly through created kinship, Trubel takes up this mantel as well. She accompanies Josh,[40] a son of a Grimm who seemingly did not inherit abilities, to protect and teach him to their ways when he returned home. She also eventually joins Hadrian's Wall, a secret government organization, fighting Black Claw, a militant and violent organization seeking to take control of the government, eradicate Grimm, and return Wesen to power and visibility. These organizations are serving as symbolic representations of progressive and conserving forces endemic to the queer social movements of recent decades, community, political, legal-policing efforts. Ideologically, Black Claw is not seeking visibility and equality but is seeking to shift Wesen into privileged social positions informed by xenophobic ideologies that may imply parallels to contemporary Neo-Nazism. Trubel is fighting to protect "innocent" Wesen and persecute the violent efforts of Black Claw. Not all Wesen are good, nor are they all bad—much like queer people, there is variation person-to-person that goes far beyond their gender-sexual identities.

Without a doubt, the casual queer audience member can readily clock Trubel as likely being queer. She is a tomboy warrior, negotiating two worlds—that which is commonly known (non-Wesen) and that which is layered with varied (queer) identities and ways of being (Grimm and Wesen). She can see both sides and actively chooses to join and identify with the queer. Further enforcing this identification is an absence of a romantic or erotic storyline—she being the only central character never linked to a romantic interest or plot point.

A final specific notable aspect of Trubel is the actor who plays her. Jacqueline Toboni is an out actor who has subsequently appeared in *Easy* (2016–19) and *The L Word: Generation Q* (2019–) in lesbian roles. The actor's identity as a lesbian, while not indicative of Trubel's identity, certainly may reinforce such an interpretation among viewers.

It Must Be Nature?

The origins of Wesen and Grimm are never fully explained within the series. Undoubtedly, the vast majority of Wesen physically appear as fully human most of the time—when unwoged, they are indiscernible. This non-distinct physicality aligns with that of many queer-identified folk— few, if any, physical distinctions denote queer or cis-status. However, there appear to be no Wesen who are not the progeny of at least one Wesen parent, indicating a genetic component. Despite limited information, genetic predisposition, perhaps even dominance, seems to be particularly linked with Wesenhood.[41] Nevertheless, not all Wesen offspring are Wesen, especially if one parent is human. Wesen may not even know they are unique until they woge for the first time, which for many appears to align with adolescence,[42] much as bodily changes and sexual awakenings do for many. In explaining the disorientation they felt upon their first woge, Rosalee and Monroe also reveal that not all Wesen children are taught about their alternate identities. This may also imply that not all children will be Wesen, even if born of Wesen parents. This said, while one might presume it important to tell children of the potential physical changes that lay ahead, we also live in a world where many girls may be surprised and confused by their first period—a seemingly obvious and unavoidable physiological adolescent transition. Here we can also draw parallels to sexual identities—heterosexual parents may not socialize or teach children about other identities; despite the variety of possible orientations with which they may later identify.

64   Part One: Identity and Identification

Among Grimm, there is also an apparent genetic predisposition. While implied throughout the series, it is eventually learned that all Grimms are descendants of an original Grimm,[43] whose mythical savior origins remain unclear and a singular event. Among their various physical abilities, perhaps the most notable is their ability to see Wesen, even in partial-woge. Specifically linked to this ability is their physiological anomaly of two additional cones in their eyes.[44] Like Wesen, Grimm abilities do not seem to manifest at birth. Indeed, it seems to vary person-to-person. They did not emerge for Nick until in his 20s, while for Trubel, it was clearly at an earlier age, perhaps at adolescence.

After Nick was sought out by Rolek Porter,[45] an elder Grimm seeking to bestow books and historic relics before his death, Trubel and Nick become acquainted with his son, Josh, who does not have Grimm powers. Despite his inability to see Wesen and prior belief that his father was crazy, he comes to accept the multiple realities of the Grimm world. As Josh becomes increasingly integrated into Grimm's knowledge, he asks Trubel if she thinks he would ever become a Grimm.

> JOSH: Do you think I'll ever become like you and Nick?
> TRUBEL: I don't know.
> JOSH: Let's hope for the best.
> TRUBEL: Whatever that is.

His ponderance parallels the cultural questions that surround queer parenting—will their children also be queer? Further, his interaction and induction to understanding this Grimm world also align with individuals who gain awareness of a queer community and question if they may one day identify as such. While portrayed as likely in his late 20s or 30s, Josh recognizes that how he "sees" the world may yet change one day. This certainly demonstrates parallels to the later-in-life coming-outs that some queer folk experience.

Over the course of the series, nearly all central characters are clearly marked as heterosexual. Nick is romantically linked to Juliette and Adalind; Hank is linked with Adalind and other women; Monroe and Rosalee are paired; Captain Renard is shown with Adalind and other women. Sergeant Wu and Trubel are the only central characters whose heteronormativity remains undetermined. Appearing in nearly every episode, Sergeant Wu, seems to stay single and of uncertain romantic orientation. This orientation ambivalence is only specifically challenged in "Love Sick."[46] Under the influence of a powerful Wesen love potion, Wu is shown to be infatuated with a woman, experiencing "love at first sight." He confesses to her that he has "been waiting for you his entire life. The only one I've ever loved is my cat."[47] Structurally, this episode offered the unique opportunity for a same-sex romantic plot path and could have easily had any character magically influenced toward such, but only does so via Hank's infatuation with *himself*. Hank's infatuation manifests upon his reflection in the mirror as "one damn fine-looking man"[48] and is accompanied by his hearing and singing "Let's Get It On"[49] to himself. It seems the possibility of same-sex infatuation, particularly by a heterosexual man, is too far a reach for *Grimm*.

A particularly poignant aspect of queer imaginary emerges through plot points where characters transform physically, via the magical spell *Verfluchte Zwillingsschwester*, to appear as someone else. Various characters undergo this spell, including Adalind, Juliette, and Nick. Most of the transformations shift a character into the body of a same-gendered counterpart. However, Eve, the later incarnation of Juliette after becoming a *Hexenbiest*, transforms into Sean Renard.[50] This cross-gender physical transformation is remarkable and can readily speak to the embodied experience some trans-persons pursue. Through these physical transformations, each can portray or "pass" as the other convincingly. The fluidity of this is further layered with sexuality when Eve/Renard,[51] previously heterosexually identified Juliette, has sex with a woman. Not surprisingly, this cross-gender, cross-orientation behavior only is portrayed by a character primarily identified as a cis-woman. Even in the Grimm world, men cannot explore the sexual fluidity deemed more acceptable for women.

Closing the Trailer Door

In many ways, the journey of Nick as a Grimm and the transformations and journeys the characters of this series began in Aunt Marie's trailer of Grimm history. It also is shown to end in the future with another trailer of Grimm.[52] Nick's son, Kelly,[53] and step-daughter, Diana,[54] both being "multi-racial" to translate to real-world parallels[55] continue to carry out the Grimm tradition of policing the supernatural world. The triplet children of Monroe and Rosalee are also mentioned to be joining them. *Grimm* here speaks to the nuance and complexity of social existence—one is rarely singular. These future characters speak to multiplicity but also remove the necessity to define this diversity. Here, the five children denote the mingling across various groups: human-Wesen, Wesen-Grimm, and cross-species Wesen (*Blutbad-Fuchsbau*). This closing sequence also speaks to the potential for various family forms. Nick's own family speaks to the diversity of family structures today, inclusive of step- and half- relationships. This diversity of family is also inclusive of created kinship via the inclusion of the triplets. While often engaging in binaries, this series has problematized this by speaking to the breadth of potentiality among identity categories. Not only are there human, Grimm, and Wesen, but within each there are numerous categories and identities possible, both known and yet to be known (especially Wesen species and various inter–"racial" categories). It also notes the critical role "family," in its many forms and symbols, plays in the journey of a queer life.

As a series, *Grimm* offers significant queer potential. Undoubtedly, it is an imperfect tale but gives perspectives about identity, visibility, social movements, and the policing of social life. Despite the often-traditional ideologies that inform many of the social institutions explored in this series, such as policing, family, racial-ethnic identity, and LGBTQ existence, the diverse and queer world on both sides of the screen is examined. Neither our world nor that of our Grimm are as simple as they may seem. Along with problematic, discriminatory, and stereotypical aspects of queer life that persist, this world of creative and evolving identities exists. Much like LGBTQ rights and queer movements of the last decades, what is to come for this *Grimm*verse remains to be seen.

Notes

1. IMDb, www.imbdb.com, last accessed 4 December 2020.
2. Wikipedia, last accessed 4 December 2020.
3. Attributed to Michelle Tauber, *People*.
4. See Benshoff; Clover; Halberstram.
5. Portland was reported second only to San Francisco in the U.S., with 5.4% rates of LGBT residents (Leonhardt and Miller ST12).
6. E.g., LGB military service restrictions in the U.S. fully lifted in 2011. Transgender military service was permitted in 2016; returned to a ban of trans personnel in 2018. Same-sex marriage was legalized nationally in 2015.
7. Inmate survey research demonstrates the self-identified LGB rates among the incarcerated is more than three times that of the U.S. population (Meyer et al.).
8. See Flores, et al.
9. Giffney 365.
10. See Becker; Keller; Keller and Stratyner.
11. See Benshoff and Griffin.
12. http://sacredscribesangelnumbers.blogspot.com/2014/06/angel-number-1710.html
13. Among his numerous roles, he may be known by many for his role of Larry in *Will & Grace* (2000–6; 2018–19).
14. See Schlatter and Steinback.
15. S2, E3: "Bad Moon Rising."
16. S2, E6: "Over My Dead Body."
17. S1, E8: "Game Ogre."
18. S4, E18: "Bad Luck."
19. First introduced in S1, E5: "Danse Macabre." The most noted being "Bud" (Actor: Danny Bruno), who appears in ~25 episodes across all seasons.
20. S2, E19: "Endangered."
21. Both are introduced in S1, E1.
22. S3, E8: "One Night Stand."

23. Introduced in episode 1.1. Monroe appears in all episodes of the series.
24. S1, E6: "The Three Bad Wolves." Actor: Jaime Ray Newman.
25. S1, E15: "Island of Dreams."
26. Actor: Rick Overton.
27. Ku Klux Klan, an American white supremacist hate group, particularly targeted African Americans. Members wore white robes to protect their identity.
28. S4, E6: "Highway of Tears."
29. A violent Wesen organization/movement, portrayed heavily in Season 5 and 6.
30. S5, E2: "Clear and Wesen Danger."
31. S2, E11: "Protect and Serve Man."
32. S2, E3: "Bad Moon Rising."
33. Pew Research Center, 2013.
34. S3, E19: "Nobody Knows the Trubel I've Seen."
35. *Ibid.*, as suggested by Nick when investigating the truck of the murdered men.
36. S3, E21: "The Inheritance."
37. Wright *Bear Book, Bear Book II.*
38. S5, E4: "Maiden Quest."
39. See Rekers; Hyde, Rosenberg, and Behrman.
40. Actor: Lucas Near-Verbrugghe.
41. In S1, E21: "Big Feet," it is learned that Wesen are parahuman, sharing two sets of DNA within the same system.
42. S3, E12: "The Wild Hunt."
43. S6, E13: "The End."
44. S4, E3: "The Last Fight."
45. S3, E21: "The Inheritance."
46. S6, E7: "Blind Love."
47. This statement could also suggest an asexual orientation but will not be explored further in this piece.
48. S6, E7.
49. Accompanying the music of Marvin Gaye's "Let's Get It On."
50. S5, E16: "The Believer."
51. To further clarify, when Eve has transformed and appears as Renard.
52. S6, E13: "The End."
53. Actor (adult) Kevin Joy.
54. Actor (adult) Nicole Steinwedell.
55. His son, Kelly, is his biological son with Adalind (a *Hexenbiest*)—whether he is part-*Hexenbiest* and part-Grimm is unclear. His step-daughter, the progeny of Adalind and Captain Renard (half-human, half-*Zauberbiest*), a multi-"racial" hybrid *Hexenbiest* of exceptional power.

Works Cited

Becker, Ron. *Gay TV and Straight America*. Rutgers UP, 2006.
Benshoff, Harry M. *Monsters in the Closet: Homosexuality and Horror Film*. Manchester UP, 1997.
_____, and Sean Griffin. *Queer Images: A History of Gay and Lesbian Film in America*. Rowan & Littlefield, 2005.
Clover, Carol J. *Men, Women, and Chainsaws: Gender in the Modern Horror Film*. Princeton UP, 1992.
Flores, Andrew R., Lynn Langton, Ilan H. Meyer, and Adam P. Romero. "Victimization Rates and Traits of Sexual and Gender Minorities in the United States; Results from the National Crime Victimization Survey, 2017." *Science Advances*, vol. 6, no. 40, 2020. Doi: 10.1126/sciadv.aba6910.
Giffney, Noreen. "The New Queer Cartoon." *Ashgate Research Companion to Queer Theory*, edited by Noreen Giffney and Michael O'Rourke, Ashgate, 2009, pp. 363–78.

68   Part One: Identity and Identification

Halberstram, J. *Skin Shows: Gothic Horror and the Technology of Monsters.* Duke UP, 1995.
Hyde, Janet S., B.G. Rosenberg, and Jo Ann Behrman. "Tomboyism." *Psychology of Women Quarterly,* vol. 2, no. 1, 1977, pp. 73–75.
Kellers, James R. *Queer (Un)Friendly Film and Television.* McFarland, 2002.
_____, and Leslie Stratyner, eds. *The New Queer Aesthetic on Television.* McFarland, 2006.
Leonhardt, David and Claire C. Miller. "The Metros Areas with the Largest, and Smallest Gay Populations." *New York Times,* 21 March 2015, p. ST12.
Meyer, I.H., A.R. Flores, L. Stemple, A.P. Romero, B.D.M. Wilson, and J.L. Herman. "Incarceration Rates and Traits of Sexual Minorities in the United States: National Inmate Survey, 2011–12." *American Journal of Public Health,* vol. 107, no. 2, 2017, pp. 267–73.
Pew Research Center. "A Survey of LGBT Americans." 13 June 2013. (Chapter 2: Social Acceptance) https://www.pewsocialtrends.org/2013/06/13/chapter-2-social-acceptance/
Reckers, G.A. "Development of Problems of Puberty and Sex Roles in Adolescence." *Handbook of Clinical Child Psychology,* edited by C.W. Walker and M.C. Roberts, John Wiley, 1992, pp. 207–22.
Schlatter, Evelyn, and Robert Steinback. "10 Anti-Gay Myths Debunked." Intelligence Report: SPLC Southern Poverty Law Center, 27 February 2011. https://www.splcenter.org/fighting-hate/intelligence-report/2011/10-anti-gay-myths-debunked
Wright, L., editor. *The Bear Book: Readings in the History and Evolution of a Gay Male Subculture.* Harrington Park Press, 1997.
_____, editor. *The Bear Book II: Further Readings in the History and Evolution of a Gay Male Subculture.* Harrington Park Press, 2001.

Grimm

Fantasy, Procedurals, and Rape Culture

Anastasia Rose Hyden

While deceptively simple, fantasy stories, especially fairy tales, frequently serve as metaphors for unarticulated social dilemmas and signify prevalent cultural dilemmas. They further encompass all-embracing themes from alienation and oppression to the struggles of puberty and sexuality, creating a space for a broad audience to explore societal issues and individual struggles. These stories pass on through generations, with each retelling importing the values of its time and place. In the recent past, these re-imaginings have manifest as television series like *Faerie Tale Theater*,[1] *Once Upon a Time*,[2] and multiple versions of *Beauty & the Beast*,[3] expanding the genre into a new, public medium and vast audiences.

Television is also home to another story form, which though more recent, mirrors the function and structure of fairy tales. Police procedurals are a staple of American television and enjoy continued popularity and longevity. Like fairy tales, procedurals also predate the small screen, beginning with novels like Wilkie Collins's *The Moonstone* (1868).[4] Like fairy tales, these stories and story forms continue to thrive, particularly in the U.S. with series such as *Law & Order: Special Victims Unit*,[5] *Chicago P.D.*,[6] and *Blue Bloods*,[7] to name only a few recent examples. The genre has also expanded beyond portrayals of traditional American police forces to include shows about FBI agents (*Criminal Minds*[8]), private investigators (the many incarnations of Sherlock Holmes[9]), military investigative units (*NCIS*[10]), and amateur detectives (*Veronica Mars*[11]). Procedurals such as these also employ an undemanding formulaic approach to storytelling to address complex social and cultural concerns obliquely—a formula often found within the telling of fairy tales.

During its six-season run on network television, NBC's *Grimm* uniquely brought the two forms together, creating an accessible and attractive platform for social inquiry. While the series addresses various issues, both "monster of the week" stories and continuations of the show's unfolding mythology take a deliberate and daring interest in exploring rape culture. This issue has traditionally been ignored or suppressed in mainstream entertainment. *Grimm* combines the tropes of fairy tales and police procedurals to bring attention to the pervasive and pernicious rape culture found in contemporary society and raise awareness of its embeddedness in traditional stories of Western culture.

Traditionally, representations and discussions of rape on television have functioned, even if inadvertently, to normalize rape culture and its negative attitudes toward women. Media scholars LeeAnn Kahlor and Michael S. Eastin have argued a strong correlation between television consumption and belief in rape myths (a term that uses "myth" pejoratively to indicate a set of mistaken beliefs that a culture holds) and the overestimation of false rape accusations. They further draw attention to a study of twenty-six storylines involving sexual assault, in which each instance contained at least one reference to rape mythology.[12] Here rape myths centered on the fallibility of the presumed victim, alleging that she was lying about the assault, wanted the assault to happen, or was to blame for it.[13] Such correlations and trends indicate the power of media to reproduce and reaffirm beliefs and suggest the potential power of mainstream shows, such as procedural dramas, to challenge rape myths and provoke discussions around rape culture.

Grimm's hybridity allows it to seize on this potential to situate rape and demystify rape myths by moving the locus of discussion about rape culture to the perpetrator while unmasking the historical forces that have perpetuated it. For this analysis, "rape culture" refers to a society where the act of rape has become normalized, making it an essentially "condoned behavior."[14] It is supported structurally by patriarchal values and strict concepts of masculinity and femininity that frame men as aggressive and macho in contrast to weak, vulnerable women.[15] Sex-role socialization practices teach non-overlapping ideas of masculinity and femininity, which empower and affirm rape culture. In the dominant, white, heteronormative culture, boys are socialized to be strong, independent, competitive, and aggressive. In contrast, girls are socialized to be gentle, vulnerable, nurturing, and physically weaker than their male counterparts. An almost complete lack of training and support for resisting rape complements female socialization as victims. The most common misconception about rape resistance is that if a woman fights back against a rapist, she is more likely to be injured than if she submits.[16] Rape researcher Karol Dean points out that the cultural context of women's resistance dictates that it is okay for a woman to avoid rape by staying home but not by becoming physically stronger. It is okay to avoid rape by being always accompanied by a man, but not to confront men who invade personal space.[17] *Grimm* employs storylines that problematize these beliefs by emphasizing the power and villainy of rapists and would-be rapists and the extent of their abilities to capitalize on woman-regulating strategies to enact their predatory behaviors.

Failures of the legal system to protect victims and punish perpetrators further perpetuates rape culture. Legal scholar Catherine MacKinnon famously said that rape in the U.S. is "regulated, not prohibited."[18] According to a national survey, only 16 percent of rapes are reported to the police. Once reported, very few go to trial. For example, a study in Philadelphia found that only 7.5 percent of reported rapes resulted in a guilty verdict. Further, the closer the relationship between the perpetrator and the victim, the less likely an arrest or conviction. Strangers are more likely than dates or acquaintances to be charged and convicted of rape, while acquaintances are more likely to be convicted than family members. American culture, therefore, functionally regulates more so than prohibits rape.[19]

Rape culture is dependent on and perpetuated by rape myths, which Kahlor and Eastin describe as the "false but persistent beliefs and stereotypes regarding forced sexual intercourse and the victims and perpetrators of such acts."[20] Martha Burt's influential theory of rape primarily focused on rape myths, as a set of irrational beliefs about women and sexuality that can act as releasers or neutralizers that elicit sexually aggressive behavior.[21] This essay examines how *Grimm* challenges rape myths and rape culture. It introduces its protagonist, Nick Burkhardt, to a fantastical world that he never knew existed while paradoxically revealing the pervasiveness of the rape culture whose existence few have acknowledged.

This examination will demonstrate how *Grimm* uses the figures of Wesen to highlight the different behaviors indicative of potential rapists. Rozee and Koss describe four critical behaviors exhibited by perpetrators of violence, which help examine fictional characters constructed as abusers. The warning behaviors are sexual entitlement, seeking power and control, being hostile and angry, and accepting of interpersonal violence.[22] While exposing these traits through Wesen, the series simultaneously employs the authority of Nick Burkhardt—both a Portland Police Detective and a Grimm who can see "the monster inside"—to unambiguously demonstrate that perpetrators are the cause of rape and victims of rape are just that, victims. While it is Wesen who are the perpetrators, *Grimm* clarifies that not all are perpetrators. In so doing, it demonstrates that choice is involved in how Wesen employ their super-human powers: some do so for good and some for evil, while others simply live quiet lives. This diversity is essential for showing that rape is not an impulse inherent to Wesen but a function of their "personalities." Although Wesen may be monstrous, their actions and motivations are represented as entirely human.

This discussion of *Grimm*'s demystification of rape culture begins with the analysis of four "monster of the week" episodes from season one to demonstrate the series' early commitment to exposing and critiquing the ubiquitous rape motifs of traditional fairy tales. A study of the role of rape culture themes, such as power, control, and consent, throughout the series, with particular attention paid to long story arcs, follows. Subsequently, how multiple characters use their powers to represent both physical and psychological rape will be examined. These various representational strategies demonstrate a commitment in *Grimm* to using fairy tales and fantasy to dismantle rape mythologies of the present and prompt further discussion of the insidious and influential role rape culture plays in the beliefs and attitudes of Western society.

The Familiar Terror of Little Red Riding Hood

The story of *Little Red Riding Hood* has proved to a flexible narrative platform for a wide array of cultural issues and themes, from parental obedience and social mores to sexual awakening. *Grimm*'s "Pilot" (S1, E1) builds upon preceding connections with sexual assault to construct an unflinching interrogation of the central themes of rape, inverting the message to women that they should not stray from the path to expose the predatory nature of sexual violence and violators. The episode opens with a quote from the Brothers Grimm's famous version of the tale, "The wolf thought to himself what a tender young creature. What a nice plump mouthful." It then follows a young woman wearing a bright red hooded sweatshirt as she leaves an ivy-covered, collegiate building to go for a run. As she runs along a wooded path listening to music on her iPod, she is distracted by a Hummel figurine on the ground, and in that momentary pause, is attacked by something that looks not quite human.

Beyond the fairy tale epigram, this scene does not differ from those of any other procedural drama. There are multiple episodes of both *Criminal Minds*[23] and *Law & Order: Special Victims Units*[24] whose openings feature women being attacked during a run. However, the details of this sequence demonstrate signifiers of the well-known fairy tale: a forest path and a red hoodie. The scene remarks on its own intermingling of fairy tale fantasy and violent reality through the use of the song "Sweet Dreams (Are Made of This)" by synth-pop duo Eurythmics playing on her iPod throughout the sequence. While the song's composer and singer, Annie Lenox, has stated that the song is about the breakup of her previous group, *The Tourists*, its invocation of dreams suggests the world of fantasy and syntagmatic links to the fairy tales read to children at bedtime. At the same time, the song features violent and aggressive language suggesting sexual predation. In the context of this scene, after the woman has disappeared, the song performs a disenchanting function, implying an off-screen, negative representation—that she has been attacked and raped. The show never says *rape*; instead, it leaves the audience to recognize a crime that so is often erased and unspoken.

Later in the show's timeline, a young girl wearing a red sweatshirt goes missing. Despite the victims' age difference, Detective Burkhardt realizes that the two cases are connected. Eventually, he becomes suspicious of Errol Ditmarsch,[25] a seemingly easygoing local postman, whom he discovers is a *Blutbad*, a wolf-like being that recalls the fairy-tale Big Bad Wolf. When a search of Ditmarsch's home deep in the woods comes up empty, Burkhardt dismisses his suspicions until he hears the suspect humming "Sweet Dreams (Are Made of This)." Hearing the tune prompts a second search, wherein a hidden door to a secret underground room is discovered. Here is where the girl is being held as a prisoner. A secret room in which sexually abused children are kept and assaulted is a common element of procedural depictions of real-life crime.[26] Including this detail further emphasizes the violence inherent to the fairy tale, and through this otherwise supernatural-themed show, makes it accessible to a real-world audience.

Using what is arguably the most famous fairy tale of all time, *Grimm* blends the tropes of fairy tales and police procedurals, preparing the audience for the nuanced and complex explorations that will follow as the series evolves. However, the use of the procedural is highly relevant for creating narratives and characters that are familiar and sympathetic. From this perspective, a woman running through the woods as if pursued renders her identifiable in television and life. She is a stock image of the soon-to-be victim in police procedurals and instantly familiar to any woman who has walked outside alone and thought she heard someone or something behind her.

The pilot quickly engages viewers because the story of *Little Red Riding Hood* fits comfortably into a procedural template. As Catherine Orenstein writes,

> Fairy tales are full of a vague dread, a catastrophe that seems to befall only little girls. Sweet, feminine Little Red Riding Hood is off to visit her dear old grandmother in the woods. The wolf lurks in the shadows, contemplating a tender morsel. Red Riding Hood and her grandmother, we learn, are equally defenseless before the male wolf's strength and cunning. His big eyes, his big

hands, his big teeth—"the better to see you, to catch you, to eat you, my dear." The wolf swallows both females with no sign of a struggle. But enter the huntsman—he will right this egregious wrong.... Red Riding Hood is a parable of rape. There are frightening male figures abroad in the woods—we call them wolves, among other names—and females are helpless before them.[27]

Orenstein's analysis applies to many procedural dramas that end with a (usually male) detective rescuing a woman—carrying her to safety while covering her with a blanket. This visual template constructs an unmistakable infantilization as the woman swaddled like an infant, emphasizing her vulnerability and impotence. She is made a child in a scene of justice and triumph, making her rescuer (and her assailant) seem even bigger, stronger, and all the more necessary by contrast. At the same time, the imagery of an innocent, abducted child gives the lie to the defamatory myths that victims are somehow responsible or not victims at all, but lied, wanted it, or were to blame. In this scenario, there is no ambiguity about who is at fault.

From Bluebeard to Lonelyhearts

The episode "Lonelyhearts" (S1, E4) subverts multiple myths about rapists, strategically disempowering central tenets of rape culture. In this episode, while investigating a woman's murder, Detective Burkhardt encounters a goat-like Wesen known as a *Ziegevolk*, Billy Capra,[28] whose first name suggests a billy-goat and last name recalls Capricornus, the "horned goat" constellation. Goats have a long history as symbols of sin and depravity, with the he-goat representing "lust personified."[29] Capra can force people to do what he wants using pheromones. He uses this ability almost exclusively to abduct women and imprison them in his basement for implied sexual abuse.

As in the Pilot, "Lonelyhearts" opens with a typical police procedural trope: a woman (in her nightgown) escaping from a building where she was held prisoner or subjected to violence. She is terrified of something unseen and runs across a bridge in darkness, where she is accidentally struck by a car. The car accident does not kill her, however. When the driver calls for help, she is left with a man shrouded by darkness. He suffocates her as she asks him for a kiss. When investigating this death, the police discover that not only had the victim been reported missing but that she is also one of a string of women who had recently disappeared in the area. The episode's epigram—"There she paused for a while thinking ... but the temptation was so great that she could not conquer it"—is taken from Charles Perrault's version of *Bluebeard*. *Bluebeard* tells the story of a woman tricked into marrying an older man, and it explicitly addresses themes of sexual manipulation and control. In this tale, the titular character murders his wives when they disobey him. While many fairy tales end with marriage as a "happily ever after,"[30] here it is the beginning of an emotionally abusive, controlling relationship that rapidly escalates. Bluebeard gives each wife a key and tells them that they have free reign over his large home, except for one "forbidden room." The key gives his wife a false sense of freedom, as she able to go into almost any room and invite anyone she pleases to stay at home. However, she is never really "free," as the key remains as a constant reminder of the "forbidden room." Ultimately, she opens the door to discover the bodies of his previously murdered wives. Perrault uses the key to symbolize Bluebeard's manipulation and control while providing her a false sense of consent and freedom. While this last wife is rescued before he murders her, chillingly, the former wives were not as fortunate.

Capra exerts similar control over and abuses his female victims to achieve total dominance. One of his most insidious abuses comes through mind control and emotional manipulation through pheromones—the women believe they are acting independently but have been tricked and trapped, not unlike the key holding wives of Bluebeard. Capra's violence departs from the story in a particularly unsettling way: he does not just rape his victims physically but also assaults their personal experiences, fears, and motivation; he breaks through their psychological resistances, giving them nowhere to hide. Moreover, he intentionally impregnates many of them so that not only will the trauma inflicted on them live on, so too will a physical reminder of it. He is both a rapist and a reproductive abuser.

While Capra is an explicit portrayal of and is referenced directly as a rapist, his psychologically manipulative behavior evokes the use of Rohypnol, the so-called "date-rape" drug, as much, if not more so, than emotional abuse. His victims lose any ability to resist his suggestions. Removing their consent, he has complete control and becomes the ultimate owner of the women and their bodies. He dictates their behavior removing autonomy; they exist only to please him. They become playthings or pets, literally portrayed by their imprisonment in kennel cages where he feeds them from what appear to be pet food bowls, reducing them to an animal state.

The banality of Ditmarsch and Capra's desires are among their most disturbing elements. Pop culture is filled with villains whose ambitions aim toward acquiring unlimited power, unimaginable wealth, or even world domination. These Wesen, however, exclusively want to dominate women. They could do just about anything with their supernatural powers but choose to abduct, imprison, and assault women and girls. Their un-extraordinariness is further reinforced by how they present themselves to the world. Ditmarsch fashions himself as a stereotypically harmless "nerd" in dress and interests, particularly notable in his collection of porcelain miniatures, while Capra dresses in expensive-looking, fashionable clothing, presenting himself as a cultured and well-educated people pleaser. Their presentations as unexceptional, professional, and respectable men mirror the reality that abusers do not have a "look"; they could be anybody.[31] By crafting the predators in this way, *Grimm* recalls the moral of Perrault's tale:

> Moral: Children, especially attractive, well bred young ladies, should never talk to strangers, for if they should do so, they may well provide dinner for a wolf. I say "wolf," but there are various kinds of wolves. There are also those who are charming, quiet, polite, unassuming, complacent, and sweet, who pursue young women at home and in the streets. And unfortunately, it is these gentle wolves who are the most dangerous ones of all.[32]

Ditmarsch and Capra are among those "most dangerous" wolves. Their unthreatening appearances subvert one of the most common rape myths, the so-called "monster myth." The monster myth claims that rapists and other abusers are not like the rest of us. Instead, they are literal monsters: the stranger lurking in the dark, the creep wearing a ski mask, and so on. The monster myth deliberately separates these men from the rest of society, enforcing the idea that there is some "otherness" about them, that they are not one of "us."[33] However, those who commit rape rarely fit the stereotype of a frightening stranger: they are most often ordinary-looking men.

The fantasy register of *Grimm*'s fairy tale landscape opens the possibility for showrunners to amplify and exploit the monster myth by expanding the sensational elements of fairy tale creatures, emphasizing the otherness or inhumanity of sexual predators. Nevertheless, most Wesen, even those portrayed as "bad guys," are the kind of anthropomorphic human and animal hybrids that would not visually be out of place on a children's show. The representation of superficially unremarkable assailants sharing the motives and strategies of real-life human predators dismisses the rapist monster myth as just that: a myth.

It further suggests an analogy between unremarkable sexual predators and the Wesen living among "normal" people, highlighting the fear and denial that many people experience when this myth is exposed. When Nick Burkhardt finally tells his long-term girlfriend, Juliette Silverton, that he is a Grimm and elaborates on the existence of Wesen, she does not believe him. She is convinced that he is suffering a psychotic break because the suggestion is inconceivable to her conception of the world.

This mindset is consistent with responses to real-life rape trials and the statistics surrounding actual convictions. For example, multiple studies have concluded that a female-dominated jury is less likely to convict a man for rape and sexual assault than other jury combinations.[34] The working hypothesis for this finding is a tendency to believe the world safe and victims are to blame or mentally unstable rather than admit the pervasiveness of rape culture its risks.[35] The initial denial of her boyfriend's supernatural revelations allows Silverton to hold onto her belief in a safe and ordinary world free of magical beings with potentially dangerous powers.

The Curse of Beauty, Another Way to Victim Blame

The construction of a "safe" world in which only identifiable monsters are predators has at its core another rape myth: that there are women who are so exceptionally beautiful that even normal men cannot control themselves. The episode "Heartbreaker" (S4, E16) addresses this mythology by inverting the gender dynamics of the fairy tale *The Frog Prince*, focusing on Bella Turner,[36] a frog-like creature known as a *Folterseele*. These women Wesen are all supernaturally attractive, making them frequent targets of sexual assault. However, when touched by the opposite sex, their skin, through an involuntary self-defense mechanism, releases a deadly toxin that kills on contact. Believing their assaults and the deaths of these men to be their fault, these Wesen often engage in self-mutilation. Traditionally, they brand their faces to be less physically attractive to would-be attackers. This tradition illustrates the inevitability of rape culture; so prevalent are rape myths that the *Folterseeles* see no other way to escape sexual assault than by trying to eliminate any sexual interest they could potentially arouse. The episode begins with Turner pursued by a male acquaintance. Catching up with her, he touches her without consent, despite her clear and deliberate refusals, and dies as a result. Burkhardt comes across Turner while investigating the mysterious poisoning death whom the audience knows would not take her cry of "don't touch me" seriously. After learning about her powers, Burkhardt decides to try to help rather than just locking her up.

The two men that die from touching Turner, despite her warnings, exemplify the multiple indicators of sexual predation laid out by Rozee and Koss in their study of rapist psychological traits, particularly entitlement. The show demonstrates this in two scenes that illustrate different forms of male sexual entitlement.[37] The first comes when Zach Blumenthal[38] follows her into the woods: after defending her from a fellow bike club member Rick Thorton's[39] sexual harassment, confessing his love

78 Part One: Identity and Identification

for her. Turner tries to brush him off, but he refuses to take "no" for an answer, leading to his death. Blumenthal's interest in Turner is framed as a typical "nice guy" narrative where a man expects or feels entitled to be rewarded for "good behavior" with sex and companionship; after all, he really likes her. Even when rejected, Blumenthal never stops acting in a mild and friendly manner because he is assured of eventually getting what he wants. After Blumenthal's death, Thorton redoubles his sexual aggression. Assuming Turner is responsible, he attempts to assault her as punishment for being a murderer and a "tease," forcibly touching her and triggering his own demise. The idea that women do things solely to tempt men positions them as objects, reinforcing the idea that their role is to please men. While his methods differ from Blumenthal's, Thorton's behavior also exemplifies male predatory entitlement—he has the right to punish and take his prize.

Even though both Turner's "victims" are men she knows, the episode plays with the "stranger danger" rape myth. Rozee and Koss emphasize that most male violence toward women is perpetuated by a male known to the female "victim-survivor."[40] There have been countless studies and texts attempting to break down the "stranger-danger" myth: the belief that women are more likely to be raped or attacked by some random stranger in a dark alley than someone they know. Studies have found that a vast majority of victims know the offender.[41] Rozee and Koss also question the effectiveness of many rape prevention strategies, such as identifying spaces as "safe" or "dangerous," and styles of "appropriate" dress, given that a known assailant commits most rapes.[42] Turner receives advice that plays into this "stranger danger" myth. The idea that being scarred prevent assault is an extension of the myth that rape happens to only conventionally attractive women because men cannot control themselves around them. Consequently, if a woman reduces her attractiveness, she will be safe from rape. However, facial disfigurement in this storyline is just a more extreme version of "don't wear short skirts," which is a way of saying that "she was asking for it." The "asking for it" myth permeates rape culture as a corollary to the mythology that rapists cannot help it or cannot accept no as an answer once provoked.

The *Folterseele* conceit problematizes the notion of female responsibility for sexual stimulation: they do not choose their appearance, how men interpret it, how men respond to them, and whether or not men will accept "no" as an answer. Nor are they strictly in control of the toxicity their skin emits: it, unlike sexual assault, is natural and involuntary. The extremeness of traditional facial disfigurement gives credence to the lie of what taking control or "helping it" (if men cannot) in the female context means. One critic observed,

> Of the various effort to explore the dark side of the Wesen world, this is one of the more effective deployments because of how little control Turner has over what happens. She cannot control her poisonous reactions any more than she can control the men who find her attractive, with both the good and bad ones meeting the same gruesome fate when they try to get too close.[43]

Of course, the only men Turner hurts are those who ignore her requests not to touch her. The early presumption that Turner's power affects "good" men, as well as "bad" ones, illustrates how deep-rooted rape myths are as women are not allowed to choose who gets physically "close" to them and the episode's "nice guy" refuses to leave her alone. Further, the episode shows that multiple men, including Burkhardt and Griffith, are unaffected by her and easily respect her autonomy.

Ultimately, Turner uses a potion to make herself less conventionally attractive, removing her skin's toxic response. It is telling that she still must find a way to "save" herself from potential rapists but doing so also means she can pursue a normal romantic relationship. It is an uneasy compromise: she distorts herself to function in a society where rape culture prevails, advancing the message that women must protect themselves from rape and beauty is a provocation; yet, it also suggests that healthy sexuality is not rooted in the objectification of female bodies.

The Mythology of Rape Culture

The theme of rape culture plays a crucial part in *Grimm*'s longer story arcs. When particular Wesen use their powers to manipulate humans sexually, this leads to long-term consequences for both. Following *Grimm*'s critical method of inverting classic tropes, Adalind Schade, a witch-like Wesen known as a *Hexenbiest*, provides a powerful challenge to traditional power relationships in sexual assault by using her powers to control men throughout the series, including raping them. In a way, she replicates the criminality of Capra in "Lonelyhearts," but with the distinction that he rapes and abuses women as an end in itself, while Adalind usually assaults men in service of a more powerful figure.[44] The first depiction of her abuse comes when she casts a spell on Detective Hank Griffith, Burkhardt's partner. While his attraction to her is apparent, her spell making him sexually obsessed. They enter a romantic relationship that includes sexual contact, all while she controls his mind and emotions. The intensity and immediacy of his feelings, however, is so unusual that he even jokes that "if she wasn't a lawyer, I'd think she roofied me," in one of the show's few explicit references to sexual assault (S1, E18: "Cat and Mouse"). Griffith suggests that her profession keeps him from suspecting her, echoing "Lonelyhearts" to demonstrate how "respectability" can mask an abuser. That Hank was drugged and raped goes unacknowledged by the characters, signaling a cultural silence surrounding female sexual abuse of men.

The silence also highlights another popular rape myth: many people, particularly men, believe that unless victims clearly and physically resist, they have given *de facto* consent to sexual contact. This mythology allows for the extenuation that rape cannot possibly be so easy and that victims must have wanted the sex. Otherwise, they would have fought harder against their attacker.[45] This myth interlinks with the belief of "token resistance": that someone says no when they really mean yes, and that "no" is merely empty performance.[46] Such logic shifts the blame onto victims for not resisting forcefully enough to prevent rape, though what constitutes forceful resistance is perceived quite variably, particularly by men and women.[47] Griffith did not put up a "fight" against Schade's advances, never mind that he was essentially drugged when consenting to sex with her.

Other Wesen are also not safe from Schade's manipulations. In season two, another spell entangles Burkhardt's girlfriend, Juliette Silverton, and his immediate boss, Captain Sean Renard. This spell causes them to become sexually obsessed with each other. Unlike most episodes where the sexual aspects are relegated primarily to allegory, their mutual fixation is overtly sexual. It is also depicted as unhealthy, violent, and undeniably unwanted on both sides. Because Schade removes their ability to consent, every sexually intimate situation is necessarily coerced.[48] Subsequently, Schade and Renard also have sex while he is still under the power of this spell, thus unable to give full, uncoerced consent.

In season three, Schade disguises herself as Silverton and has sex with Burkhardt, in effect, raping him. The assault takes away his powers and identity as a Grimm. Nick's loss of a Grimm identity mirrors the loss of self that many rape survivors, both male and female, report (S3, E22: "Blond Ambition"). Even though he was a detective before manifesting his *Grimm* powers, he became much more powerful and effective at his job afterward. He enjoyed this "special" status and is distraught when it disappeared. While the show depicts Nick's feelings of identity violation, it never uses the term "rape," focusing instead on Silverton's feelings of betrayal. This elision suggests the show's discomfort with women as rapists. Later, when Schade reveals she is pregnant as the result of this assault, Burkhardt not only agrees to co-parent their child, but eventually develops romantic feelings for her. This progression bolsters the rape myth that victims *want* to have sex with their perpetrators (S5, E1: "The Grimm Identity"). It also actively demonstrates the double standard regarding female-on-male sexual assault.

Shortly after Schade assaults Burkhardt, he and Silverton re-enact his rape as she magically assumes the body form of his rapist (Schade), thus restoring his powers as a Grimm. Despite their feelings for each other, both make it clear that neither want to have sex, under those circumstances, ultimately making this sex compelled or coerced by Schade as well. The sexual encounter also culminates in Silverton's loss of self. Her personality changes, and she gains the magical powers of a *Hexenbiest*. Eventually, she calls herself "Eve" and distances herself from her old identity completely, leaving behind everything from her job to her relationships.

However, in yet another inversion, it must be recalled that Schade is herself a victim of the rape culture in the *Grimm* universe, well before her assault on Burkhardt, a trauma that sets in motion her future predatory acts. Schade is sexually degraded by her mother and Captain Renard, who pressures her into coercing Griffith and Burkhardt into sex. Both sexual assaults serve as a weapon of war in which she is an instrument. They are not acts that bring her pleasure, and indeed, are acts in which Schade is not a fully willing but coerced participant. Her victimization by rape culture escalates during a violent conflict with Burkhardt when he pins her to the ground, climbs on top of her, and kisses her against her will, penetrating her mouth with his tongue. Biting him in defense, she ingests his blood, thereby stripping her *Hexenbiest* abilities (S1, E17: "Love Sick"). To be clear, at this moment, she ceases to be a *Hexenbiest* fighting a *Grimm* and becomes a woman fighting off a sexual assailant. He exerts his control over her, takes away her ability to resist, and strips her of her magic, forever changing her both mentally and physically.

The act and its unfolding aftermath resemble the pathology of sexual assault. When Schade reaches out to loved ones expecting sympathy, she is instead brutally rejected. Her mother even blames her, asking, "How did he get his blood into you?" implying that Schade must have done something that "made" Burkhardt do this to her, mirroring the victim blaming reported by many rape survivors. Schade is romantically involved with Renard at the time, and he discards her because she has been violated, and, without her powers, she is no longer of use to him. This process emulates the experience of many rape victims who frequently describe being rejected by others after disclosing their assaults, with more than half the respondents in one survey of women who experienced sexual assault in college reporting such experiences of rejection.[49]

Adding to her pain and isolation is Burkhardt's status as a "hero." His drive to be a hero, no matter the consequences, motivated him to strip Schade of her powers, regardless of the means or how it would affect her. His actions highlight the role of savior, often positioned by society and themselves as exonerating of any action as heroic and necessary. This role parallels that of a rapist: both make choices for women based on traditional male socialization and ideas of masculinity and are exonerated by them.

Conclusion

This essay has identified several significant ways *Grimm* challenges and explores rape culture and the prevailing rape myths that shape much of the dialogue surrounding sexual assault. *Grimm* uses the specter of Wesen employing their powers to abuse and control women, mirroring the actions of rapists and demonstrates how male entitlement problematically positions women as objects of male pleasure. It also gives critical and demystifying depictions of the various abuse tactics, such as victim blaming and control, while challenging narratives such as the monster and savior myths and ideas surrounding active resistance. Despite being a fantasy-driven show, *Grimm* depicts, deconstructs, and complicates modern rape culture by displacing these mythologies into a fairy tale landscape where their violence and abuse are made clear. Art and entertainment can shape social views and significantly influence cultural perceptions. When writers use rape metaphorically or otherwise, they open sexual assault and rape culture discussions as a plot device. There is great value in telling the stories of survivors and interrogating the structure of rape myths and the culture that perpetuates them. *Grimm* is thus exemplary in its attempts at engaging with and deconstructing rape culture in its fairy tale revision of the police procedural.

Notes

1. Showtime, 1982–1987.
2. ABC, 2011–2018.
3. The most recent being *Beauty & the Beast* (The CW, 2012–16).
4. Deirdre 179.
5. NBC, 1999–present.
6. NBC, 2014–present.
7. CBS, 2010–present.
8. CBS, 2005–2020.
9. The most recent being *Elementary* (CBS, 2012–19).
10. CBS, 2003–present.
11. UPN, 2004–06; The CW, 2006–07; Hulu, 2019.
12. See Kahlor and Eastin 215.
13. See Kahlor and Eastin 215.
14. See Rozee and Koss 295.
15. See Rosee and Koss.
16. *Ibid.* 299.

17. *Ibid.* 298.
18. See MacKinnon.
19. See Rozee and Koss 303.
20. See Kahlor and Eastin 216.
21. See Burt 217.
22. See Roser and Koss.
23. One example is Episode 6.7, "Middle Man."
24. One example is Episode 14.24, "Her Negotiation."
25. Actor, Tim Bagley.
26. Ariel Castro, John Thomas Jamelske, and Gary Michael Heidnik all famously kept their victims locked in basements for years.
27. See Orenstein 58.
28. Actor, Patrick Fischler.
29. See Cooper 111.
30. Cinderella ends up happily married at the end of Perrault's and The Brother's Grimm's versions of the story.
31. See Moffett.
32. See Perrault.
33. See Moffett.
34. These include: Hanly, Healy, and Scriver; Koss.
35. *Ibid.*
36. Actor, Leah Renee.
37. Rozee and Koss define "sexual entitlement" as: "touching women with no regard for their wishes, sexualizing relationships that are not sexual, inappropriately intimate conversation, sexual jokes at inappropriate times or places, or commenting on women's bodies, preference for impersonal as opposed to emotionally bonded relationship context for sexuality, and endorsement of the sexual double standard" (299).
38. Actor, Josh Mead.
39. Actor, Max Artsis.
40. *Ibid.* 296.
41. See Wells and Motley 157.
42. See Rozee and Koss 297.
43. See Chappell.
44. She is repeatedly shown updating Renard on her "progress" with Griffith and takes direction from him to manipulate him, implying that it was done at Renard's behest.
45. See Rozee and. Koss 300.
46. *Ibid.* 302.
47. *Ibid.* 300.
48. Even the necessity that Renard kiss an unconscious Silverton to awake her from her magically induced comma is a form of sexual assault.
49. See Guerette and Caron 46–47.

Works Cited

Burt, Martha R. "Cultural Myths and Supports for Rape." *Journal of Personality and Social Psychology*, vol. 38, no. 2, 1980, pp. 217–230.
Cooper, C.J. *Symbolic and Mythological Animals*. Aquarian, 1992.
Chappell, Les. "TV Review: *Grimm*: Heartbreaker." *AV Club*, 03 Mar. 2015, https://tv.avclub.com/grimm-heartbreaker-1798183583. Accessed 1 Mar 2020.
Grimm, The Complete Collection. Created by Stephen Carpenter, David Greenwalt, and Jim Kouf. Perf. David Giuntoli, Russell Hornsby, Silas Weir Mitchell, Bitsie Tulloch, Sasha Roiz, Claire Coffee, Bree Turner. NBC, 2011–2017. Blu-ray. Universal Pictures Home Entertainment, 2018.
Guerette, Sarah M., and Sandra L. Caron. "Assessing the Impact of Acquaintance Rape: Interviews with Women Who Are Victims/Survivors of Sexual Assault While in College." *Journal of College Student Psychotherapy*, vol. 22, no. 2, 2007, pp. 31–50.

84   Part One: Identity and Identification

Hanly, Conor, Deirdre Healy, and Stacey Scriver. *Rape and Justice in Ireland.* Liffey, 2010.

Kahlor, LeeAnn, and Matthew S. Eastin. "Television's Role in the Culture of Violence Toward Women: A Study of Television Viewing and the Cultivation of Rape Myth Acceptance in the United States." *Journal of Broadcasting & Electronic Media,* vol. 55, no. 2, 2011, pp. 215–231.

Koss, M.P. "Blame, Shame, and Community: Justice Responses to Violence Against Women." *American Psychology,* vol. 55, no. 11, 2000, pp. 1332–1343.

MacKinnon, Catharine A. "Feminism, Marxism, Method, and the State: Toward Feminist Jurisprudence." *Signs,* vol. 8, no. 4, 1983, pp. 635–658.

Moffett, Helen. "Stemming the Tide: Countering Public Narratives of Sexual Violence." *Womankind Worldwide.* 2003, www.womankind.org.uk.

Orenstein, Catherine. *Little Red Riding Hood Uncloaked: Sex, Morality, and the Evolution of a Fairy Tale.* Basic Books, 2002.

Perrault, Charles. *Little Red Riding Hood.* Translated by W. Heath Robinson, Everyman's Library, 1996.

Rozee, Patricia D., and Mary P. Koss. "Rape: A Century of Resistance." *Psychology of Women Quarterly,* vol. 25, no. 4, 2011, pp. 295–311.

Wells, Christina, and Erin Elliott Motley. "Reinforcing the Myth of the Crazed Rapist: A Feminist Critique of Recent Rape Legislation." *Boston U Law Review,* vol. 81, no. 1, 2001, pp. 127–198.

Part Two
Justice and Social Spaces

Grimm

Disillusioning Privilege and Developing a Practice of Listening

MATTHEW GRINDER

As children, the phrase "Once upon a time" prepares the mind for fantastical stories of magical beings and heroes—likely princes—who pit their warrior skills and cunning against monsters, witches, and dragons to save a princess. Other stories overflow with thievery, betrayal, and revenge, yet somehow end with a happily ever after for those who dream big enough and work to overcome obstacles. Generally, the "happily ever after" (HEA) ending entails achieving goals, acquiring wealth and power, and the triumph of what is good or moral over that which is considered evil or immoral.[1] As exemplary stories for children, fairy tales create frameworks to understand the world and how it functions. Such constructions are often built on principles of gendered social conditioning, giving boys and girls specific attributes that lead to their often stereotyped HEA.[2] They also reify a status hierarchy connecting moral and economic work where rivals are punished while the innocent or heroic gain happiness—and often kingdoms—through marriage and wealth. *Grimm*, this essay argues, disrupts these hierarchies by questioning "happy ending for who?" and envisioning a very different process for achieving them.

The traditional HEA framework persists in modern culture through varied mediums and is exemplified and interrogated through television programs from the 1990s that incorporate fairy-tale elements. Two successful programs of this nature are *Buffy the Vampire Slayer* (1992–2004) and its spinoff *Angel* (1999–2004). Both series laminate the fairy-tale framework of an ancient evil in a youthful California landscape to situate transgressions of the wicked within contemporary cultural conflicts aimed at teenagers and young adults. Predicated on the strong emotions of their protagonists, these shows illustrate the punishment of the wicked through frameworks of supernatural violence. *Buffy* tells the story of a teenage girl in a suburban high school who slays vampires with her friends. *Angel* tells the story of the eternally twenty-something-vampire and his motley collection of young adult sidekicks fighting crime in a noir Los Angeles. Both employ the vampire or demonic trope to represent oppressive forces violently seeking to marginalize and consume identities before they are realized. As a "Slayer," Buffy[3] rises to fight these forces while Angel,[4] a vampire with a soul, seeks redemption for his part in the violence of historical oppression. What *Buffy* and *Angel* both retain is discrimination between good and evil, heroes and monsters. While both series address social injustice by bringing violent retribution to demons and monsters who represent oppressive forces consuming the marginalized, they also leave little room for redemption, reconciliation, or personal growth. The dominant narrative is that evil things must be punished or destroyed to achieve the hero's happiness: a zero-sum game.

The simple fairy-tale framework of good and evil yields binary happy endings that mirror the reductiveness of the fairy-tale ontologies. *Buffy* and *Angel* only partially seek to overcome such limitations in the complexity of their protagonists. Members of their creative teams, however, directly challenge this reductiveness in their later show *Grimm*. Perhaps un-coincidentally, *Grimm* focuses on characters in their early thirties who are firmly established in their adult lives and identities. Building on characters who are not adolescents but socially-established adults who, as Nietzsche would say, have become who they are, allows for a different and ultimately more successful critique of the HEA through their character Nick Burkhardt. When the show begins, Nick exemplifies how deeply the privileged mythology of HEA pervades mainstream American culture and the degree to which its illusions are rooted in reductive othering and supersession of the different, vulnerable, and marginalized. Nick is about to fulfill one standardized version of the western HEA by proposing to his girlfriend Juliette Silverton, with whom he lives in dreamy domesticity. Nevertheless, this normative fantasia is disenchanted and dismantled, leading to the demystification of the simplistic dichotomy of good and evil on which the supernaturally-themed shows like *Buffy* and *Angel* had rested. *Grimm* critiques such dichotomies by unmasking the troubled hegemony of a singular history and normative narrative, allowing various historical, cultural, and marginalized voices to speak while the hero listens, reflects, and engages in dialogues about counter-histories.[5]

Nick serves as a model for developing a practice of listening, serving as a proxy beginner in redressing the ongoing marginalization and persecution of vulnerable populations.[6] *Grimm* presents a fairy-tale format that demystifies the trope of HEA, revealing its imperviousness to critique within an echo chamber of privilege. Through subversion of this fairy-tale form, *Grimm* provides a foundation for exploring contemporary questions and rationalizations of privilege, such as: "Why is it my problem that marginalization happens?," "Don't all lives matter?," and "Why do I need to change when none of this is my fault?"

These questions are not easy to answer, mainly because they seize upon the privileged position of the questioner as an unquestionable given. There are no answers because they are the wrong questions. Instead, the series models Nick's growth beyond the HEA, engaging a complex awareness of cultural diversity and personal development. Reformulating the fairy-tale "hero" as a questioner, listener, and thinker creates a protagonist designed to invite mainstream Americans into an honest engagement with marginalized populations by promoting an ongoing reconciliation process.[7] Nick is a white, middle-class, heteronormative American man struggling honestly to listen, recognize his internal biases, and become more than the stereotypical, decapitating Grimm. This essay considers Nick to be a radically transformed hero for the contemporary moment, a hero who learns to listen. While his heroic status may vary within the series, he demonstrates the complex and challenging process of leaving a privileged narrative to recognize and dismantle social injustice in the real world.

Part 1: A Hero of Dialogue

Grimm departs from the heroic monologue of the often-repeated one-story fairy-tale structure or what Joseph Campbell has called the Monomyth. As an alternative, the series presents a complex world where the hero, Nick, interrogates his beliefs and understanding of the world. As his identity shifts into that of the Grimm, he questions his values as both a member of normative white American culture whose job is to enforce cultural laws to keep the peace and as a Grimm whose role has historically been to violently kill those designated as "evil" in the name of what has been culturally identified as "good." Nick experiences a process of becoming that is radically different from predecessors such as Buffy and Angel. These characters reproduce a binary moral logic of right and wrong, acting on the authority of their impulses, emotions, and opinions without nuanced discernment.

While both Buffy and Angel are supernatural heroes who fight against supernatural evil, they represent heroic origins that cast good and evil within a presumed history of innocent victims who are primarily human or human-conforming and evil predators who are supernatural.

Buffy inherits the role of "Slayer" to fight against vampires. However, as the final season reveals, this role is established through historical victimization: the first Slayer was an indigenous woman of color who was magically abused and tormented by radical monks who wanted to use her as a tool to fight evil.[8] Her superhero inheritance is thus also the inheritance of a historically suppressed double-victim status that fights the first evil that spawned creatures like vampires and necessitated the formation of slayers and the patriarchal evil that made slayers by turning a woman into a weapon without her consent. The show terminates with her fighting to overcome the victim history by perpetuating it: She makes more non-consensual slayers for fighting monsters while avoiding the racial violence of the Slayer's origin entirely.

By contrast, Angel's history begins as an established member of the patriarchy reveling in his white male privilege as the son of an 18th-century Anglo-Irish, nouveau riche silk and linen merchant, and described as *"A drunk, whoring layabout and a terrible disappointment to your parents."*[9] His sexualized conversion to vampirism during an evening of extreme intoxication renders him the unambiguously evil Angelus. Within the show's mythology, his early life is dismissed as simple buffoonery—an Oedipal struggle with his father. It gives as little attention to the political populism that financially promotes his mercer father and the sexism that socially condones his "gentlemanly" lifestyle as does the character. As Angelus, he develops a reputation for unspeakable psychopathic violence toward humans. He then is cursed by the Kalderash with a soul allowing him to become consciously aware of all the evil he did as a vampire.[10] Notably, his soul remains utterly unconscious of any pre–Angelus misdeeds beyond the occasional moment of filial regret. After the curse, Angel ceases his predation. He becomes a hero for trying to atone for his vampiric past by killing those who engage in the same violence he had once so gleefully perpetrated.

Neither of these shows addresses the complexities of their fictional histories or alters the fundamental dichotomy of good and evil in any meaningful way, with the exception that *Buffy* extends what counts as evil from supernatural to transcendental misogyny. However, if it enlarges the scope of evil, then *Angel* articulates its absolute status by shifting from "evil" to "good" via magic that is meant to make him suffer, leaving no space in between. A significant cross-over character who unites the two series, Spike,[11] also demonstrates another kind of shift from evil to good, seeking out a soul. His transformation, however, is sought out not because he feels he did anything wrong but because he wants to impress Buffy. As with Angel, however, magic plays a strong hand in perspective changes. Spike, it turns out, is a singularly prophesied figure for fighting the evil in which he was previously complicit—not because he was evil but because of the woman hero he loves and the larger supernatural framework in which their fictional world exists desire it. In the end, both *Buffy* and *Angel* share a crucial framing of the evil Other. There is no nuance or flexibility in the categories of good and evil. No remedy to their conflict exists beyond violent suppression, if not extermination of the evil other. Neither is there any genuinely independent desire demonstrated to assess the individual's complicity in "evil" systems; instead, it is always a kind of supernatural compulsion. Theirs are fairy-tale worlds of absolutes of clearly heroic and villainous behaviors where the hero's call is magically compelled. The way to a happy ending requires the violent removal or overthrow of the villain to benefit the innocent and the good.

Grimm, by contrast, presents a protagonist who takes a critical stance toward the fairy-tale world to consider the possibility of greater complexity in concepts of justice than mere good and evil. Nick emerges as a hero who approaches the social other beyond self-affirming emotions or binary logic. While he can fight with supernatural power against what is perceived as evil, he can and does choose to listen and thereby reconsider what constitutes evil or good. This choice makes him a more complex hero than his predecessors, different in kind rather than degree.

Buffy and *Angel* are shows in which the hero fights to protect the social status quo of a normative white America. Nick begins by embodying that culture as its gatekeeper, a police officer, following his path to the socially codified HEA of marriage and financial stability. When he is confronted by what exists on the borders of that tableau and the dark history that helped to craft its privilege and its ignorance, Nick begins to ask questions about the structure of good and evil and the role he plays within it: "How should I live with those that are different from me?" and "How can I live tolerantly with those I do not agree with?" By promoting questions about how to begin creating a more tolerant and just society, *Grimm* problematizes the need for education about the physical and cultural violence of the past and an expanded understanding of the realities surrounding the fantasy of the innocence and the goodness of white, middle-class American HEA. In turn, it dismantles the fairy-tale framework in which there is a clear villain or evil to be fought or killed and replaces the HEA paradigm with an invitation to reflect, reconcile, and listen.

Part 2: Beyond "Happily Ever After"

Grimm's disruption of "happily ever after" allows for an awareness of a world that exists beyond the hegemonic, mainstream American vision for society. In *Grimm*'s first episode, Nick's lifestyle reflects a familiar white middle-class ideal that unwittingly separates itself from marginalized populations.[12] He must grow beyond this worldview as he examines and acknowledges his internal biases fostered by cultural conditioning.[13] Raised by his librarian Aunt Marie after what he believes to be his parent's accidental death, Nick remains subject to the particular social blindness of middle-class life. After graduating high school, Nick most likely completed a college education then pursued a career as a Portland homicide detective. Such a job provides a substantial enough salary to live in a beautiful house in an affluent neighborhood with his highly educated veterinarian girlfriend, Juliette Silverton. The series opens as Nick buys an unmistakable symbol of HEA, an engagement ring. In nearly reaching his HEA, Nick foresees his life leveling out onto a plateau of a comfortable existence.

The attractive framework of HEA limits Nick's worldview to the bubble of middle-class existence and its laws of absolute right and wrong. Nick is living in the illusion that everything is perfect because everything conforms to these middle-class ideals. Even his vocational life reflects a sense of perfect equilibrium: Nick has never had to draw his weapon in the line of duty; nor has any conflict within his racially and ethnically diverse police department arisen; nor are there any conflicts regarding unfair wages, affirmative action, or gender politics. Markedly, men rule this police department unproblematically, intimating a tacit acceptance of separate spheres: active regulation for men and sentimental complementarity for women. Everything and everyone have a place. Nick's world becomes a mirror of mainstream American reality as he remains comfortably unaware of social conflicts from within the security of HEA. As long as everything remains in place, Nick retains his secure HEA ontology.

Nick's comfort is radically disrupted with the arrival and eventual death of his Aunt Marie.[14] Most strikingly, he begins to perceive the faces of everyday people contorting into monstrosities. Understandably, he at first believes himself to be experiencing a psychological break with reality. When his aunt engages him regarding the visions, she explains that he is a Grimm, and it is his genetic/familial duty to police the Wesen or fairy-tale monsters and "hunt down the bad ones."[15] Nick is disoriented by his newfound abilities and their socio-historical implications, as well as the death of his aunt from cancer (further aggravated by a Wesen assault). As a result, he slips into a space between identities, confronting what he wanted to be, his HEA, and what he is expected to be as a Grimm.[16]

Initially, Nick resists the idea of his supernatural Grimm heritage that marks him as a police enforcer of the Wesen community. Because his Grimm identity is unseen by humans and feared by Wesen and Royals alike, Nick is outside the communities with which his identity intersects. Throughout the series, a hierarchy of supernatural beings emerges. The Royals, who discovered and enslaved the Wesen in ancient times, fear their strength and numbers, employing the Grimms as enforcers and overseers of their population. Understood as more than human, Grimms became the iron fist of the Royals. They struck fear in the Wesen community, acting in the roles of intelligence officers and executioners who observe, record, and kill in the name of progress, empire, and civilized human safety, compelling Wesen to live in the shadows.[17]

Feeling anxious and lost in his newfound power, Nick needs a teacher who can help him learn to use such powers responsibly. Unfortunately, such a teacher cannot be found in the comfortable world of HEA. Acting as a homicide detective, informed in part by his Grimm senses, Nick discovers Monroe while investigating the kidnapping of a young girl wearing a red jacket. With an unmistakable social awkwardness, Monroe appears while checking his mail. He sniffs the air as two children ride past on bicycles, briefly revealing his *Blutbad* nature to the supernaturally Wesen-sensible Grimm (S1, E1: "Pilot"). Understandably, Nick reacts to a stereotypical "creep" factor by trying to arrest Monroe. Hereafter, through a series of conversations, Monroe begins to teach Nick what it means to be a Grimm—as a story told from the side of the victims that departs from the briefly uttered absolutes of his Aunt. Monroe's perspective yields a counter-narrative wherein Grimms are the story-time monsters who live under the bed of Wesen children or act as threatened agents of discipline: the Grimm comes in the night to chop off the heads of little Wesen who do not behave. More gruesomely, they are also the force that has indiscriminately murdered his kind for centuries. Monroe reveals that Aunt Marie had a bloody reputation of such violent beheadings in her younger years that make the children's stories so scary but without the morally didactic function.[18]

Nick quickly realizes that Monroe understands the "real world" better than he does, and in his fear, *demands* an answer from Monroe, as any self-respecting, however self-centered, student might. Specifically, Nick wants to know how to "cure" himself to return to his ordinary life: he does not want to know what he does not know. Nick is neither ready to reconcile neither with his new identity nor his new reality. From the second episode onward, however, as he sees how his powers and newfound knowledge can be used to protect the innocent, Nick dedicates himself to learning all he can about Grimm and Wesen history. He reads ancestral journals left to him by his aunt, and he pursues Monroe until he essentially agrees to be his mentor and, ultimately, his closest friend. He listens to his traditional enemies' views and goes so far as to serve as the best man at a Wesen wedding. However, the more he learns about the violence and oppression of his Grimm heritage, the more guilt, anger, defensiveness, and helplessness he feels, reflecting fear about and for his own identity. This fear reinforces a desire for the simple, normative HEA and a return to the state of ignorance. Nevertheless, he increasingly engages with the newfound information he discovers surrounding his identity and begins to craft a new role that he can play in the world. Eventually, he wholly rejects the former HEA just as he rejected the role of the Grimm in episode one, carving out a more informed, tentative path.

As Monroe explains, once one is aware of the "real world," there is no going back, and there is no cure for ancestry or identity.[19] Coinciding with his realization that there is no return to ignorance, Nick does what no Grimm in history had ever done. He asks Monroe, a Wesen, to teach him what it means to be a Grimm and how to change Wesen perceptions of Grimms. Shocked, Monroe eventually agrees, and, to his credit, Nick listens. Not only does he listen, but he begins to engage with Monroe by asking questions so that Monroe acts as a dialoguer. As Nick listens, he begins to understand better the nature of the crimes of his ancestors and the necessity to reform the Grimm reputation in order to lead Wesen and Grimms toward a truthful, ongoing process of reconciliation.[20] The process, however, is not strictly limited to the world of the Wesen, and reaches toward the atrocities committed by Western European and Euro-American in the past. Like the history of the Grimms, these dominant narratives are unmasked by giving voice to the experience and oppression of the "Other."

Part 3: How a Grimm Learns to Listen

For Nick to develop a practice of listening, he must first recognize that his viewpoint had previously only extended to the world as he knew it. Through the Grimm journals and Monroe's tutelage, his worldview expands, allowing Nick to recognize a world beyond the illusions in which he had lived. Once his awareness expands, he enters a process of listening and dialogue that guides his actions better to understand the issues present in the Wesen community while recognizing them as an equal cultural group deserving of his assistance and protection. Through the process of listening, Nick cultivates lasting relationships with the Wesen he encounters; most notably Monroe (a *Blutbad*), Bud[21] (an *Eisbiber*), Rosalee (a *Fuchsbau*), and, eventually, one of the more prominent "villains" in the show, Adalind (a *Hexenbiest*). Similarly, when Nick listens to the *Eisbibers*, he discovers their gentle and anxious dispositions and how they have made them a target for harassment and persecution by humans and Wesen.[22] With this information, he can protect this population from exploitation by empowering the *Eisbibers* to send their assailants to prison with a murder conviction. He both realizes and demonstrates to the community that their lives matter to a Grimm. Nick develops strong friendships and reliance on Rosalee (the romantic interest of Monroe), winning her trust by investigating and arresting her brother's murderers. He begins to reevaluate Adalind through insight into her past and the complex power constellations of her present. These meaningful relationships in the Wesen community set Nick apart from his blood-thirsty ancestors.[23] His change in perspective affects Wesen's perceptions of him as a Grimm and the potential for what such an identity could entail.

Nick's potentiality is exemplified further in his diplomatic influence with other Grimms. Notably, Nick has a significant influence on Trubel and, to a lesser extent, his mother, Kelly, on how they view and relate to Wesen. Through his example and encouragement, they can move from positions from which all Wesen must be killed to one that suggests that Wesen are individuals, not all of whom are evil. As their opinions change, so do their views that Wesen deserve the same, and in some cases, even more protection than humans.[24,25] In these cases, Nick sets the example for other Grimms that mindful listening leads to a change of opinion, leading to better understanding and better outcomes for everyone.[26]

Nick's listening practice enables him to confidently self-fashion a new identity and departs from the inherited identity of the Grimm. It enables dialogue concerning his past and how that past affects his present.[27] On a larger scale, it also opens up discussion on how histories sculpt unequal identities that have devastating impacts on communities that surround him. One powerful example of this practice arises when a local school calls him and Hank to investigate the murder of a custodial staff member, leading to the discovery of racist graffiti sprayed on a young Native American student's locker.[28] Examining the case in detail highlights the power and potential of this listening model.

While investigating Simon George,[29] a young Native American student of Ojibwe ancestry, Nick and Hank visit the nearby reservation. Here they discover that Simon, seeking to connect with his tribal heritage, has embarked on a power quest for holistic healing from the trauma of witnessing the racially motivated murder of his father by three white men. Part of the healing process in the power quest involves communion with his guardian spirit animal that brings him a new name and a new identity and healing for his soul.[30] However, this healing cannot be achieved alone: it is not solely the work of the oppressed individual to recover from collective historical traumas. A full recovery requires public acts of legitimation and justice. If Simon's father's murderers escape justice, his identity will remain violently divided between revenge and becoming. To aid Simon, the *Mishipeshu*, a mythic water cat originating in Lake Superior, becomes Simon's spirit animal. It possesses him to bring inescapable justice to the murderers for his father.[31]

Neither Monroe nor the Grimm journals can explain the nature of the *Mishipeshu* since it is more spirit than Wesen. Seeking to understand leads Nick to Hector,[32] a reservation museum curator, and spiritual guide.[33] Although he comes from a Western United States tribal tradition (an important but subtle point that resists simple ethnic reductionism in the show), he generally understands Simon's ceremony. He acts as a dialoguer with Nick to give context to Simon's experience and situate his father's death in a larger story than simple homicide. To find Simon, Hector suggests a ceremony. Hector excludes Nick, explaining that he has darkness within, and participation in the ceremony would dishonor the ceremony and degrade Nick's spirit.[34] Rather than demanding access or forcing his participation out of a sense of egoism or entitlement, Nick listens and watches, demonstrating respect for Hector, Simon, their judgment, and their sacred ceremonies and traditions.

Unlike other episodes where Nick, like a Buffy or Angel, strong-arms his way through intense and challenging violent conflicts, his pursuit of the *Mishipeshu* leads to a revelation. As a law enforcement agent, he wants to prevent the vendetta of justice of the *Mishipeshu's* vengeance. However, he recognizes how utterly justice has failed people and how they have been marginalized, victimized, and dehumanized by public institutions. This failure is something his original HEA never needed to consider and perhaps needs to suppress in order to exist. This episode explores the systematic failures experienced by Simon and the offensive, racist stereotypes and harassment of Native Americans.[35] Simon and his victimization are as invisible as Wesen as they are to the fairy tale of normative American life. The only difference is that in Native American subjugation, it is not that people cannot see; it is that they will not bother to look. As a result of this insular ignorance, Simon's humanity is dismissed by the justice system, his school, and mainstream America generally, reducing him to a mere "Indian" and its pejorative usage. In its current use by mainstream Americans, "Indian," suggests not a person but a mystical savage, a relic of nature existing in the past but now extinct in the present. In his invisibility, Simon's world became real the night of his father's murder, and the only way to achieve justice is through the spirit of *Mishipeshu*.

While Nick can never fully appreciate Simon's "nobodiness," he can approach Simon empathetically. After all, he is also striving for self-understanding.[36] Feeling empathy is all Nick can do since the Grimm exists to police Wesen and, implicitly, any other supernatural threat. His listening leads to recognizing that the *Mishipeshu* will only stop once all three murderers have been brought to justice. In his capacity as a detective in the current case, Nick is helpless. Arresting Simon will only solidify his nobodiness, and the *Mishipeshu* will inhabit another body to finish the work. Attempting to prosecute the murder so many years after the failure of justice is also impractical: two of the murderers had already died when Nick takes the case, and the other is finished off by the *Mishipeshu* before Nick can arrest him and gamble for justice in the courts.

In the end, Nick's listening attitude protects Simon's life by keeping him out of prison and by opening up a dialogue within the show while also communicating a disturbing reality to viewers. Through the idea of American exceptionalism, mainstream Americans continue to marginalize specific populations by redefining humanity, forgetting the guilt of past atrocities, and even rewriting history to make their legacies seem more heroically legitimate. Simon embodies a history of racialized abuse, trauma, nobodying, and violence from white "heroes" and their institutions at all levels of Native American history since the first European contact. In his listening, Nick performs a suspension of judgment that allows for uncomfortable, often painful conversations. He thereby presents an example of listening as a new heroic paradigm, suggesting that sometimes justice begins with learning, empathizing, and being willing to take critical instruction. Nick strives to empathize with Simon without labeling him, even as his experience parallels a quest for identity. Listening brings the social "nobody" from the margins into a dialogue where difficult conversations must happen for the change to occur.

Part 4: Creating Monsters at Home

While Nick is willing to champion racially marginalized populations, he is not a consistent heroic exemplar or archetype. While Nick struggles with moments of internal bias by which he regresses into typical tropes of righteous violence, he also tends to return to the taxonomy of pre-determined good and bad as well as fantasies of entitlement particular to the HEA. Nick's most evident HEA fantasy is his long-held and idealized domestic image of life with Juliette. As the series progresses, Nick begins treating her first as a domestic caregiver and later as a monstrous woman.[37] Despite examples of listening within the world of *Grimm*, it reflects a reality where women remain "other," whether Wesen or human. Juliette represents a sentimental identity that Nick instrumentalizes, sacrificing her humanity to restore his powers. Unlike Wesen communities, Juliette's community has already diminished her because of her gender, eventually abjects her as a loathsome, unassimilable entity when she becomes a *Hexenbiest*.[38]

Nick has tended to see Juliette as an extension of himself. He fails to recognize that, as an independent individual, she has attitudes and beliefs that diverge from his own. His desire to preserve her pre–Grimm identity frames her as a professional occupying a feminized domestic space in their relationship (S4, E22: "Cry Havoc"). Nick stops listening to Juliette after she restores his powers as a Grimm, partly because he does not want to hear anything threatening how he understands her. Juliette's independent identity empowers her to reject his marriage proposal, realizing her identity transformation and independence as a *Hexenbiest*. As she begins to contradict the imagined identity openly, Nick more strongly limits her to the identity of subordinate caregiver and recoils from her personal growth and change. He still does not kill Juliette when he has the chance, but this is more to protect his memories than to affirm her value.[39] At the apex of his new heroism, he is still plagued by remnants of old ideologies that have yet to find resolution beyond self-reflection.

Overall, Nick's stickiest bias throughout the first four seasons of *Grimm* is entangled with *Hexenbiests*. As female figures, they become the antithesis of Nick as a Grimm and represent feminism that is still considered monstrous by mainstream Americans, especially men, who seem to fear strong and independently-minded women outside patriarchal control measures. Rather than submitting to domestic imperialistic dictates, these women pursue ambitions beyond the domestic space or family. Representative of ambitious women, *Hexenbiests* have strong wills and bodies that allow them to hold their own against Grimms.[40] Their power is generally feared even amongst the Wesen community, and they have in-depth knowledge of the natural world and its cycles.[41] Because it is intimately connected with nature, *Hexenbiest* power is generally feared amongst the Wesen community. While they are considered treacherous, they are also incredibly loyal to those they claim to love and serve.

Adalind is the first *Hexenbiest* Nick encounters, and instead of listening to her or trying to understand her, he immediately regards her as an enemy. She is the opposite of Juliette and challenges Nick's expectations for women. She is comfortable in her skin and is primarily independent, representing women who are demonized for gravitating away from stereotypes of feminine expectations.[42] Even outwardly, Adalind embodies a feminine ideal. She is blond, slender, beautiful as well as intelligent, which leads to her professional success. Overall, Adalind demonstrates both the real-world mistrust of the independent, ambitious female professional and the mistrusted *Hexenbiest* feared by nearly all Wesen in the Grimmverse. Nick decides Adalind is not worth listening to as she embodies the most monstrous of female qualities.

Primarily guided by the opinions of Monroe, the Wesen community, and the Grimm journals, Nick allows himself to become prejudiced against all *Hexenbiests*. This prejudice develops into skirmishes with Adalind, leading to the loss of his Grimm powers (S3, E22: "Blond Ambition"). Not only does Nick hate Adalind for taking his powers, but he also encourages others to hate her as well. It is not until Adalind tells Nick that she is pregnant with his child that he begins to soften and listen (S4, E13: "Trial by Fire"). While Nick eventually learns to accept and even love her, he understood her as evil until she became the mother of his child.

Hexenbiests reveal an unacknowledged bias in Nick's new awareness as a hero that listens since he would have women, especially Juliette and Adalind, change to suit his needs. However, what Nick fails to realize concerning *Hexenbiest*s is that their identity is based on self-definition first and, secondly, on their ability to complete tasks for those to whom they are loyal. From the day Nick became a Grimm, his HEA dissolved, as does Juliette's. At the same time, Nick only truly hears Adalind after she is pregnant with his child, as he again can foresee a new potential HEA. Nick, perhaps inadvertently, presents another consideration for mainstream Americans: spouses/partners are not static possessions. Instead, they are individuals with lives, thoughts, beliefs, ambitions, and experiences that deserve an audience.

Conclusion

Fairy tales can provide a valuable interface to shape the awareness and development of individuals, teaching them to consider the world they inhabit and provide a means for evaluating norms and morals for living in a better world. The format of the modern fairy tale presents social justice issues that expand the awareness of mainstream Americans. *Grimm* offers a representation of mainstream American life reaching beyond the illusion of the "happily ever after" as Nick exemplifies a process for developing a practice of listening to marginalized and persecuted people. He demonstrates a genuine internal struggle of a privileged white, straight, middle-class, American man who seeks to accept the truth of his actions and pursue reconciliation by learning to listen, dialogue, and act to change the privileged and marginalized perceptions.

At the same time, Nick demonstrates that heroes are imperfect, requiring constant development. Internal biases guide his perceptions even as he struggles to overcome his preconceptions. He demonstrates that marginalization is not just something historical but also actively happening closer to home. *Grimm* offers a glimpse of how predominately white, heteronormative, middle-class Americans, particularly men, can use a practice of listening to discover internal biases and remediate them beyond "happily ever after." In the end, *Grimm's* pairing of fairy tales with social justice enables it to educate viewers. It provides an example of how privilege, however well-intentioned, can create marginalization. It also suggests a solution: develop a practice of listening to discover and dismantle the systemic evils hidden within "happily ever after."

Notes

1. See Churchwell.
2. Bettelheim 25.
3. Actor, Sarah Michelle Geller.
4. Actor, David Boreanaz.
5. Definitions of counter-history have been drawn from Gabriel Rockhill's interpretation of Michel Foucault's concept from "Society Must Be Defended." Counter-history "counters the moralizations of history by developing a multidimensional account that is recalcitrant to categorical moral judgments from a single vantage point within a system of values that is at least partial de-historicized. In other words, it resituates *all* values within ongoing collective struggles" (109).
6. Row 2.
7. Bettelheim 25.
8. *Buffy the Vampire Slayer* S4, E22: "Restless."
9. *Angel* S1, E15: "Prodigal"
10. *Ibid.* S1, E7: "Angel"; *Ibid.* S2, E13: "Surprise."
11. Actor, James Marsters.
12. Derald Wing Sue's *Microaggressions in Everyday Life* pages 250–254 illustrate this process of internal bias.
13. Nick reflects the tyrannical history of mainstream American policy designed to marginalize minority populations while living in ignorance of marginalization. Carol Anderson's *White Rage* provides a wonderful overview of these policies that construct mainstream American conditioning through policy.
14. *Ibid.*
15. See Festinger.
16. It is noteworthy that many of Nick's ancestors were conquistadors, anthropologists, explorers, and detectives whose journals reflect early considerations of human hierarchies being apparent in the nineteenth century. The Grimm brothers, in the context of the show, were considered the most brutal, collecting folktales for the express purpose of killing Wesen (S1, E1: "Pilot").
17. Sue 250–254.
18. *Ibid.*
19. Kristeva provides a fuller view of this horrific identity: 4, 15, 65.
20. *Ibid.*
21. Actor, Danny Bruno.
22. The concept of an art or philosophy of listening can be found in Eric Fromm's *The Art of Listening* (192–193) where "art" deals with the living voice of another. Mortimer J. Adler in *How to Speak How to Listen* (85–136) and Derald Wing Sue (253) provide templates for how listening must be done in an attitude of complete focus without an agenda.

23. Haroutunian-Gordon provides a consideration for the place of dialogue between students and teachers.

24. Nick's developing sense of listening reflects David Bohm's dialogic method in *On Dialogue* as well as F. David Peat's *A Gentle Action Theory* that both use the process of dialogue that gently allows difficult conversations to take place where everyone involved is acknowledged and affirmed all the time as being worth listening to. Through this process, Nick becomes an example of how listening becomes a force for positive change as he models how the world should take action.

25. S1, E19: "Leave it to Beavers."

26. S1, E15: "Island of Dreams."

27. S3, E19: "Nobody Knows the Trubel I've Seen"; S2, E1: "Bad Teeth."

28. For example, S2, E9: "La Llorona"; S2, E18: "Volcanalis"; S4, E4: "Dyin' on a Prayer"; S6, E9: "Tree People" all have various natural spirits of retributive justice, but they are largely inconsistent in their behavior and motives, especially *La Llorona* and *Volcanalis*, providing no specific motivation for their actions.

29. Actor (teenager), Booboo Stewart.

30. This is presented well in S4, E18: "Mishipeshu."

31. The concept of *Mishipeshu* reflects concepts of justice connected to identity in Native American literature such as Sherman Alexi's *Indian Killer*, Leslie Marmon Silko's *Almanac of the Dead*, or Janette Armstrong's *Slash* which all present a picture of Native American justice for stealing of land, culture, and, ultimately, lives by American colonialism.

32. Actor, Gregory Cruz.

33. While Simon's citizenship of a particular nation is not specifically mentioned in the episode, the use of the *Mishipeshu* suggests that Simon is from the Great Lakes Region of Indigenous communities.

34. Realistically, Nick's inability to participate in the ceremony reflects his inability to shed the darker connotations of his colonialist considerations of others. While he is allowed to watch, he could never fully participate since his identity remains fractured, struggling to understand how to live as a human and Grimm. Participants seem to know themselves.

35. This is summarized from Gerald Vizenor's *Narrative Chance* centered on cultural schizophrenia developed by terminal creeds (249) and institutional power (187) that use science and cultural studies that use stereotype as acceptable definitions of Native Americans.

36. Octavio Paz *The Labyrinth of Solitude and Other Writings*, Chapter 5 "The Conquest and Colonialism" presents this idea of nobodiness as the definition of the conquered who are beneath the notice of the colonizers, especially considering the conquest of the Americas by Europeans relegating Native Americans who were treated worse than animals.

37. Jeffery Cohen, *Monster Theory: Reading Culture* suggests that monsters, while marginal, may find freedom on the margins, and Juliette certainly pursues that freedom as she suddenly becomes a cultural body defined through fear and desire (14–15). Deleuze and Guittari's concept of "nomad thought" in *A Thousand Plateaus: Capitalism and Schizophrenia* provides a sense of freedom that Juliette may experience as well since mainstream thought presents a probabilistic system based on faulty logic that propagates probabilistic systems (15). Juliette can only find freedom of identity beyond mainstream American conceptions of "woman," and that makes her monstrous.

38. This can be observed in S4, E18: "Mishipeshu" Sarah Churchwell, in "Justice and Punishment in Fairytales," suggests that the role of male/female dichotomies are designed for women to submit to men. Sometimes, it can be women becoming content and complacent suggested by Colette Dowling in *The Cinderella Complex*.

39. Women can be ambitious as suggested in Peggy Orenstein's "What's Wrong with Cinderella" and her book *Cinderella Ate My Daughter*. There is a sense in which maturity of women also brings a sense of ambitious desire that goes beyond social definitions and norms.

40. Episodes that demonstrate this strength: S1, E17: "Love Sick"; S2, E2: "The Kiss"; S2, E13: "Face Off."

41. For *Hexenbiest* pursuit of power, "The Believer" (S5, E16) provides a good example. For their natural magic they have access to a recipe book that only opens with *Hexenbiest* blood, and mirrors have special locks on them that are similar. See S3, E20: "My Fair Wesen"; S4, E15: "Double Date"; and S6, E12: "Zerstörer Shrugged."

42. Nick's desire to keep Juliette in a domestic care role is an observable framework of Western Civilization; concepts of women can be seen beginning with St. Jerome's theology of women as evil in the early medieval era (*Principle Works*) to the early Modernist Rousseau's *Emile* (568–579), through Kant's era describing women in *Observations on Feeling of the Beautiful and Sublime*. Within nineteenth century American fiction, women can be observed as overgrown children in need of a patriarchal hand of guidance in Gilman's *Yellow Wallpaper* or Glaspell's *A Jury of Her Peers* that all provide insight into the abuses Juliette suffers based on conceptions of the feminine.

Works Cited

Adler, Mortimer Jerome. *How to Speak, How to Listen*. Macmillan, 1983.
Alexi, Sherman. *Indian Killer*. Open Road Media, 2013.
Anderson, Carol. *White Rage: The Unspoken Truth of Our Racial Divide*. Bloomsbury, 2017.
Angel. The WB, 5 Oct. 1999.
Armstrong, Jeannette. *Slash*. Theytus Books, 1995.
Bettelheim, Bruno. *The Uses of Enchantment: The Meaning and Importance of Fairy Tales*. Vintage Books, 2011.
Bohm, David. *On Dialogue*. Routledge, 2009.
Buffy the Vampire Slayer. The WB, 10 Mar. 1997.
Campbell, Joseph. *The Hero with a Thousand Faces*. New World Library, 2008.
Churchwell, Sarah. "Justice and Punishment in Fairy-tales." *The Guardian*, 15 Oct. 2009. www.theguardian.com/books/2009/oct/15/churchwell-justice-punishment. Accessed 16 May 2020.
Cohen, Jeffrey Jerome. *Monster Theory: Reading Culture*. U Minnesota P, 1996.
Deleuze, Gilles, and Felix Guattari. "Desiring-Production." *Anti-Oedipus: Capitalism and Schizophrenia*, translated by Robert Hurley, Mark Seem, and Helen R. Lane, Penguin, 2009, pp. 1–8.
Festinger, Leon. "Cognitive Dissonance." *Scientific America*, vol. 207, no. 4, 1962, pp. 93–106.
Foucault, Michel. *Society Must Be Defended*. Picador, 2003.
Fromm, Erich. *The Art of Listening*. Continuum, 2009.
Gilman, Charlotte Perkins. "The Yellow Wallpaper." *Points of View: An Anthology of Short Stories*, edited by James Moffett and Kenneth R. McElheny, Mentor, 1995, pp. 138–54.
Glaspell, Susan. *A Jury of Her Peers*. Kessinger Publishing, 2010.
Grimm. NBC, 28 Oct. 2011.
Haroutunian-Gordon, Sophie. "Plato's Philosophy of Listening." *Educational Theory*, vol. 61. no. 2, pp. 125–39.
Kant, Immanuel. *Observations on the Feeling of the Beautiful and Sublime and Other Writings*, translated by Patrick Frierson and Paul Guyer, Cambridge UP, 2011.
Kristeva, Julia. "Power of Horror: An Essay on Abjection." Columbia UP, 1982.
Orenstein, Peggy. *Cinderella Ate My Daughter: Dispatches from the Front Lines of the New Girlie-girl Culture*. HarperCollins, 2013.
_____. "What's Wrong with Cinderella?" *New York Times*, 24 Dec. 2006. www.nytimes.com/2006/12/24/magazine/24princess.t.html. Accessed 6 Nov. 2020.
Paz, Octavio. *The Labyrinth of Solitude: And, the Other Mexico; Return to the Labyrinth of Solitude; Mexico and the United States; the Philanthropic Ogre*. Grove Press, 2001.
Peat, F. David. *Gentle Action: Bringing Creative Change to a Turbulent World*. Pari Pub., 2008.
Rockhill, Gabriel. "Foucault, Genealogy, Counter-History." *Theory & Event*, vol. 23, no. 1, 2020, pp. 85–119.

Rousseau, Jean-Jacques, and Roger D. Masters. *The Collected Writings: Emile or On Education: Includes Emile and Sophie, or the Solitaries*. UP of New England, 2010.
Row, Jess. *White Flights: Race, Fiction, and the American Imagination*. Farrar Straus & Giroux, 2019.
St. Jerome. *The Principle Works of St. Jerome*, translated by W.H. Freemantle, Amazon Digital Services LLC, 2010.
Silko, Leslie Marmon. *Almanac of the Dead*. Simon & Schuster, 2013.
Sue, Derald Wing. *Microaggressions in Everyday Life: Race, Gender, and Sexual Orientation*. Wiley, 2010.
Vizenor, Gerald, editor. *Narrative Chance: Postmodern Discourse on Native American Indian Literature*. U Oklahoma P, 1993.

The Wesen Next Door
The Racial Dynamics of Grimm
Melanie D. Holm

The role of race in *Grimm* is as complex as it is omnipresent. The series is rooted in a history of animosity between two closely related species—races for the purposes of the show—Humans and Wesen, yet this division multiplies in several nuanced relationships and conflicts: racial divisions and hierarchy within Wesen society; the dual identity of the Grimm as a protector of people and genocidal agent of traditional royal families; the effects of biology on personality; the value and legitimacy of ethnic tradition; the credibility of assimilation; the relationship of humans as a race and their own racial divisions; and the friendships and romances that traverse biological and socio-cultural boundaries. This essay will explore the multiple and overlapping approaches to race and ethnicity in *Grimm*. The goal is to open for discussion its many modes and layers of engagement with racial, racist, and ethnic concerns, not to evaluate the show in terms of contemporary moralities. Nevertheless, *Grimm* operates in a continual dialogue with the lived-world reality of viewers and their histories. It creates a mirroring fantasy realm that employs the supernatural in order to displace and think through the very real concerns and troubling legacies of racial and ethnic conflict in the "real world."

The fantastic mode in which *Grimm* participates has its own troubling entanglements with histories of racism and racial hierarchy. As Helen Young has noted, "Fantasy formed habits of Whiteness early in the life of the genre-culture, and is, in the early decades of the twenty-first century, struggling to break them."[1] Innovators of the fantastic J.R.R. Tolkien, C.S. Lewis, and H.P. Lovecraft and contemporary inheritors like George R.R. Martin and the legacy of Disney princes and princesses "habitually" construct "the Self through Whiteness and Otherness through an array of racist stereotypes, particularly but not exclusively those associated with

Blackness."[2] Similarly, the Brothers Grimm fairy tales from which the fictional world of *Grimm,* or the "Grimmverse" springs, "exemplif[y] early European associations of black skin with nonhumanness."[3] Without suggesting that it has "the answer," *Grimm* provides a number of overlapping racial dimensions that illustrate the difficulty and necessity of thinking seriously about the grim realities, present and past, of racial discrimination and violence.

The White Grimm's Burden

Grimm begins with Detective Nick Burkhardt's discovery of his true ancestral past, the legacy of power it bestows upon him, and the obligation he inherits to destroy Wesen as humanity and royalty's protector. He discovers not only that he is physically distinct from other "people," but that he has physical advantages over them. At the same time, he is the recipient of valuable knowledge whose power resides mainly in its secrecy: the existence of Wesen, his identity as a Grimm, and the Grimmlore couched in Aunt Marie's trailer. Throughout the series, Nick wrestles with what it means to be a Grimm—to be given power, knowledge, and resources denied to others—and how to do so responsibly. His position in the Grimmverse signals a variety of metaphorical ties with contemporary inquiries into racial privilege and power—particularly the position of white, European-descended men in modern America. Allegorically, it serves as a site of awakening to the position's complexity and an inquiry into the obligations to the past, the present, and the self it bestows.

In *Grimm,* power is not the social positionality of inherited racial privilege *per se* but a mystical, "natural supernaturalism"[4] wherein Nick is differentiated by distinct physical abilities that surpass natural human limits, as well as access to occult history and knowledge of Wesen and how to fight them. Throughout the series, he maintains a controlled distribution of this knowledge among select people, diffusing the locus of power *qua* knowledge. Nevertheless, as a descendent of the Grimm line, there is no getting away from the necessary observation that Nick's power and authority derive from physical, racial inheritance. Thus, a troubling network of associations with traditions of racial superiority is unavoidable, mainly because Grimms are portrayed as "superior" in a way that gives license to determine the life or death of others—namely the Other: *Wesen.*

However undesirably or unintentionally, the Grimm structurally intersects with strands of white supremacy concerning the historically discredited myth of the Aryan race. Aryan mythology formed in Europe's early 19th century, and then Germans "in the later part of the century, avidly adopted the myth as dressing for ... the doctrine of a race of supermen, destined to dominate the world with the ruthlessness of ancient savagery."[5] Initially, in the series' mythology, Grimms are portrayed as Germanic in descent, linked to the Brothers Grimm and their German nationalist project of accumulating folktales, which were later valorized in Aryan and anti–Semitic propaganda by the Third Reich. The Grimm connects more than nominally with atrocities of modern European history and the stories that engender them. However, these stories are always subject to historicized interpretations. Even the term "Aryan" signals more than a historically fictitious genocidal race, indicating nobility, illustriousness, and aristocratic lineage etymologically. These concepts are racially portable but power-asymmetric along hereditary lines. When Marie Kessler tells Nick, "The stories are true," the claim potentially extends beyond the magical creatures of the tales to an ideal of the Germanic heroic code, as described by Tacitus, of revenge, obligation, courage, and reciprocal loyalty reflected in characters such as Beowulf and other romance heroes.[6]

The pre-history of Grimm heroism within the series evinces undeniable brutality that is not easily digested by modern sensibilities, not least because every Grimm represented in the series is of white European descendent. In the strictest interpretation, Grimms are or have been racially self-designated agents of genocide with a mystical destiny to eliminate the world of the Wesen race. Their mandate reflects the United Nations war crime of "Genocide": actions committed with the "intent to destroy, in whole or in part, a national, ethnical, racial or religious group, as such."[7] The term, derived from the Greek *genos* (race or tribe) and Latin *cide* meaning killing, was developed by Polish lawyer Raphael Lemkin in 1944 in response to atrocities, including the Nazi Holocaust.[8] Therefore, it should come as no surprise that the showrunners quickly distinguish the Grimm from any connection with a Nazi or German nationalist ideal. In the first-season episode "Three Coins in a Fuchsbau" (S1, E13), Nazism is directly tied not to Grimms, but the problematic Wesen race, a trend that will continue throughout the series. In his Aunt's trailer, Nick discovers antique footage of Hitler at a Nazi rally, where he wears the mystical coins of Zakynthos on his lapels. He watches in fascinated horror as the image of Hitler melts into a *Blutbad*, one of the most dangerous Wesen. In a moment of etymological comedy—Adolf means "noble wolf"—the unmasking of the Nazi leader and Nazism displaces one of the most shocking episodes of modern history, absolving human beings from its inhumanity. "Eve" (earlier Juliette Silverton) later reveals that Hitler was not only Wesen, but his ultimate design was akin to something like Aryan dominion—a world ruled by Wesen. Genocide is thus characteristic of a problematic humanoid race that it is Nick's destiny to police, subdue, and destroy. His mandate is not to commit genocide but to rid the world of those who would—however compromised his methods may be.

The logic of "Three Coins in a Fuchsbau," however, troubles easy displacement. The impulse of world domination linked to genocide appears to be neither strictly Wesen nor Germanic; instead, it is a magical curse associated with coins that infect whoever possesses them with irrepressible desire for power and domination, regardless of racial particularity: A *Steinadler* (a Wesen hawk), Nick's partner Hank Griffin, an African American (human) police detective, and the police captain, Sean Renard, who in the mythology of the show is half-royalty (human) and half–*Zauberbiest* (or warlock, the male complement of the *Hexenbiest*), are all susceptible— only Grimms can resist. Here, the desire for dominion extends beyond racial supremacy, subordinating it to a larger category of enchanted megalomaniacal control. This supernaturalism denaturalizes genocide by making its existence merely contingent upon the bad luck of someone having encountered a few impressive coins. It is withdrawn from the historical and social asymmetries of human history. Beyond the enticing picture this paints of humanity as incapable of large-scale monstrosities unless controlled by dark enchantments, the complex displacement of this kind of racial genocide separates Nick's actions as a Grimm from violent histories of authoritarianism, colonialism, genocide, and other atrocities.

The series constructs an environment in which Nick as a Grimm is absolved of the Grimms' collective past crimes. Nevertheless, he struggles with his cultural inheritance and the legacy of colonialism, racism, religious intolerance, and imperialism throughout the show in a manner analogous to modern reflections on whiteness. In the series, early ignorance of the more extensive Grimm-Wesen history distances Nick from whatever negative associations may linger in the identity. As he becomes exposed to Grimm lore, he increasingly challenges its doctrine. Moreover, his distinct and familiar identity as an "American" distances him from the show's exoticizing of the White European/German. While much of the Grimm lore is written in German (increasing multicultural for later episodes), German identity links directly with Wesen. This is not least because the first Wesen with whom Nick interacts, the Hässilch, speaks German, is of German descent, and is embedded in his Germanic heritage, while pan-European, imperial identity is ascribed to the nefarious Royals.

The character Monroe exhibits a similarly complex but inverse relationship with white European legacies. He has an oddly Gaelic name but lives in a house that draws from motifs of the German *Schwartzwald*. At the same time, his character reflects object cultures of Germanophone nations such as Austria and Switzerland in his vocation as an artisanal caretaker of watches and clocks. Thus, Monroe introduces the "old world"

108   Part Two: Justice and Social Spaces

of Europe to the series, particularly Germany, as Nick does the modern American male identity, a distinction made clear by his need to have Monroe translate Wesen-Human history linguistically and culturally. These are utterly foreign to him and thereby have nothing to do with who he is as the modern individual, Detective Nick Burkhardt. Instead, he must discover and evaluate based on his independent judgment. In so doing, he disavows colonial and racial violence, as illustrated in scenes of emotionally charged reactions to ancestral accounts of Wesen slaughter. At the same time, his day-to-day Wesen friendships and alliances refute racial ideology. Thus, Nick becomes a hybrid that disenchants some old-world ideologies regarding Wesen and race while unflinchingly enforcing those with which he agrees and align most closely modern American values of human rights and universal equality. And yet, Nick is decidedly not equal.

The Grimm conceit draws from mythologies of superior warriors, superheroes, and above all, the prince whose quality in a hierarchy of beings places him at the top of the social order, invested with political and martial power while materially, or as we might say in modern parlance, genetically, superior to others. At least in part, this physical difference manifests as a retinal genetic mutation that allows Nick to see Wesen (S4, E3: "The Last Fight"). While some aspects of Nick's powers imply a supernatural origin (for example, that his Grimm powers can be taken away through sexual intercourse with the supernatural femme-fatales, *Hexenbiests*), scientific possibility admits biological distinction. He is sufficiently different from mere humans in so far as he can absorb powers of a Wesen from a parasitic infection that is fatal to others and has intensified reactions to biological compounds, such as the venom of the *Cracher-Mortel*.[9] Medical tests even confirm that Nick's body has metabolic rates that are substantially beyond the norm. He is physically supra-human.

Nick is thus emblematic of a superhero, as conceived in the American tradition of Superman (as opposed to racial mythologies of the Aryan), while also occupying the social and political position of *übermensch* ("overman" or "superman") as a result of those "super" powers.[10] As described by Nietzsche, the *übermensch* is the man of superior intellect who consequently exists beyond the boundaries of conventional morality and thereby is free to impose values of his own. In the case of *Grimm*, Nick ascends to *übermensch*, not because of his superior intellect but his superior power and knowledge. He rejects several Grimm values and is discretionary about which traditions he enforces based on his own immediate, individual judgment. The same behavior translates from the fantasy realm of Wesen to the mundane human condition through selectivity about which laws to enforce and what to report as a police officer. He is in an unbidden position of racial, historical, and what we might call ethnic if Grimm is an ethnicity, power that allows him to act beyond any impersonal or universal notion of good and evil. This power has cognates in our non-magical world, and yet, any metaphorical translation can never be genuinely didactic or symmetric. Unlike in this present moment of #BlackLivesMatter and post-colonial struggles for equity, the secrecy surrounding Wesen existence and their enduring, predatory threat to human and Wesen lives alike complicate Nick's struggles with and exertions of his privilege. His struggle is thus private and personal. In the personal and the private, the value of individualism in resolving dilemmas is endorsed, which depending on the nature of the individual, can bring either great social benefit or great social cost. What would the show look like, we can speculate, if the burden fell upon different shoulders?

Cry! The Beloved Portland

While Nick battles with questions of Grimm power and privilege, the city in which he lives suggests a fantasy space of integrated racial plurality. That the fantasy should be located in Portland directly repudiates its racist legacy. Oregon was founded as the first "only whites" state in 1859: its constitution banned black people from living, working, or owning property there, and it was not until 1926 that the state permitted black Americans to move there as a place of residency. Whether intentional or not, the racial plurality and harmony of modern Portland in *Grimm* starkly contrast with Oregon's racist past. *Grimm* creates a multicultural, multi-ethnic space in which characters of different races and ethnic identities mingle in workplaces, social settings, and romantic relationships without distinction. In 1972, psychologist Cedric Clark developed a "Stage Model of Representation" for the portrayal of African Americans in a white-dominant media culture that consisted of four stages—non-recognition, ridicule, regulation, and respect—which map increasing levels of equity and dignity granted to the minority group.[11] In an application of these categories, Michael Ray Fitzgerald, who renamed them the "Evolutionary Stages of Minorities in the Mass Media," has demonstrated their applicability to all minority groups.[12] The first stage, non-recognition, presents a reality in which the minority group is non-existent. In the second stage, group members are introduced only to be diminished and dehumanized; they are made visible but coded as inferior. The third stage reflects an integrationist perspective, in which minority characters are featured as enforcers of the dominant, which is to say, white, social norms as, for example, judges or police officers. Finally, in the fourth stage, respect, minority characters are represented no differently than characters of the dominant group, and interracial personal and romantic relationships are not treated as different or significant from any other. In its representation of human Portland, *Grimm* tends to the level of "respect" by not only featuring an array of races and ethnicities but by doing so in a way that emphasizes the quality of representation, disembedding characters from mere racial signification.

Grimm's Portland of the present is a space of diversity without distinction. Different races work together, live together, and form romantic partnerships without remark, yielding "ethnoracial politics [that] are progressive for an American-made show."[13] While the male leads Nick and Monroe are "white," the supporting and episodic casting is markedly interracial: Sergeant Wu is Filipino, Detective Hank Griffin is African American, and Captain Sean Renard is European-born. Notably, Renard is later revealed to be a descendent of human royals and the mystical *Hexenbiests* (any intolerance of his mixed identity, however, is located in the antiquated thinking of a failing and evil aristocracy). It is difficult to draw a line between respect and regulation as levels of representation in a police procedural in which a majority of characters will be police officers. Nevertheless, the officer characters expand beyond regulatory acts, expressing distinct personalities and increasingly complex character narratives that allow for growth and change as the series unfolds. Beyond these core characters, *Grimm* establishes a tableau of racial integration. In a significant detail of the early episode "Lonelyhearts" (S1, E4), Nick and Hank investigate a bed and breakfast where the first couple they encounter is interracial, but unremarkably so—no attention is paid or explanation offered. Interraciality in Hank and Nick's partnership never receives comment and appears only incidentally in Hank and Adalind's ill-fated romance, in which it is the question of her undisclosed status as a *Hexenbiest*, not as a "white woman," that raises Nick's suspicions and contempt. With details such as these, *Grimm* normalizes racial integration and acts as a counter-model for the reality from which its fantasy departs.

The series also goes to lengths toward elevating multilingual and multicultural representation by integrating the supporting and episode casts in racially non-specific roles. Examples include casting Haitian American actress Garcelle Beauvais (*The Jaime Fox Show*, *NYPD Blue*) as the powerful *Hexenbiest* Henrietta without an exotic backstory. In addition, episodes featuring traditional stories from various nationalities and cultures feature spoken languages associated with those traditions, including Spanish, Tagalog, Japanese, and Russian, as well as German, French, and Latin. This last instance is a spoken language of an ancient Wesen species, the *Gelumcaedus* (S3, E7: "Cold Blooded"); the lingual inclusion gestures toward the historicity and multiplicity of language and culture, which is complemented by the lingual diversity of the Grimm-lore books.

Being multilingual and seeking guidance beyond one's own ethnic group is generally rewarded, as in the case of Juliette consulting Pilar[14] regarding her memory loss (S2, E18: "Volcanalis"). This particular sequence of exchanges is critical for establishing a presence for Pilar in the show that exceeds racial cloistering: the knowledge Juliette seeks from her is not racially or ethnically coded. Her role is not as translator of her culture to a white audience. Rather, she is a giver of sophisticated information that transcends national or cultural borders. In other instances, such as "Chupacabra" (S4, E8), episodic characters who bear a racial or cultural tie to the monster of the week are stationed in prestigious social roles rather than stereotyped occupations. Here, the character infected with the disease that creates *Wældréor*, the condition popularly known as *Chupacabra*, is the physician Diego Hoyos,[15] introduced to viewers while on a charity medical mission in the Dominican Republic. He emerges as the hero of the episode not just from his extraordinary humanity as a devoted volunteer doctor, but also from his self-sacrifice to save his wife Bélam[16] from succumbing to the disease. Notably, his wife is also a person of color, rather than white, as is often the case in representations of minority men in status positions.

The terms "post-racial" and "post-ethnic" generally signify a social existence where race and ethnicity are socially indeterminant. As David Hollinger describes, "post-racial" or "post-ethnic" indicate:

> a possible future in which the ethno-racial categories central to identity politics would be more matters of choice than ascription; in which mobilization by ethno-racial groups would be more a strategic option than a presumed destiny attendant upon mere membership in a group.[17]

The racial diffusion of Portland reflects the aspirations of the post-racial or post-ethnic society. It is not a race-free society, but one envisioned as passed or moving past the legacy of racism. "Race" is rarely a topic among the main human characters or the human population of Portland, except for an investigation into a thirteen-year-old, racially-motivated murder of an Ojibwe man, Gus George, and the harassment of his son, Simon[18] (S4, E18: "Mishipeshu"). While the episode approaches racism, it does so by representing racism as a diminishing relic of the past, not unlike the intolerance of the Royals. Furthermore, though the perpetrators of the racially-motivated murder survive the thirteen fictional years to play a role in the episode, their role is to symbolize the destruction of racism, its eradication from the current moment, as they are slain by a vengeance spirit, the Ojibwe *Mishipeshu*.

The absence of racism in Portland correlates with its near absence of serious human crime. In *Grimm*'s Portland, human criminality is rare and primarily limited to Season one. "Let Your Hair Down" (S1, E7) recounts attempted child molestation, kidnapping, and drug-running, but these crimes are by no means exclusively human in nature. Similarly, the Pilot features kidnapping and attempted child molestation by a Wesen postman. Furthermore, the violence of Wesen drug culture is the locus of Rosalee Calvert's narrative pre-history. It is further responsible for the death of her brother, Freddy,[19] introducing her to the show (S1, E15: "Island of Dreams"). It also provides the conditions under which she and Monroe form a romantic attachment. Human-on-human violence is more-or-less limited to petty shoplifting in "The Twelve Days of Krampus" (S3, E8)—a crime to which Wesen are no stranger[20]—fraud and conspiracy to murder by brothers profiting from the conceit of a lake monster in "A Reptile Dysfunction" (S5, E8), and attempted rape—though here it is ultimately undecided whether the impulse toward sexual assault was authentic or supernaturally induced by the *Folterseele*'s charms—in "Heartbreaker" (S4, E16). These are merely a handful of episodes. The Wesen world, by contrast, is rife with internal Wesen-on-Wesen violence, discrimination, segregation, and degradation. It is also identified as the source of the majority of violence perpetrated on the human world. The dissonance between the post-racial utopia of human Portland and the dystopian prejudices of and surrounding Wesen suggests that while they may be fairy-tale creatures, the non-presence of racism in Portland is its own aspirational fairy tale within the show.

The Blutbad *Who Came for Dinner*

Grimm displaces critical explorations of race, racism, and ethnic division from the human world into the realm of fantasy creatures, examining the relationships between humans and Wesen and among Wesen themselves. These complex relationships provoke critical questions about race, ethnicity, and racial relations. The categories of race and ethnicity are often intertwined. For this section, "race" will refer to phenotypical, biological designations, while ethnicity will refer to cultural practices and identities. The most fundamental racial division in the show lies between humans and Wesen, but the nature of this relationship is asymmetric. On the one hand, Wesen are universally aware of human beings, while, except for Grimms and the rare *Kehrseite-Schlich-Kennen*, human beings are ignorant of Wesen existence.[21] Wesen can pass for humans in their un-woged state and, again, except for Grimms, cannot be seen unless they want to be. Those few humans who *do* see an un-woged Wesen, unless the encounter is contextualized, are at risk of thinking themselves to be or being thought mentally ill, seeing things that are not there, or losing touch with reality. Sgt. Drew Wu's experience is exemplary in this respect, insofar as he is institutionalized after his encounter with an *Aswang* (S3, E14: "Mommy Dearest"). The woge is therefore frequently used as a tool to manipulate or prey upon humans, as with the cannibalistic *Wendigo* in "To Protect and Serve Man" (S2, E11). Monroe also uses it to his advantage to escape the pursuit of policemen in the woods, setting the stage for Hank Griffin's later PTSD in "Big Feet" (S1, E21). However, when contextualized, the experience of horror can be mitigated to one of simple fear, as in the Halloween episode "La Llorona" (S2, E9) where Monroe woges to get revenge on kids who egg his house, or, more profoundly, in Wesen "coming-out" woges, particularly in the case of Juliette Silverton's encounter with Monroe and Rosalee. The initial surprise is followed by interest and acceptance of difference (S2, E21: "The Waking Dead"). In the case of the *Kehrseite-Schlich-Kennen*, preparation and context allow for a smooth exposure, minimizing the shock of what is otherwise thought an impossibility. However, as a model for race relations, this proves to be a tendentious allegory because of the particularities of knowing and not knowing and the extreme difference between the two parties involved. Nevertheless, in the case of Grimms and a larger human cultural network, there are exemplary models and cautionary tales offered by human-Wesen relations.

The relationship between Nick (and, later, Trubel and Kelly) and Wesen, namely Monroe, suggests a more applicable model insofar as both sides possess an element of knowledge and secrecy: they are aware of the existence of the other, yet can keep their own identity hidden, at least partially, passing as everyday people. The historical relationship between Grimms and Wesen is unambiguous: Grimms are charged by the Royal families with the task of ridding the world of Wesen and, in turn, Wesen have either an immediate "fight or flight" reaction when they see a Grimm or cower, begging for their lives. The root of the conflict undoubtedly arises from two sources: a history in which predator Wesen preyed upon humans, a practice that continues in what Monroe, who intimates past participation, euphemistically calls "The old ways"; and a history of human beings terrified by unexplained Wesen encounters, framing them in various superstitious contexts. The force of this superstition leads to retaliation on all Wesen kind in occasional violence and more historically pronounced movements such as the witch trials and the Inquisition (which the series thereby incorporates seamlessly into the augmented history of the Grimmverse). However, it is suggested that in pre–European, ancient history, a less violent but differentiated understanding existed between Wesen and humans, namely, that in ancient Egypt, Wesen were worshipped as gods (S3, E15: "Once We Were Gods").

Nick and Monroe's friendship creates an aperture for a different kind of interracial partnership. What makes it possible is their weak ties and non-identification with the conflict. Nick has only just found out he was a Grimm upon meeting Monroe and is not yet integrated into the Grimms' genocidal culture. Monroe, on the other hand, has renounced the violent practices of his ancestors. He is a reformed *Blutbad*—Wesen in kind, but not in cultural expression. Because neither Nick nor Monroe embraces inherited ethnic beliefs, they encounter one another as individuals, and a partnership emerges, ultimately becoming an endearing, lifelong friendship. However, even this model is fraught with power asymmetries, as it is clear that Nick uses his position as a detective and as a Grimm to gain Monroe's cooperation early in the first season. Neither seeks out the other for any intentional racial reconciliation; instead, the friendship is contingent on the relationships each has with his culture, their personalities, their immediate needs (namely, Nick's need for information and Monroe's unarticulated, but nevertheless real need to not be murdered by a Grimm), and the pure coincidence that Monroe happens to have the same size and model of the boot as the more traditional, murderous, and pedophilic *Blutbad* who Nick is after.

While their contact is contrived by circumstance and, initially, gentle compulsion, a friendship and mutual respect emerge that become exemplary among Wesen and Grimm. Nick gains trust among the Wesen world and expands his friendships while serving as a model for tolerance among his fellow Grimms. At the same time, Monroe uses his influential position as a *Blutbad* to convince other Wesen that Nick is not like "other Grimms," and serves as an ad hoc ambassador to the human world. A secondary, similar figure is Bud,[22] an *Eisbiber*, who takes a clear social risk vouching for Nick's difference, heroism, and friendship at his lodge's emergency meeting (S1, E19: "Leave it to Beavers"). Notably, both Nick and Monroe have to intervene and reject the murderous intolerance of their parents to protect the other (S2, E1: "Bad Teeth"; S3, E13: "Revelation"). Nick defends Monroe from his mother Kelly, while Monroe is forced to intervene when his father, whose inter–Wesen intolerance is only surpassed in anti–Grimm rage, attacks Nick when he comes to see Monroe. The parents eventually come around, and tolerance unfolds, intimating a future potential for at least partial integration in which Grimms and Wesen can abide side-by-side with both identities cloistered from the human world.

And yet, it cannot go unmentioned that Nick continues to kill Wesen, and Wesen generally rank lower in his estimation than human beings. Sean Renard plays a significant role in scenes that pertain to the problematic status of Wesen concerning Nick and human society. Renard is a suitable character to frame these disclosures because of his own delicate, bi-racial status. He generally attempts to pass as fully human—keeping the secret of his powers and status, and for the excellent reason of a childhood plagued with assassination attempts on himself and his mother. His personal history and influential position within the police force enable his keen observations of human-Grimm-Wesen relations. Similar to the Grimms, he too is more powerful than a mere human and most Wesen. He wields a high degree of social capital as a Royal that subordinates Wesen and *Hexenbiests*, who were traditionally in royal service, as were Grimms.

Early in the series, it becomes clear that each case Nick works implicates Wesen and usually ends with their death, though occasionally there is an arrest. In the Grimmverse, the uncomfortable reality on display is that most inmates in prisons are Wesen, as shown in "To Protect and Serve Man." Indeed, we are shown that the one human inmate directly encountered is falsely convicted and is himself a victim of Wesen violence. When asked by Wu how much crime is related to Wesen, Renard echoes the prison tableau, responding, "most crime in most places is Wesen related" (S2, E11). The remark, while seemingly explanatory, retains a troubling ambiguity. That crime "is Wesen related" need not be understood merely as "Wesen commit most crimes," though this is certainly the interpretation that satisfies Sgt. Wu. The conceit that Wesen might be victims of crimes and crimes perpetrated by humans at that, or that they would qualify as victims in such a circumstance is a second rebarbative possibility, one typical of the Captain's grasp of language and irony. The question appears: "Is a crime committed by a human against a Wesen really a crime at all?" Renard puts the question to Nick in a form that demands recognition of the Wesen subalterity in Nick's ideology. While in a *Cracher-Mortel*-induced rage-trance, Nick goes on a spree of violence, destroying a bar, terrorizing a family, and killing a man who wielded a knife.

By getting Nick to admit that he is "bothered," as Renard frames it, by having killed the man, Renard unsparingly reveals the inequity of his guilt: "Let me ask you something, Nick. What's really bothering you, the fact that you killed somebody or the fact that you killed somebody who wasn't Wesen? Because God knows you've killed plenty of them. That's what you Grimms do, isn't it?" (S3, E3: "A Dish Best Served Cold"). Thus, while Nick is willing to risk his life for his friend Monroe, he shows no remorse or hesitation when it comes to killing Wesen that—unlike Monroe—do not assimilate into the dominant social order of modern human Portland. In this way, Wesen are made not part human but sub-human in a manner similar to native populations of imperial dominion or suppressed racial groups within a country. Their lives are *prima facie* understood as lesser in value than those of a dominant class, here the Grimms as superior members of the human race.

The value of an individual Wesen's life is established by their willingness to assimilate humanity, a process of deculturalization. In its most general form, "deculturalization is a conscious attempt to replace one culture and language with another that is considered 'superior.'"[23] This can be accomplished through soft methods such as education or more violent such as corporal or capital punishment for those who fail to assimilate to the dominant cultural mores. Deculturalization allows for the separation of the good from the bad among ethnic and racial groups as seen in mythologies such as the "model minority" or the "good negro," where goodness reflects adherence to the dominant cultural values and rejection of one's "group." Along these lines, Wesen, like Monroe, and to a lesser extent, Rosalee and Bud, are "good" Wesen. Monroe disavows his past, while Rosalee and Bud contribute to modern human American society while keeping their Wesen culture hidden.

Bad Wesen are those who refuse to disengage from their cultural practices and ethnic traditions. These traditions conflict with the values Nick upholds and thus mark those Wesen as objects for discipline or punishment. In the first season, the conflict between ethnicity and modernity provocatively plays out in "Bears Will Be Bears" (S1, E2) when a *Jägerbar* (bear-like Wesen) participates in a *"Roh-hatz"*—a male rite of passage that involves disemboweling human prey with an artisanal bear claw. In all other respects, the *Jägerbar* family are model citizens. It should not go unnoticed, in a compelling irony, that the young men of the family do not pick human beings at random for ceremonial prey. Instead, they select a criminal who has broken into and defiled their home. Nevertheless, they are charged with and convicted of kidnapping and attempted murder. In indicting response, the mother, or momma bear of the family declares, "You have to respect your heritage," and the father, who admits what the boys did was wrong, extenuates their behavior: "She wanted them to know their heritage. She never understood the danger of it. It isn't easy to give up your history. You haven't had to give up yours." Wesen ethnic practices often mark the "bad" Wesen in ways that justify Grimm violence in much the same way the British Empire featured the practice of *Sati* or "bride-burning" as a justification for their political and cultural imperialism of India. Human Sacrifice, incestuous gang rape, and gender-based mutilation are thus become the Grimm fantasy-world equivalent, in Gayatri Spivak's imperial grammar, of "white men saving brown women from brown men," fused with the southern racial imperative of protecting white women from brown men via lynching.[24] Nevertheless, it cannot be denied that these are intolerable crimes in any social construction that claims universal human rights. Cultural relativism has its limits, and here, that limit seems to be secrecy and benignity: Wesen and their practices are tolerable, only so long as humans are not bothered.

Secrecy in this respect requires the suppression of racial identity or compulsory passing. For Wesen, this has been mandated by their internal government, the Wesen Council, for fear of what humans would do to them if Wesen were exposed. Therefore, it is unsurprising that the Wesen revolutionary group of later seasons, Black Claw, adopts as its mantra: *Occultatum Libera*, or free what is hidden. Their objective is to have a world dominated by "out" Wesen, inverting the dominance of human culture over Wesen. Again, it is no surprise that fighting this cause unites all humans, Grimms, and "good" Wesen (including select *Hexenbiests*) in a multi-governmental, secret coalition, Hadrian's Wall. The name is telling as Hadrian's wall was a martial barrier separating the Romans from northern tribes, or the "civilized" from the "barbarians." Truly, Black Claw's objective to take over the world and violent means are deplorable, but what makes them "barbarous" in this analogy is not their ambition to power or violence—human history is full of its own all-too-human atrocities—but their refusal to remain under or acknowledge human supremacy. The Wesen uprising is quelled, but the fundamental conflict it reflects goes unresolved. Can Wesen be out and live alongside humans? Is integration without deculturation possible?

West Side Wesen

While the equity between humans and Wesen looms as a yet unrealized and perhaps unrealizable dream, cultural and racial equity is as undesired as it is unrepresented within the Wesen world. Wesen are grouped into communities based on their bodies and self-identify racially and ethnically along these lines. According to one fan-driven source, there are 132 different types of Wesen, each with its own differentiating physical characteristics.[25] These physical characteristics are frequently linked to animal correlatives. *Blutbaden* have wolf-like fur, claws, and most significantly, teeth—often killing their prey as wolves do by biting the throat to tear it apart. *Löwen* have leonine manes and imposing teeth. *Mauzhertz* are generally smaller, mice-like creatures with whiskers and short fur when woged. *Seelengut* are covered in white, wooly fur with sheep-ears and enlarged eyes. Such physical characteristics also correlate with behaviors that are more often than not linked with the natural or metaphorical attributes of different creatures. These behaviors dictate personalities inherent to the species, allowing for broad racial characterizations that are often negative and totalizing. A form of biological essentialism dominates Wesen thinking. Biological determinism theorizes that "the belief that certain biological traits and social behaviors were linked and constitute the 'essence' of a certain racial group."[26] Such essentialism has historically enabled Social Darwinism and racial hierarchies: it performs a similar function in the Wesen world. However, unlike the simple good and bad division Nick comes to embrace, Wesen see each other through the lens of ethnic stereotypes expressed in both comical and tragic ways.

The most dramatic and sustained effects of essentialism emerge in the *Blutbad-Bauerschwein* (pig-like Wesen) feud, rooted in *The Three Little Pigs'* wolfish antagonism. As Monroe explains to Nick, "this *Blutbad-Bauerschwein* feud goes back centuries. We get blamed for every *Bauerschwein* death" (S1, E6: "The Three Bad Wolves"). The series twice gives *Bauerschwein* the chance to strike back, declaring *Blutbaden*-superiority "part of an old-world order" that they will overturn (S3, E3). The feud is symbolically resolved when a chef who has been poisoning *Blutbaden* is set up to confess his murders and surrender to human law or be served up to that very same old-world order embodied in a large Wolfpack hungrily staring him down. That *Bauerschwein* are represented as antagonists and arrested in each episode quietly affirms the preceding hierarchy in which *Blutbaden* are superior, as one might consider, in an absolute state of nature, wolves to be superior to pigs. This extends to moral superiority as well, where the representative wolves are ready to make peace while the pigs are out for revenge.

Less dramatically, Wesen's descriptions are rarely, if ever, complicated by the individual character *pace* Monroe. *Klaustreichs*, related to the alley-cat, are always low-life jerks prone to controlling behaviors such as domestic violence and hate crimes. *Eisbibers* are involved in bridge building, crafting, and other maker activities, demonstrating that they are "busy beavers." *Lausenschlange*, a Wesen-snake, are simply put evil, but in an "underbelly" fashion, operating as hitmen or henchmen in organized crime, and decidedly "cold-blooded." *Skalengecks* are lizard-like creatures and "cold-blooded," but considerably less powerful than *Lausenschlanges*, and appearing more often than not as drug-addicted thieves. *Seelenguts* are timid, gullible creatures who function by groupthink. Perhaps the most damning of these essentialist ascriptions are made by Monroe toward the *Schneetmachers*, an unfeatured Wesen whose name is always and undisputedly invoked as the lowest of the low. Ironically, this essentialism arises as Monroe disabuses Nick of negative Wesen stereotyping. When Nick is startled that Wesen have retirement homes, Monroe replies, "Yeah, we're not savages. Except for Schneetmachers" (S1, E11: "Tarantella"). Moreover, when Nick is surprised that Wesen own and run restaurants, Monroe retakes the opportunity to defend while diminishing, "Lots of Wesen own restaurants. I mean, I would never frequent a place run by a *Schneetmacher*, or for that matter, that served *Schneetmacher*" (S3, E3). The double rejection of the *Schneetmacher* as a conscious being and a material body to be consumed demonstrates the reductive identification of the body as being.

So dominating is this body-being hierarchy that the series features three self-loathing Wesen. On the one hand, there is the genetic manipulation of a *Genio Innocuo* whose DNA is blended with *Löwen* to make him more aggressive and more of a leader (S2, E8: "The Other Side"). This results in several murders, a suicide attempt, and an embrace of violence in incarceration (S4, E7: "The Grimm Who Stole Christmas"). There is also the case of Ryan Smulson,[27] a *Lebensauger*, or leach-Wesen, who so thoroughly loathes his Wesen form that he self-identifies as a slayer of Wesen, the Grimm, with the credo that "All Wesen must die" (S2, E10, "The Hour of Death"). This, too, ends in a tragic suicide attempt and incarceration, signaling the complex caste hierarchy of the Wesen world: *Blutbaden* and *Löwen*, and other apex predators at the top, and loathsome or weak creatures, the *Reinigen*, *Lausenschlanges*, and *Lebensaugers* at the bottom. From the top of this hierarchy, Monroe confronts a more complex essentialist dilemma. It is clear that he is proud of and enjoys being a *Blutbad*, yet actively fights against being the creature that he was born to be—essentially, a killer. Other *Blutbads* also demonstrate this ambivalence, and struggle against biological and psychological drives, taking advantage of support groups, and even castrating chemical implants to suppress undesired behaviors—yet these ultimately end up killing those who tried not to be what they are.

So deeply imprinted is this essentialist hierarchy that characters not only assign identities and values to bodies, the Grimmverse features racial-power groups who enforce segregation and species purity, namely the *Secundum Naturae Ordinem Wesen* or "*Wesenrein*." As the names suggest, the group is dedicated to an ideology of racial purity that mirrors a perceived Natural Order. Reprising the association of genocide with Wesen, the *Wesenrein* represent a conflation of Modern Neo-Nazi and White Supremacist groups while drawing from the iconography and dramaturg of the Nazis, the Ku Klux Klan, and the Spanish Inquisition. They wear robes and masks and participate in elaborate rituals. Further, their logo or rallying symbol is a *Wolfsangel*, the sign of a wolf trap that resembles the Nazi swastika and doubles as a Klan-like cross when placed ablaze on Monroe's lawn in retribution for their interspecies marriage (S4, E5: "Cry Luison"). The connection is underscored by Hank Griffin's especially emphatic reaction and urgency to be the one who extinguishes it (S4, E6: "Highway of Tears"). The *Wesenrein* reflect the racial hierarchy they enforce. In their unwoged state, *Wesenrein* members are white males; in their woged state, they are *Klaustreichs*, *Blutbads*, and *Löwen*; however, it is clearly the *Blutbads* who are the elites and make up the leadership whereas *Klaustreichs* reflect a rank and file, working-class membership reproducing the physical and sentimental superiority of the wolf to the cat. Nevertheless, it is also *Blutbads* who are the victims of mock trials and violent, ritualized executions, which points toward especial anxiety toward keeping the apex race "pure" in terms of ethnic practice more than any general concern with inter-species alignment.

Conclusion

The bloody, extralegal defeat of the *Wesenrein* sends an unambiguous message against racism, particularly in such an organized, mobilized fashion. But if the fall of the *Wesenrein* indicates an argument against racial or ethnic hierarchy, it also upholds Nick's authoritative position as the Grimm authority who signs their death warrant. A hierarchy is affirmed that places the Grimm at the top, with Wesen, Humans, and Royals beneath, however cooperative and invested they may be in the same goals. In a similar ambiguity, although the show celebrates the inter-species alliances—the marriage of Monroe and Rosalee, the Wesen-Human friendships that Nick forges, and the birth of two human-*Hexenbiest* babies (Diana and Kelly)—there is a clear biological distinction between humans, Wesen, and Wesen offspring through which species and races are always conserved. There are no wolf-fox or *Blutbad-Fuchsbau* hybrid children. They must be one or the other, conserving racial distinctions. Further, the series retains the secrecy or suppression of Wesen and Grimm populations, preserving a social world where everyone passes for merely human.

There is no indication that this version of the Grimmverse is one that the series endorses as an ideal for our own world. Instead, it appears as an impasse or invitation for the audience to do better. Perhaps, it is the case that after the main characters come together to save their shared world from the phenotypically Aryan aggressor, the *Zerstörer,* the series leaves it to the audience to write the next episode, to fantasize about what the future looks like in the Grimmverse, and to consider what we might be able to achieve among ourselves.

Notes

1. Young 10.
2. Young 11.
3. Schmiesing 211.
4. The term "natural supernaturalism" arises in William Carlyle's *Resartus,* but finds its major literary expression in Abrams's work. Abrams uses the term to describe "diverse degrees and ways, to naturalize the supernatural and to humanize the divine" (68). Nick

and the Grimms, indeed, the fictional world of Grimm participates in this tendency, albeit with more literalism than the Romantic metaphorical understanding of the imagination as the location of divinity in humanity. Nick suggests an altogether different expression of a naturalized supernatural, but one that nevertheless makes something magical or superhuman embedded in the natural human among an elect, or as Percy Shelley might say, fit but few.
    5. Dunlap 296.
    6. Scholars have clarified that the connection between Tacitus's depiction of the German hero in *Germanicus* with any actual historical people is highly suspect and is much more likely invented for a satirical critique of his contemporary politics (Niles 137–8). Nevertheless, the mythology Tacitus creates, whether "Germanic" in origin or not, has a profound influence on cults and representations of heroism in heroic romances and continues its influence through the nineteenth and early twentieth centuries. Such was the influence of the idea that it "became one of the principal texts of Arian xenophobic nationalism and part of the hour code by which war was to be pursued" (Toswell 503).
    7. United Nations 1948.
    8. Lemkin 79.
    9. S2, E15: "Mr. Sandman"; S3, E1: "The Ungrateful Dead."
    10. Nietzsche 5.
    11. See Clark.
    12. Fitzgerald 368.
    13. Rudy and Greenhill 168.
    14. Actor, Bertila Damas.
    15. Actor, Max Arciniega.
    16. Actor, Alyssa Diaz.
    17. Hollinger 1033–34.
    18. Actor, Booboo Stewart.
    19. Actor, Randy Schulman.
    20. See S3, E20: "My Fair Wesen"; S5 E3: "Lost Boys."
    21. *Keirseite-Schlich-Kennen* is a term used by Wesen to refer to humans who know of their existence—it roughly translates from the German to those who know the secret of the other side or the other-siders who know our secret.
    22. Actor, Danny Bruno.
    23. Spring 1.
    24. Spivak 129.
    25. See "Wesen." *Grimm Wiki*, grimm.fandom.com/wiki/Wesen.
    26. Byrd and Hughes 10.
    27. Actor, Michael Grant Terry.

Works Cited

Abrams, M. H. *Natural Supernaturalism: Tradition and Revolution in Romantic Literature.* W. W. Norton, 1971.
Byrd, W. Carson, and Matthew W. Hughey. "Introduction: Biological Determinism and Racial Essentialism: The Ideological Double Helix of Racial Inequality." *The Annals of the American Academy of Political and Social Science*, vol. 661, 2015, pp. 7–22.
Clark, Cedric. "The Concept of Legitimacy in Black Psychology." *Race Relations: Current Perspectives*, edited by E. G. Epps, Winthrop, 1973, pp. 332–354.
Dunlap, Knight. "The Great Aryan Myth." *The Scientific Monthly*, vol. 59, no. 4, 1944, pp. 296–300.
Fitzgerald, Michael Ray. "'Evolutionary Stages of Minorities in the Mass Media': An Application of Clark's Model to American Indian Television Representations." *Howard Journal of Communication*, vol. 21, no. 4, 2010, pp. 367–384.
Hollinger, David A. "Obama, the Instability of Color Lines, and the Promise of a Post Ethnic Future." *Callaloo*, vol. 31, no. 4, 2008, pp. 1033–1037.

122   Part Two: Justice and Social Spaces

Lemkin, Raphäel. *Axis Rule in Occupied Europe: Laws of Occupation, Analysis of Government, Proposals for Redress*. Carnegie Endowment for International Peace, 1944.
Nietzsche, Friedrich. *Thus Spake Zarathustra*. edited by Robert Pippin, Hackett, 2011.
Niles, John D. *Old English Literatures: A Guide to Criticism with Selected Readings*. Wiley-Blackwell, 2016.
Rudy, Jill Terry, and Pauline Greenhill. *Fairy-Tale TV*. Routledge, 2021.
Schmiesing, Ann. "Blackness in the Grimms' Fairy Tales." *Marvels & Tales*, vol. 30, no. 2, 2016, pp. 210–233.
Spivak, Gayatri C. "Can the Subaltern Speak?" *Marxism and the Interpretation of Culture*, edited by Cary Nelson and Lawrence Grossberg, U Illinois P, 1988.
Spring, Joel. *Deculturalization and the Struggle for Equality: A Brief History of the Education of Dominated Cultures in the United States*. Routledge, 2016.
Toswell, M. J. "Tacitus, Old English Heroic Poetry, and Ethnographic Preconceptions." *Studies in English Language and Literature: 'Doubt Wisely,' Papers in Honour of E. G. Stanley*, edited by M. J. Toswell and E. M. Tyler, Routledge, 1996, pp. 493–507.
United Nations, General Assembly, *Convention on the Prevention and Punishment of the Crime of Genocide*. 9 December 1948.
Young, Helen. *Race and Popular Fantasy Literature—Habits of Whiteness*. Routledge, 2016.

Folk Creatures

What Can Justice Do with These People?

Fernando Gabriel Pagnoni Berns *and* Emiliano Aguilar

At the end of the episode "Twelve Days of the Krampus" (S3, E8), Nick, Hank, and Monroe face a dilemma: a perverse Santa-like figure (the *Krampus*[1] of the title) is responsible for a string of teenagers, specifically delinquents, who go missing. They identify the creature as the *Krampus*, a mythological obverse of Santa Claus who punishes naughty children. In this incarnation, punishment includes whips, kidnappings, and consumption of the offenders. Nick and his team seek out the *Krampus* to stop him before he can eat the kidnapped teenagers; this, however, is when the real problem begins: what is to be done with him once he is found?

Unlike other Wesen, there is no relationship between the creature who emerges at Christmas and the everyday man who exists the other days of the year. *Krampus* is not the individual but a pagan spirit that overtakes a wholly innocent and ignorant man for twelve days during the Christmas holidays. After the period of supernatural possession ends, the human host returns to normal: in this case, a mild-mannered citizen who makes a living as a wedding photographer. Nick and his friends are at a loss for how to proceed. It is clear, due to his innocuous, mild appearance that he can't credibly be taken to police headquarters. No one feels comfortable letting him go; however, the alternative, executing him, which promises to eliminate any potential for repetition of the crime, fails to gain traction. Nobody wants to be the one to kill the Krampus because of an underlying discomfort with the act; they know they would be ending the life of a man who was not aware or in control of his actions. *Krampus* is a supernatural monster guided by seemingly unquenchable desires and impulses beyond the purview of common justice. Nick and Hank cannot arrest and incarcerate him, nor can they reeducate him. Nevertheless, they are hesitant to release him because he will go on to harm more people. Hank and Monroe insist that killing the *Krampus* is the only solution to the problem. Yet, killing the monster means killing his human host, who is in no way responsible for the crimes. An ethical quandary thereby arises: how can society respond to someone who is truly not responsible for their actions but at the same time cannot control them?

The episode raises this question only to give a partial and ambiguous resolution. As an innocent man only circumstantially transformed into a Wesen, he goes unpunished. However, he should remain under the careful surveillance of the police though to no specific end, with execution at the holidays left as an open possibility. The episode thereby concludes with explicit ambivalence about the nature of justice where seemingly unreformable but involuntary criminals are concerned.[2]

One of the most striking aspects of *Grimm* as a series is the uneasy intermingling of human justice and supernatural justice. By the former, we mean that Nick is a human police detective obliged to enforce human laws and rules designed to increase the protection of society from harm. By the latter, we refer to the supernatural nature of Wesen, creatures that exist outside the human sphere. As a police detective who is also a Grimm, Nick is obliged to do his best to translate/transfer human laws into a terrain entirely foreign for humans, creating and applying trans-species justice. This scenario brings to light questions about humanity, monstrosity, and dehumanization, as human laws are, in the series, applied to inhuman creatures that cannot reform or act differently because of their incomplete or non-human nature. To try to apply human laws to them may be read as an act of violence rather than justice. Still, many of the Wesen engage in acts of hostility and violence; therefore, something must be done to protect the community, both human and Wesen alike. This being the case, it is not merely the episode "Twelve Days of Krampus," but the entire series that poses the difficult ethical question: How can humans protect themselves from these unregenerate, involuntary "criminals?"

This inquiry mirrors concerns about criminality in the real world rather than being merely a question for navigating the waters of speculative fiction and horror genres. As argued by Laura Hubner, "the classical fairy tale is entirely unreal, fundamentally located in the imaginary zones of enchantment and magic, and yet vitally it is also seen as providing a basis for approaching real life."[3] The Grimm/police dilemma at the end of "Twelve Days of the Krampus" resonates with contemporary social scenarios where worries about delinquency are increasing. What to do with unreformed criminals? Is there a possibility of reeducation? What to do with the "monsters" that psychology designates as unable to assimilate to everyday social life? When understood as a "nasty Santa," the figure of the Krampus reorients our attention to children and the reward system for good behavior that Christmas symbolizes in the U.S. The *Krampus* kidnaps and consumes, which is to say, executes teenagers who appear sufficiently and persistently naughty. It is an extreme solution to the problem of increasing delinquency when it seems that reformation is not entirely viable. Vigilantism—a topic to which this chapter will return—is thereby embedded in the episode as a possibility through the actions of the *Krampus* concerning persistently problematic teens.

Reeducation and reintegration measures are practiced every day on a global scale as a way to control criminality. However, sexual predators, hate criminals, mentally ill offenders, and serial killers test the limits of the criminal system, provoking cultural anxiety regarding what to do with these seemingly less-than-human or "inhuman" criminals. In the United States, where the legal system has "become more punitive over the past 30 years,"[4] worries about criminals popularly depicted in both media and the justice system as "nonreforming savages" have turned the potential rehabilitation of offenders into a controversy because of a tendency to perceive monstrosity as innate.[5] As with Nick's struggle, society does not know what to do with them. The conversation among Nick, Hank, and Monroe reproduces in miniature the significant debates on criminality in real life.

In this sense, it is not by chance that *Grimm* started with an episode that evokes the tale of Red Riding Hood, a story inextricably linked to the sexual assault of minors (S1, E1: "Pilot.").[6] The opening quote, "The wolf thought to himself, what a tender young creature. What a nice plump mouthful…" uneasily conveys undertones of child molestation and sexualization. "Little Red Riding Hood," like many fairy tales, is a cautionary tale. Specifically aimed at youth, a cautionary tale "is a narrative that demonstrates the consequences of wrongdoing and thus reinforces moral and behavioral norms."[7] Essentially, the cautionary tale tries to keep the children "on track" while staging rites of passage.[8] As the story of "Little Red Riding Hood" taps into contemporary cultural fears about pedophiles and strangers ("big bad wolves") that people may pass in the streets, *Grimm*'s pilot implicitly stages a scenario connected to issues of rehabilitation and reeducation of sex criminals. It does so by comparing two wolves: an active criminal and one claiming reform.

Grimm's pilot opens up the possibility of criminal rehabilitation through Monroe, a *Blutbad*—a Wesen featuring characteristics associated with wolves—who has chosen to no longer live the violent lifestyle typical of his kind. Previously a Big Bad Wolf, he has undergone a self-disciplining transformation and is no longer controlled by his wild impulses.

Maintaining this suppression and reform requires a strict regimen of a vegan diet, Pilates, and the use of drugs (What drugs precisely? Magical or chemical in nature? The show leaves this issue cloaked in darkness). Monroe will become Nick's best friend: thus, the show's pilot and arc teach viewers that bad creatures can reform if they so desire and assimilate peacefully into the community. Other Wesen helping Nick, such as Bud,[9] an *Eisbiber* or beaver-like creature, socially assimilate and "pass" rather effortlessly because their characteristics are helpful and non-threatening. However, Wesen of his kind tend to be preyed upon by others. Rosalee, a *Fuchsbau* with fox-like characteristics, straddles in between, with a temptation to criminality exhibited by her brother Freddy's[10] illegal trade in Wesen drugs and human organs and her own stint in jail for drug-related crimes. This is tempered by a desire for sociability and generally non-lethal, if aggravating, predatory potential. There is a reason we do not speak of the big bad fox. Perhaps the most significant example of reformation in the series comes with Adalind Schade, a *Hexenbiest*. During the early seasons, she revels in her magical, witchy powders and potions. In the end, she becomes Nick's ally, partner, and co-parent, ostensibly reformed through the powers of maternity and a stable heteronormative domestic partnership.

Can the different creatures be rehabilitated into good citizens? If not, what can the law and ordinary people do with them? *Grimm* stages the tensions taking place between crime and rehabilitation in our current society. It addresses the question of rehabilitation and unregeneracy metaphorically through the lenses of horror and fantasy. Rather than offering a univocal solution, Grimm addresses concerns on a case-by-case basis and remains ambiguous on how to cope with monstrous criminality. While some episodes advocate for rehabilitation, others support or promote vigilantism and extralegal responses. Nevertheless, some offer no closure, ending with monsters free to roam the streets. What *Grimm* does offer, however, is a platform in popular culture for exploring the otherwise invisible questions of justice and potential rehabilitation for society's involuntary "monsters."

Rehabilitation, Reeducation, and Reformation: Issues on Criminality

The American preoccupation with cruel treatment, capital punishment, and violence was on the rise in the last decades of the 20th century. The late 1980s saw a renewed interest in incarceration and crime, emphasizing the possibility for "fatal miscarriages" of justice, such as executions of wrongly convicted men and women.[11] The system was depicted as "error-prone"[12] and increasing concerns about overcrowded prisons[13] and political activism around racial inequality[14] that shaped new concerns and conversations about the punitive nature of imprisonment and the state of prisons in the 1980s and 1990s. Currently, "the alchemy between the perceived urgency of reversing existing crime trends and the promise of effective rehabilitation programs has fueled the public's desire for nonpunitive, rehabilitative responses to crime."[15] Thus, many Americans feel that education and vocational programs are the best way to reduce crime; drug addiction is a medical problem that asks for treatment rather than punishment; and the primary purpose of prison should be rehabilitation rather than deterrence.[16]

In response to these views, politicians have begun to focus on rehabilitation. This shift, however, has generated concern about rehabilitation's feasibility because some criminals seem to exist outside the sphere of recuperation. While drug addiction and gang criminality can be attended to with varying degrees of success, some offenders seem unable to rehabilitate. Hate criminals, offenders with mental illnesses, and sex offenders seem resistant to complete rehabilitation as their cases present a complex amalgam of psychological and sociological issues. For example, many communities are reluctant to provide aftercare in the medical treatment of paroled sex offenders even when they need it the most[17] and the indices of employment after prison are low for this type of crime. Programs to deal with offenders with mental illnesses, meanwhile, are underutilized. Serial killers, in turn, may be rehabilitated. However, even advocates for reeducation have serious doubts about the potential for total recuperation and whether such efforts "should ever be made."[18]

Contributing to the contemporary discourse is increased media coverage and depictions of sexual offenses that sometimes offer "a simplistic and an incomplete picture" when presenting sex offenders as "monstrous individuals who prey incessantly on children and are impervious to punishment or rehabilitation."[19] America still does not know what to do with sex offenders. The effectiveness of psychological treatments to reduce sex offender recidivism has not been convincingly demonstrated. There is support for the efficacy of behavioral conditioning techniques in decreasing pedophilic sexual arousal, but the long-term maintenance of such changes is unknown. It is possible that offenders can learn to control their sexual arousal, but the underlying sexual preference for prepubescent children (and motivation to engage in sexual behavior with them) may remain unchanged,[20] leaving the potential for re-offending a serious concern.

Currently, a dubious "solution" comes with the instauration of places such as Miracle Village, a community in South Florida where over half the population are registered sex offenders. A place to live or "dump" those deemed irrecoverable is necessary for people who sometimes have difficulty finding housing because of strict regulations limiting where sex offenders can live. Additionally, "community notification laws, in charge of warning about the offender amidst a community, sometimes fail to discriminate between those capable of rehabilitation and those whose deviancy may be permanent,"[21] thus grouping an indiscriminate cluster of criminals and "monsters." For some, solutions such as chemical castration are not considered rehabilitation but incapacitation akin to mutilation.[22] Rather than justice, both chemical-castration and Miracle Village are explicit acknowledgments that actual rehabilitation is impossible for some offenders and that the State does not know what to do with them.

While some criminal behaviors suggest an offender-pathology, another problem emerges with offenders who repeatedly re-offend, serving multiple prison sentences with no evidence of reformation. They appear impervious to reformation and reeducation efforts. Their time in prison appears instead to intensify and multiply deviancy via accumulated contempt for "normal" society and exposure to or socialization in more insidious forms of crime. Selective incapacitation, meaning targeting criminals for incarceration whose inability to rehabilitate makes them especially suitable for long imprisonment, is one approach to repeat and escalating offenders. However, it "raises several moral and ethical questions"[23] as there is no common ground about what type of offense, number of offenses, or constellations requiring this approach; at what point, is someone appropriately labeled as bad and only capable of getting worse?

A third consideration arises for offenders with mental illnesses because they may not fully understand the scope of their actions' consequences or legality. Approaches to treating these kinds of offenders often include "participation in cognitive-behavioral programs, participation in restorative justice programs, and involvement in coerced or mandated treatments."[24] While cognitive-behavioral programs have shown some success,[25] there is little documented evidence or analysis of the results of participation in restorative justice programs, the latter emphasizing collaboration with the community, dialogue between offender/victim, and reintegration rather than coercion and isolation. "Restorative justice programs use a range of strategies to facilitate participation from victims, offenders, and communities," including dialoguing "about the consequences of injustice" and "a pluralistic approach to defining the very terms of justice, which builds on dialogue among distinct cultural traditions."[26] Coerced or mandated treatments, in turn, present unclear conclusions; "Studies have found that some individuals who are coerced into treatment see the need for treatment … whereas others who supposedly entered treatment voluntarily felt coerced to do so by pressure from the criminal justice system."[27] While showing some effectiveness in the willing, the effectiveness of health treatments entered through coercion has yet to be established, raising concerns about patient autonomy and best interests.

This unsettled debate of what to do with unregenerate criminals (or what to do for them) is based in part on a dehumanizing perspective. Scholars have defined and studied dehumanization in many different ways. Rebecca Hetey and Jennifer Eberhardt divide processes of dehumanization into many types. These include dehumanizing language use such as pejorative animal metaphors indicating something less-than or sub-human and collective dehumanization via differences in race, ideology, and religion.[28] These approaches share a double process that first transforms the subject to be dehumanized into an Other (somehow less-human) and then transforms the Other into a creature with monstrous traits. The monstrous is not human or, at least, not wholly human: the savage, the deformed, the grotesque, the irremediable evil, the unreformed criminal. Like the unregenerate criminal, the monster is characterized as threatening, predatory, and devoid of humanity. Indeed, in a series of in-depth interviews with victims of serious crimes, a familiar image of criminals as animals, savages, or beastly monsters prevailed among the points of view.[29] Such imagery is fueled, in part, by media representations that conjure images of monstrous criminals that are innately undeserving of public compassion. The offender is thereby "thingified," i.e., turned objects of/to hate, fear, and loathing.

Jeffrey Jerome Cohen's *Monster Theory: Reading Culture* argues that the monster embodies otherness within a concrete culture in a specific historical time and space. The monster is shaped by what a culture conceives as threatening, foreign, and, as such, potentially dangerous. "The monster's body is a cultural body."[30] Judith Halberstam agrees: "Monstrosity (and the fear it gives rise to) is historically conditioned rather than a psychological universal."[31] The monster is not universal and ahistorical but culturally localized. Even more interesting, "the monster works as a kind of trash heap for the discarded scraps of abject humanity."[32] Within this discursive context, the unreformed criminal becomes "the lowest of the low" and "prison staff members, prisoners, sex offender programs, and manifold media forms enact institutional abjection"[33] exposing the criminal to the world for harassment. Dehumanization prevails when the apparently irrecoverable criminal is turned into an abject object, something loathsome, to be jettisoned or confined far away from human sight (as in Miracle Village). If they cannot assimilate into normative social life, then they can only be a monster.

Grimm periodically allows unregenerate Wesen to respond to such a charge, perhaps most poignantly voiced in the *Blutbad* Angelina's[34]

130 Part Two: Justice and Social Spaces

outraged exclamation to Nick: "we are not things!" (S1, E6: "The Three Bad Wolves"). Though it centers on supernatural creatures chased by two detectives of the Portland Police Department, *Grimm* demonstrates how monstrous conceptualizations offer essential insights into crime and policing. In this scenario, the monsters populating the series metaphorize questions and issues of criminality and uncertainty into how criminality should be addressed, particularly when pairing the conceptualization of criminality with a racial minority. In *Grimm*, Wesen are indeed a racial minority. As creatures of legends and myth surviving in modern America, they embody racial differences. Though many of them come from European countries like Germany, where whiteness prevails, these "monsters" are nevertheless marked by physical difference: their bodies and faces are monstrous. They are either animalistic, resembling wolves,[35] pigs,[36] lions, and mice,[37] or they are entirely monstrous, as is the *Krampus* (which, nevertheless, is depicted as a goat-like creature). As a racial minority, they are more susceptible to being coded as "sub-human" and, as such, are often victims of discriminatory laws and practices. This discrimination intensifies if the Wesen belongs to a societal group whose visibly human form is also a minority group member. Differential models of dehumanization are related to the violence and the nature of the different crimes according to the race of the perpetrators, creating a link between public attitudes toward offenders and higher incarceration rates of racial minorities.[38] For example, the episode "El Cucuy" (S3, E5), highlights the functions of racial prejudice. In one scene, a witness tells the police about a crime. She describes having gotten off the bus and seemingly being stalked by a Latin-looking man who, by chance, got off at the same stop. However, her actual attacker is a white-skinned man: her fears reveal preconceived ideas about the Latino community. In this brief scene, the show embeds a framing concern for how Latinos themselves are socially coded as potentially monstrous.

Such demonstrations of dehumanization complement the show's concern for the fallibility and bias of the justice system. This is particularly the case when the law looks to discredit differences, leading to bias within the justice system. A nuanced version of the discrediting phenomenon appears in the episode "To Protect and Serve Man" (S2, E11) which draws on mental illness as the locus of difference. Ironically titled, the actual victim is initially regarded as the criminal and the criminal as the victim because a history of PTSD renders the victim sufficiently Other to negate his credibility. The episode starts with Hank recalling a seeming double-homicide, wherein the shooter screams about how the two men were monsters with "teeth like needles, twisted lips, yellow eyes" that were going to eat him. Occurring pre–Grimm, it was Hank's testimony that sent a man to death row. After learning about Wesen, however, he reconsiders the case, now suspecting the monsters may have been real. Because Ferren is to be executed in less than two days, Hank asks for Nick's help investigating the case. After describing to the detectives military service and PTSD had impacted the man, leading to alcoholism and self-abnegation, the inmate's girlfriend articulates the irony that when he was a victim, he was treated "like a monster" by society. The show vindicates Ferren, yet Hank regrets and apologizes for having dragged Nick into this complicated case. Nick replies, "You didn't. My family did." This brief exchange of words highlights two important things. On the one hand, the origin of Nick's participation is motivated less by his status as a law enforcement officer than the hereditary duty of being a Grimm. Grimm justice couples with human justice, but uneasily so (something different from the law) uneasily overlap. On the other hand, there is Hank's apologetic necessity to act and seek extrajudicial help because legal justice itself, with his participation, has monstrously condemned an innocent man, sentencing him to death through its Othering bias. As in many episodes, Grimm-justice and human-justice uneasily overlap. When dealing with monsters of any kind, justice loses its purchase on objectivity, leading to or in this case almost leading to monstrous miscarriages of justice.

Monstrous Criminality

The tense relationship between criminality and monstrosity is present from the beginning of the series in the architecture of its pilot episode. The episode starts with a young co-ed in a red sweatshirt going running through the woods, where a beast assaults her. Detectives Nick and Hank are called to investigate this murder, which turns out to be just one more in a string of crimes where female victims wear red clothes. This adaptation of the Red Riding Hood unfolds as a metaphor for sex crimes with big bad wolves preying on young women. In a similar scenario of predation, a humanoid attacks Nick's Aunt Marie in the street. Nick as a cop, defends himself and Marie, shooting and killing the monster. The killed Wesen's criminal background includes "assault, rape and murder" in many states, signaling the relationship between recurrent criminality, particularly in sex offenses, with Wesen monstrosity. He is the first Wesen killed in the series, and his beastly appearance and legal history establish his fundamental monstrosity. Nick, in turn, is sent to visit a psychiatrist to cope with the fact that he has killed a man. While he is coded completely "human" because of his feelings and sensibility after killing, the Wesen is made both materially and legally monstrous. That he is a rapist and a murderer has no additional weight in the episode's narrative; his file exists solely to allow Nick to describe him as a "beast." Further in the episode, the Wesen who murders women wearing red kidnaps a little girl, an action that contradicts his previous modus operandi of onsite attacks of adult women. When faced with an underage girl, he kidnaps her and takes her to his home in the woods, linking the Wesen predator with predatory sexual offenders such as pedophiles.

The pilot introduces a fundamental question that the series never fully resolves: what to do with monsters like the *Blutba*d-pedophile[39] at the center of the show's pilot? This is repeated in various forms throughout the series, such as in "One Angry Fuchsbau" (S2, E17) whose premise rests on the impossibility of bringing human justice to a monster that escapes actual rehabilitation. This episode starts with the crime: a wealthy and abusive male *Löwen,* Don Nidaria,[40] kills his Wesen wife as the final escalation in a violent tirade. To defend him in court, Don's lawyer, Barry Kellogg,[41] uses his Wesen powers as a *Ziegevolk*[42] to supernaturally seduce the jury into agreeing with all his statements. Kellogg is unmasked as an extremely dangerous Wesen with supernatural charm, but neither Nick, Monroe, nor Hank knows what to do with him, as a proper arrest will mean telling the world the truth about these creatures. Because they cannot deal with him in a "legal" way, they at least try to incapacitate him through an elaborate ruse resulting in his "chemical castration." Kellogg superficially continues his life as a well-regarded citizen. However, his seductive ability to persuade is now disarmed through chemical intervention.

Grimm signals approval of nonconsensual chemical castration to bind some irrepressible criminal actors. However, it shows less certainty on addressing potentially criminal mental illness in minors. Reprising the question of credibility in "To Protect and Serve Man," the beginning of "El Cuegle" (S6, E4) portrays a mother, Haley,[43] who sees a man with "three arms and three eyes" (the *Cuegle*[44]) kidnapping her baby, Auggie. Her experience is dismissed by her husband, who also scolds the detectives for encouraging her delusion as they question her about the monster she believes she saw. The trope of dismissing claims of the unusual as a sign of mental illness serves as a minor, complementary concern to the episode's more significant focus on the question of sociopathology and criminal mental illness in the young. The Wesen who kidnapped the child has visions that predict the potential future of some newborn babies to become criminals. It therefore takes the child for three days, and unless something significant changes in the immediate context during this holding period, the child is eaten—though the *Cuegle* loathes this task. On one level, he acts as a metaphor for people who harm children due to a mental illness making them feel omniscient or compelling them toward grandiose acts of violence for the greater good. In his human form, the *Cuegle*'s erratic behavior, complete with outbursts of migraines, further codes him as a sufficiently mentally unstable man to be deemed by a jury as not guilty by reason of insanity.

The monster-of-the-week formula makes it attractive to see the *Cuegle* as the threat. However, the episode complicates this easy closure by intimating that Paul,[45] Hayley's husband, may be the real monster and a hereditary source for his son's potential future criminality. He is a man who dismisses and diminishes his wife without empathy—be it toward her fears of the *Cuegle* or her joy in posting pictures of her son on social media. In this scenario, the *Cuegle* serves as a stymied vigilante while the father and potentially the son suffer from socio- or psycho-pathology. The episode further suggests that if Auggie becomes mentally ill, it will likely have been inherited, and aggravated by his unsuitable home environment. If that is the case, then Auggie[46] reprises the dilemma of the man possessed by the *Krampus* and the episode's ambiguities surrounding culpability and Wesen.

Many episodes of *Grimm* refrain from suggesting the potential of rehabilitation modeled by Monroe. Instead, they tend to emphasize how difficult it is to determine if observed Wesen nature is innately monstrous or if it is a suppressible, perhaps even revisable set of behaviors and instincts. In "El Cucuy" (S3, E5), the titular Wesen is a Bogeyman from Latin-American folklore, reframed as the vigilante who kills criminals who escape human justice, particularly in Latino communities. Moreover, the vigilante is sought and summoned, arriving in the community only after being called by a sufficient percentage of the community. After investigating many suspects, Hank and Nick learn the identity of the Wesen executing criminals but are unable to proceed without a confession. This killer is quite confident in a *de facto* immunity from prosecution because convicting a Wesen with a non-monstrous woged form would necessitate revealing the existence of supernatural creatures. The admirable cleverness of the vigilante creates an ambiguous effect for the audience who is unsure of whether to see the Wesen as a criminal or hero.

Vigilante Justice

El Cucuy presents one of few cases of vigilante Wesen who predate upon human criminals. Throughout the series, the most common responses to Wesen marked as unreformed criminals are vigilantism and extralegal action. The potential for vigilante justice such as

134   Part Two: Justice and Social Spaces

the series demonstrates, as well as public harassment and harm, loom in sex-offender registration lists[47] and (social) media publication of names, faces, addresses, and associates of criminals and suspected criminals whose putative inhumanity denies them the privilege of privacy and protection. Resilient criminality creates public fear, and in some instances, "those fears were warranted. Every year, there are numerous crimes, including murder, against convicted sex offenders who comply with registration laws."[48] *Grimm* features many episodes in which there is no ready answer for what to do with a Wesen offender, reflecting the offender's precarious and ambiguous status in a community. When unable to bring the monstrous criminals to legal, institutional justice, Nick, Hank, and Monroe are often obliged—or feel obliged—to act extralegally, leaving a trail of abandoned, brutalized bodies behind them.

Vigilantism shares with the phenomenon of wrongful prosecution and conviction a "battered and misguided pursuit of devils—drug dealers, child molesters, environmental polluters, white-collar criminals, and terrorists—, all of whom must be rounded up at all cost,"[49] enacting a civil war on crime. Public shaming may lead to vigilante attacks by vengeful community members on former criminals or people who have been released from prison after conviction.

A challenging form of Wesen vigilantism unfolds in "Inugami" (S5, E17) when a teenage boy, Brian Johnson,[50] is beheaded with a katana by an *Inugami*, or ghost dog-like Wesen. Along with his friend Roger Voorhees,[51] Johnson had been charged with the first-degree murder of another boy but received probation. This episode addresses two moral questions: 1) what is the culpability of boys who kill a friend while "playing" with a loaded firearm; 2) what functions as justice for a dead child. The samurai-styled *Inugami* are responsible for protecting families, enacting a custom of vendetta justice when human justice has been ineffectual, uncomfortably mirroring the actions of Nick as both detective and Grimm.

Vigilantism unites both Grimm and Wesen: Grimm effect justice upon Wesen, and Wesen serve their own brand of justice to other Wesen and, occasionally, humans, acting with secretive impunity. The problem for Nick is his ambiguous status as an agent of the police who enforces human criminal law and his familiarity with Wesen that emblematize the conceptual limitations of the legal system. Thus, Nick behaves as both a police officer and as a vigilante in some episodes. In "El Cucuy," Florez,[52] a former marine with a pronounced sense of duty and justice, lives in the neighborhood and attends crime scenes to protest the insufficiency of the police. He approaches the patrol car when Nick and Hank investigate and tells them, "Somebody is doing your job, cleaning up the streets," referencing the murders done by *el Cucuy*. If *el Cucuy* acts, it is to answer the call of those who need justice, to punish criminals that justice had left unpunished. Nick, Hank, and Monroe effectively share this motivation and act extralegally because they, too, believe something must be done with the unreformed and unreformable criminals. As Nick becomes more comfortable in his role as a Grimm, this becomes less and less surprising. By nature, a Grimm is something of a vigilante: he or she kills Wesen because they might be potentially dangerous for the community without giving the subjects a fair trial.

Is Reformation Possible?

The show's pilot implies that criminal reformation is possible but challenging, and it is unclear how exactly a Wesen can reform, to what extent, and what this entails. Monroe gives an example of extreme rehabilitation efforts that mirror measures advocated by criminology on sex offenders and the general methods of cognitive-behavioral therapy regarding addictions. Though the precise nature and extent of Monroe's rehabilitation is uncertain, he tells Nick that he has been cured, in part, by Pilates, yoga, vegetarianism, and a support group. The rehabilitation, however, has limits. When Nick and Monroe approach the house where the young girl is held captive, Monroe leaves the situation rather than continue with Nick because he is afraid of what he may do in the house if tempted by the unpredictable interactions of his Wesen side and the situation. Monroe fears being unable to control himself before a little girl, a clear allusion to the myth of the Big Bad Wolf and its connections with the criminal impulses that come with pedophilic sexual perversion. This potential perversion is later resolved in the series when he marries Rosalee Calvert, finally accessing (hetero)normativity as a (monogamous) citizen. However, when he finds out about some morally atrocious fact or injustice against someone helpless, his eyes turn red as if possessed by his Wesen instincts (as seen in "El Cuegle"). This physical response indicates that although reformed, rehabilitation for a *Blutbad* is never permanent. The impossibility of complete rehabilitation characterizes Monroe as well as Rosalee. Upon learning that Monroe has been kidnapped Rosalee states, "I would hunt them and kill them all [the culprits]," flashing her Wesen side (as a *Fuchsbau*) as a form of wish fulfilling threat (S4, E9: "Wesenrein"). Later in the episode, the wife and husband woge into Wesen form and together tear apart their enemies as animals in an orgy of vigilante violence.

The connection between unreformed criminals and Wesen intensifies in "The Three Bad Wolves" (S1, E6). In this episode, three *Blutbad* brothers are hunted down and killed one-by-one by a *Bauerschwein* (a pig-like Wesen) as revenge for past family crimes. Monroe knew the victims from a shared treatment program years ago. The treatment was conceived to re-educate *Blutbads* into "good" people, free of violent, criminal "impulses." On the one hand, Monroe's ex-girlfriend, Angelina, mentions that Monroe is now a "clean" man, a term that evokes different forms of rehabilitation; on the other, Lt. Peter Orson,[53] the *Bauerschwein* claims that these kinds of monsters cannot change. Because he is a cop, his actions suggest vigilantism—a person who brings criminals down by any means necessary (even going so far as to tell Nick that they are alike and on the same side). Lt. Orson evokes anxieties about the quality and longevity of rehabilitation for criminals living released into society. When the public holds negative attitudes toward the law system, it is much more likely to engage in vigilante forms of justice.[54]

This position brings viewers back to the question of the *Krampus* with which this essay began: what can people do with the unreformed criminal?

Conclusions

This brief review of episodes from *Grimm* demonstrates the series' ambivalence or uncertainty about the fundamental nature of criminality, especially when viewed through the lens of rehabilitation. However, it is clear that neither Wesen nor Grimms have a secure protocol to address the problem of crimes committed by "monsters" that cannot be rehabilitated. This is not least because violence is thought to be an essential part of their nature. The options that recur through the series are either letting them go free or acting as vigilantes, exterminating those thought irredeemable. Rehabilitation seems possible in fits and starts, but only a fraction of characters can do so[55] and only to some extent as their feral natures always lurk behind the human surface. One solution to what to do with those monstrous Others is proffered in "Stories we Tell our Young" (S3, E6). In this episode, a (human) child kills a priest during an exorcism. The Wesen council (a Wesen-disciplinary body interested less with criminality than maintaining secrecy) calls for the execution of the child because it is deemed a dangerous abomination, while the condition is later determined to be non-essentialist and treatable. After a battle of wills, the council leaves the treated child alone, choosing to trust Nick as a Grimm. The episode hints at the possibility of trusting the Other *because some Others hold the capacity to behave differently.* The man tasked with killing the boy informs the council that Nick is "different," a Grimm, who in this case, is adamant in his advocacy of communication and cohabitation over routine extermination. Like Monroe, Nick also works heavily to hear the Other and respect them, which becomes the basis of their friendship. This discussion model facilitates and enhances awareness of the individual potential and community responsibility (as demonstrated by Monroe and Rosalee). Such integration, trust, and projection of broader humanity may contribute to decreased criminal behavior.

The show oscillates between progressive and reactionary philosophies: the Wesen must be placed under surveillance—even if vigilantism is needed—because they possess a series of characteristics that make them potentially dangerous. The show brings forward an emphasis on questions about the limits of the law and the impulses to destroy what it seems cannot be reformed and how prejudice is an influential factor that should be addressed. The law, in fact, is not so fixed as it tries to naturalize itself, and its practices and applications are still trying to answer what to do with those coded as impossible to reform. Perhaps we should be asking whether it is not just the law but also our methods of rehabilitation and the limitations we imagine for "cause" of such behavior that needs to be reformed

As a metaphor for addressing the problem of potentially irrecoverable criminals, the Wesen populating *Grimm* are signposts of anxieties and failings within the fabric of communities and law. At the end of its six-season run, *Grimm* remains unable to answer the question about what justice can or should do for or with these "monsters." Rather than a flaw, however, this indeterminacy is its strength. The show stages the difficulties still haunting society regarding monstrous criminality while hinting at the possibility for rehabilitation and integration through confidence in the capacity that the Other can change.

Notes

1. Actors, Derek Mears (Wesen form); Darius Pierce (human form).
2. Other episodes revolving around innocent citizens transformed against their will into predatory monsters are "Lycanthropia" (S5, E14), which analyzes the case of a Wesen's disease that would cause the *Blutbaden* to become feverish and eager to hunt during each full moon. "Quill" (S2, E4) is another story about the possibility that a virus or a disease—which turns out to be a kind of yellow plague that has affected supernatural beings since ancient times—infects Wesen and forces them to have very violent attitudes. In "The Waking Dead" (S2, E21), a drug produced by a *Cracher-Mortel* causes its victims to become zombies whose behavior is aggressive.
3. Hubner 19.
4. Vasiljevic and Viki 130.
5. Ibid.
6. Beckett 39.
7. Valk 170.
8. Hubner 121.
9. Actor, Danny Bruno.

10. Actor, Randy Schulman.
11. Haines 87.
12. Zimring 158.
13. Hallet 56.
14. Guevara Urbina and Álvarez 290.
15. Farabee 8.
16. *Ibid.*
17. Farabee 42.
18. Harmening 7.
19. Craissati 13.
20. Seto 190.
21. Stohr, Walsh, and Hemmens 423.
22. Halevy 136.
23. Todd Clear, Cole, and Reisig 69.
24. Linhorst, Dirks-Linhorst, and Sy 96.
25. Linhorst, Dirks-Linhorst and Sy 98.
26. Leebaw 121.
27. Linhorst, Dirks-Linhorst and Sy 98.
28. Hetey and Eberhardt 136.
29. See Madriz.
30. Cohen 4.
31. Halberstam 6.
32. Halberstam 143.
33. Ricciardelli and Spencer 46.
34. Actor, Jaime Ray Newman.
35. S1, E1: "Pilot."
36. S1, E6: "The Three Bad Wolves."
37. S2, E17: "One Angry Fuchsbau."
38. Vasiljevic and Viki, 122.
39. Actor, Tim Bagley.
40. Actor, Phillip Keiman.
41. Actor, Brian T. Finney.
42. A Wesen denomination linked to serial rape in a previous episode, "Lonely Hearts" (S1, E4).
43. Actor, Ellen Wroe.
44. Actor, Carlos Sanz.
45. Actor, Jeff Branson.
46. Actor (adult) Samuel Elliott Summer.
47. Meloy 95.
48. Hudson 32.
49. Stevens 53.
50. Actor, Kyler Morrison.
51. Actor, Christopher Meyer.
52. Actor, Manny Montana.
53. Actor, Daniel Roebuck.
54. Vasiljevic and Viki, 120.
55. Monroe and Rosalee; That Adalind turns into a "good mother/wife" in the last couple of seasons could also be taken as an example of a character who can move between both sides, human and Wesen.

WORKS CITED

Beckett, Sandra. *Red Riding Hood for All Ages: A Fairy-tale Icon in Cross-cultural Contexts.* Wayne State UP, 2008.

Clear, Todd, George Cole, and Michael Reisig. *American Corrections*. Thomson & Wadsworth, 2009.
Cohen, Jeffrey Jerome. "Monster Culture (Seven Theses)." *Monster Theory: Reading Culture*, edited by Jeffrey Jerome Cohen, University of Minnesota Press, 1996, pp. 3–25.
Craissati, Jackie. *Managing High Risk Sex Offenders in the Community: A Psychological Approach*. Routledge, 2004.
Farabee, David. *Rethinking Rehabilitation: Why Can't We Reform Our Criminals?* AIE Press, 2005.
Guevara Urbina, Martín, and Sofía Espinoza Álvarez. *Hispanics in the U.S Criminal Justice System: Ethnicity, Ideology, and Social Control*. Charles C. Thomas, 2018.
Haines, Herbert. *Against Capital Punishment: The Anti-Death Penalty Movement in America, 1972–1994*. Oxford UP, 1996.
Halberstam, Judith. *Skin Shows: Gothic Horror and the Technology of Monsters*. Duke UP, 1995.
Halevy, Gabriel. *The Right to Be Punished: Modern Doctrinal Sentencing*. Springer, 2013.
Hallet, Michael. *Private Prisons in America: A Critical Race Perspective*. U Illinois P, 2006.
Harmening, William. *Serial Killers: The Psychosocial Development of Humanity's Worst Offenders*. Charles Thomas, 2014.
Hetey, Rebecca, and Jennifer L. Eberhardt. "Cops and Criminals: The Interplay of Mechanistic and Animalistic Dehumanization in the Criminal Justice System." *Humanness and Dehumanization*, edited by Paul G. Bain, Jeroen Vaes, and Jacques-Philippe Leyens, Psychology Press, 2014, pp. 136–154.
Hubner, Laura. *Fairy-tale and Gothic Horror: Uncanny Transformation in Film*. Palgrave Macmillan, 2018.
Hudson, David, Jr. *Sentencing Sex Offenders*. Infobase, 2009.
Leebaw, Bronwyn. *Judging State-Sponsored Violence, Imagining Political Change*. Cambridge UP, 2011.
Linhorst, Donald, Ann Dirks-Linhorst, and Jolene Sy. "Criminal Justice Responses to Offenders with Intellectual and Developmental Disabilities." *The Wiley Handbook on Offenders with Intellectual and Developmental Disabilities*, edited by William R. Lindsay and John L. Taylor, Blackwell, 2018, pp. 86–104.
Madriz, Esther. "Images of Criminals and Victims: A Study on Women's Fear and Social Control." *Gender and Society*, vol. 11, no. 3, 1997, pp. 342–356.
Meloy, Michelle. *Sex Offenses and the Men Who Commit Them: An Assessment of Sex Offenders on Probation*. Northeastern UP, 2006.
Ricciardelli, Rose, and Dale Spencer. *Violence, Sex Offenders, and Corrections*. Routledge, 2017.
Seto, Michael. *Pedophilia and Sexual Offending Against Children: Theory, Assessment, and Intervention*. American Psychological Association, 2008.
Stevens, Dennis. *Media and Criminal Justice: The CSI Effect*. Jones and Bartlett, 2011.
Stohr, Mary, Anthony Walsh, and Craig Hemmens. *Corrections: A Text/Reader*. SAGE, 2013.
Valk, Ülo. "Cautionary Tale." *The Greenwood Encyclopedia of Folktales and Fairy Tales: A-F*, edited by Donald Haase, Greenwood, 2008, pp. 170–171.
Vasiljevic, Milica, and Tendayi Viki. "Dehumanisation, Moral Disengagement, and Public Attitudes to Crime and Punishment." *Humanness and Dehumanization*, edited by Paul Bain, Jeroen Vaes, and Jacques-Philippe Leyens, Routledge, 2014, pp. 129–146.

Witches, Stepmothers, and Princesses

Rethinking Gender and Money in Grimm

Sarah Revilla-Sanchez

Witches, stepmothers, and princesses are prominent figures in the Western cultural imagination. Their relative moral status has often been associated with adherence to or transgression of normative gender values of self-sacrifice, passivity, and beauty, with deviance manifesting in several disdainful behaviors from cannibalism and child abuse to merely jealous cruelty.[1] While witches and stepmothers are aberrant, princesses emblematize a fairy-tale collection of female virtues physically and behaviorally.[2] The NBC series *Grimm* (2011–2017) adds an explicitly economic dimension to the fairy-tale taxonomy of feminine virtue and villainy by representing the intersections of gender and capital in two of its most-memorable first-season Wesen: the *Geier* and the *Murciélago*. In the episodes "Organ Grinder" (S1, E10) and "Happily Ever Aftermath" (S1, E20), female Wesen villains commit crimes that mirror components of their origin fairy-tale stories, "Hansel and Gretel" and "Cinderella," respectively, but do so with monetary desire at the heart of their motives. "Organ Grinder" extends the witch of "Hansel and Gretel" into an organ trafficking, murderous female physician. "Happily Ever Aftermath" ironically flips the nature of its Cinderella and her evil stepmother, portraying the evil stepmother as a successful businesswoman and the princess as a socialite who murders her step-family to maintain her privileged lifestyle. In both cases, Detective and Grimm Nick Burkhardt investigates these crimes, but he is not the agent of justice. Instead, the female villains die violently at the episodes' ends by other means, which raises questions about the nature of their crimes and what is being punished.

The gender roles and traits associated with the figures of the wicked witch, the evil stepmother, and the good princess have received significant attention from scholars, as has the nature of fairy-tale villainy. Jack Zipes asserts that fairy-tale villains "have no respect or consideration for nature and other human beings, and they actually seek to abuse magic by preventing change and causing everything to be transfixed according to their interest."[3] Robin Briggs complements this reading of fairy-tale villains in her historical view of European witchcraft, finding that "the witch is an incarnation of the 'other,' a human being who has betrayed his or her natural allegiances to become an agent of evil."[4] In traditional fairy tales and North American popular culture, wicked stepmothers tend to embody the same negative characteristics as witches: jealous, greedy, vain, selfish, and cold.[5] They also have no natural love of children as such, though often overly fond of their own. Both stepmothers and witches are often unmarried, widowed, or sexually non-compliant older or contentious women: they are the opposite of the princess, which, in traditional gender roles, makes their very being dangerous long before they have committed any crime.[6]

The fairy-tale princess, by contrast, is Western culture's quintessential figure of female passivity and benignity.[7] As an extension of this passivity, the female protagonist of Grimm's fairy tales is the embodiment of obedience and self-sacrifice.[8] Moreover, her happiness is generally framed within patriarchal rules insofar as she requires a man for wealth and protection, frequently through marriage.[9] This brief overview of fairy-tale witches, stepmothers, and princesses begins to tease out some of the continuities between evil women and gender deviance. The continuity is emphatically apparent when it comes to age and sexual deregulation. Unlike the young princess in a tower (or coffin) awaiting her prince, these more dangerous women contravene hegemonic structures, which is to say, no one is in control of them.[10] They are unregulated and on the margins, which is itself a sufficient threat.

Just as female villains often share specific characteristics, they also share the same fate: death, usually a violent one. In the Brothers Grimm version of "Hansel and Gretel,"[11] for example, both the witch and the stepmother are dead by the end of the story. The story begins with two siblings who are twice abandoned in a forest by their impoverished parents. In later editions, the stepmother prompts this decision, indexing her as a bad wife who oversteps her role by dominating her husband.[12] After wandering for days, the children find a house made of gingerbread—a trap set by a witch who eats children after fattening them up. However, Hansel and Gretel outsmart the witch: Gretel rescues her brother by tricking the witch in the oven, burning her to death. In the end, the siblings make their way home to their father and find out that their evil stepmother had passed away. The malevolent women are gone, dead. Likewise, in some variants of "Cinderella," the stepsisters are blinded by birds as punishment when they attend the royal wedding (and presumably wander off into obscurity and death) and the stepmother is often forced to dance in burning hot iron shoes until she dies. However, the passive and innocent Cinderella is given magical assistance by her fairy godmother as a reward for her submissive virtue, which allows her to be visible to the prince, who rewards her beauty with royal marriage. As with the traditional origin stories, *Grimm* reproduces the imperative to punish the gender-deviant female villain with death. However, their crimes are demonstrably embedded in a much larger socially-directed discourse of gendered economic enfranchisement that though ubiquitous, is not part of the moral economy of the original stories.

This essay explores these female-villain narratives through gendered and economic lenses to argue that the crimes they commit are not merely their ostensibly criminal acts, such as murder. They also commit the social crimes of gender transgression to pursue a gender inappropriate motivation: money. Exploring how these episodes depart from their origin stories demonstrates how the 21st-century adaptations portray female villains who are doubly villainous. First, they commit horrific crimes. Second, committing these crimes demonstrates an independent desire for capital that is itself criminal in a woman. Each episode establishes a contrast between tolerance for economic dependency and disenfranchisement that accords with female virtues of passivity, generosity, and nurturing, and a decidedly criminal desire for money layered on top of lesser gender transgressions, making villainous women monstrous. These monstrous villains are brutally punished by a narrative economy that requires penalties for both their crimes and transgressions of a fairy-tale relationship between gender and money. With this fate, *Grimm* depicts them as scapegoats of a more extensive patriarchal system of economic inequity that requires women's infantilized financial dependence and behavioral discipline.

The Wicked Witch in the City

Through its treatment of murder victims, "Organ Grinder" initially guides the audience with allusions of vampires and occult imagery. By the end of the episode, the primary homicide is connected to an organ trafficking crime network. It had been hiding in plain sight because of an unexpected criminal mastermind and victims that were already socially invisible. The organ trafficking network operates throughout Portland, overseen by Dr. Levine,[13] a female *Geier*, a vulture-Wesen, practicing adolescent medicine at the city's free clinic serving the homeless and runaways.[14] Her position as a devoted caretaker has gone unquestioned because it fits the nurturing aspects of female gender roles, allowing her to select victims at will. That the victims are missing is never ascertained because of their community's indifference to child-homelessness.

The similarities between "Organ Grinder" and "Hansel and Gretel" extend to its villain, who structurally parallels the fairy tale's evil witch. But the villainy here is double: first, her criminal activity and, second, her defiance of approved female stereotypes and motives. An initial and gruesome connection appears between the cannibal witch of the Brothers Grimm and the *Geier* who traffics human organs for Wesen consumption: both reduce the human being to a material commodity. There is, however, a sharp distinction between how the children become their prey. Both narratives feature vulnerable children, but their paths are quite different. Hansel and Gretel leave home due to extreme poverty. Their parents can no longer feed their children or, for that matter themselves. They are put into the hands of fate out of desperate self-preservation. By contrast, the brother and sister of "Organ Grinder" are explicitly portrayed as runaways from a grossly abusive home. They are not alone in a dark forest but in the center of a populous city. Further, they are but two of countless homeless youth in Portland living in a state of danger and precarity tolerated and reinforced by broad social apathy.

Just as they become vulnerable for different reasons, a different mechanism puts them in the hands of their witches. In the traditional Brothers Grimm version, the children wander into the witch's dangerous territory: she does not seek them out. Moreover, though her house is a trap, it requires the initial transgression of the children eating it upon sight. In "Organ Grinder," however, Dr. Levine selects children at the health center. They are then lured to the organ harvesting center by the promise of a job and room and board, or they are kidnapped from the street with no one seeming to notice. In the fairy tale, the children walk into a well-designed trap. In *Grimm*, they are actively stalked, coerced, and hunted for profit.

Electing to harm children is the epitome of female deviance from the traditional maternal role. Both witches are guilty of this. However, there is more intensely hypocritical dissonance between Dr. Levine's self-portrayal as a female caregiver who works at a free clinic (rather than private practice) and her greedy consumerism of vulnerable lives for profit. The witch in traditional versions of "Hansel and Gretel" may be read as an elderly, marginal woman who ate children for survival because she lived alone without income: she too was in a state of precarity. In direct contrast, Dr. Levine's evil has no extenuation; rather, it is intensified by its volition. Her participation in organ procurement is for wealth and advanced economic power. Unlike traditional witches who lived in the outskirts of society, Dr.

Levine is not geographically marginalized but highly visible. Thus, *Grimm* complicates its "witch" by simultaneously deviating from and reinforcing traditional paradigms associated with witches. These contrasts demonstrate that Dr. Levine's crimes exceed the fairy-tale witch with gender transgression coupled with economic overreach.

(Un)Healthy Business: Healer or Dealer?

Grimm's presentation of this witch challenges the traditional valuation of the maternal role as a paramount female expectation, which Dr. Levine mimics as an apparently nurturing physician. To detectives Nick and Hank, Dr. Levine appears as a caring, hard-working doctor saving vulnerable lives out of innate goodness. She demonstrates a caring rapport with her patients, making it easier for her to lure the victims, echoing the fairy-tale witch's false generosity feeding Hansel. While not "fattening up" her victims, Levine is working to assure the health of her patients to later harvest their organs for sale. The nurturing portrayed is for self-serving, nefarious reasons, not altruism.

Dr. Levine's deviance is communicated aesthetically through her continuous visual presentation as a doctor. When she harvests organs, she retains her white coat and medical authority rather than reveal herself as a *Geier,* reinforcing a continuity between her evil *Geier*/witch self and her urban identity as a doctor. At the clinic, however, she codes herself as feminine: she has long, curled hair and wears a V-neck blouse and a necklace under her coat. By contrast, her hair is neatly tied up at the cabin, and she is almost entirely covered by surgical scrubs. Wearing surgical attire suggests that Dr. Levine does not need to woge (transform) into a monster because there is something about a powerful female doctor who intentionally kills children that is terrifying or monstrous itself. More broadly, the witch's job as a doctor transgresses gendered social order: she inhabits the public urban space as a doctor and businesswoman, reflecting the nature of cities as sites for both deviant and liberated femininities, as well as representations of the working woman.[15]

Dr. Levine's role as an urban doctor is overdetermined and communicates the narrative's ambivalent relationship to gender expectations. However, the witch's greedy motives and lack of sympathy amplify her villainy. Her seeming indifference to her victims grows into interpersonal cruelty in the episode's organ harvesting dénouement. She intentionally disrupts a tender moment between Gracie and her previously abducted crush Kevin[16] by choosing her as the next victim. That she chooses the girl and not the boy, in contrast to the fairy-tale witch, implies a kind of feminine acrimony—perhaps contempt for or jealousy of romance and female youthfulness, reinforced by her unmarried status. A single woman who navigates the public space as an independent professional is dangerous to traditional femininity. Being the head of any organization, traditional or illegal, also transgresses gender roles: she is in charge with power over others who are almost exclusively men.

From Cannibalism to Capitalism

Dr. Levine is an active member of the economic and political black-market system, an offshoot of capitalism. She has a network of accomplices, for instance, the driver, the men who recruit victims, and another woman doctor. Similarly, many *Geiers* work at the clinic and in the organ trade, complicating the web of perpetrators. From this perspective, the witch's motives may be understood as purely profit driven. Sergeant Wu's quip underscores this significance in a larger socio-political context. When one detective says they are dealing with crimes of cannibalism, he corrects: "it is pronounced capitalism." Laminating capitalism over cannibalism suggests the ultimate terminus of capitalist logic: anything can be a commodity if there is a buyer, and profit is the arbitrator of ethics. In this context, children's lives are only inconvenient obstacles in the collection of their profitable parts. The disregard for human life is shocking, but as the episode shows, it is not the witch alone who holds this perspective: instead, it is the entire society.

What makes the organ trafficking work is not the villainy of the witch alone but her accomplices, both in the business and complicity of the surrounding society. Within the business of organ trafficking, there are her many employees, from the receptionist at the faux-free clinic to the drivers transporting organs, to the distributors who bring the wares to the public. In turn, there are the customers who buy the illegal goods, some of which are renowned for their "Viagra-like-effect." This claim arises in conversation between Nick and his *Blutbad* friend Monroe, who knows a lot about this trade but seems embarrassed to admit he may have consumed such organs himself. Looking at consumers as perpetrators of this evil trade raises questions about where the blame lies and how far it extends. It also raises questions about the trade's notoriety and tolerance in the silence of those aware of but indifferent to its existence.

Complementing the business end of the organ trade is the more extensive social neglect that supplies its raw materials: homeless children. Dr. Levine could not run her enterprise if there were not an already ample supply of disregarded homeless youth in Portland. That Hanson[17] and Gracie are runaways from an abusive home represents a problem of children's dependence on parents and protective social institutions: they cannot survive on their own, but when this system fails, they put themselves into the hands of fate, taking their chances in a large city. Here they are malnourished, sick, and vulnerable to the elements and exploitation. Nevertheless, no one seems to do anything about it. They are not taken to social services; they are not taken to a foster home; they are not taken to Nick and Juliette's guestroom. They are sent back to the streets. Being dependent on their parents and *in loco parentis* social programs, and both failing them, they are left to fend for themselves. Like so many others, no one is particularly concerned about their lives until their bodies turn up dead.

While this systematic network of violence does not diminish the witch's crimes, it does open the discussion about who the perpetrators are. Like traditional villains who seek to wrong others, this witch harvests human organs for profit, occasionally evincing a sadistic pleasure in the pain she causes. The *Geier* falls to her death in a corpse fire pit at the episode's end. It is in an ironic allusion to the fairy-tale witch burnt to death in her oven. Here, the witch's death gives symbolic closure and satisfaction as justice served. However, given the expanse of the criminal participation from abusive parents to Wesen who tolerate the existence of the trade, to police offers who turn children back onto the streets, to unconcerned passers-by, the question arises: why is Dr. Levine the one who suffers capital blame? Unlike traditional witches who defy the norm, Dr. Levine is deeply engaged within a political and social system that perpetuates violence against the vulnerable. Her deviance from society, however, is embedded in her socially constructed identity. She is a powerful, single, professional woman—deviant from hegemonic codes of femininity. The role of men as perpetrators and consumers of illegal business is undeniable, as is their role as abusers of children. Nevertheless, lack of concern for children, violence, an emphasis on business, and chemically protecting the male orgasm all fit within the boundaries of gendered male behavior. The witch is not innocent, but others are entangled in her criminal guilt: what sets her apart is not her crimes but her transgression into male spaces of evil.

The (Not So Passive) Princess and Her (Evil?) Stepmother

"Happily Ever Aftermath" (S2,E20) unfolds as a critical rethinking of the Cinderella tale that questions the gender roles and materialism of "happily ever after" fairy-tale tropes in a modern context of wealth and beauty. It does so by altering enough details of the story to focus not on female virtue rewarded but deviance punished. In so doing, it raises questions about the constructed identity of "princess" or its modern cognate, the child-like trophy wife, as well as the gendered economic relationships that regulate the fragile narrative teleology of happily ever after.

At the center of the episode is Lucinda,[18] a complex parodic Cinderella figure whose connection to the iconic figure is signaled by the "cind" their names share. Unlike her namesake, Lucinda was not abused and neglected by a stepmother and sisters after her father's death, forced to do menial tasks and later rewarded for her virtuous submission by a fairy-godmother. On the contrary, while still having lost both her parents, her godfather Spencer[19] supported her as she grew up with her step-family, fulfilling a promise to his former business partner, Lucinda's father. Spencer granted her every material desire until her marriage to Arthur,[20] who takes on the responsibility of her provider and protector. The princess's portrayal in a modern urban setting is similar to representations of the "Real Housewives" in popular culture who have become emblems of leisure and luxury.[21] Importantly, however, Lucinda seems to believe that her female step-family did threaten and deprive her and that she needs protection from them: she seems to have relatively little understanding of her relative privilege in the world. Yet, it is not a story consciously fabricated for sympathy. Instead, her fantasy of childhood cruelties provides insight into how Lucinda's reality has been contoured. Male economic power and control have artificially shaped her experience, creating a perfect woman that embodies the most significant Western gender ideals: beauty, passivity, dependence, and, notably, no negative emotion to express beyond trivial fears that her prince can lovingly assuage.

Lucinda's mediated understanding of herself, her husband, and her world joins a host of other fantasies about gender and economic power that unravel when Arthur loses their money—his family money and Lucinda's inheritance—in a Ponzi scheme. His foolishness with money is directly juxtaposed to the success of Lucinda's stepmother, Mavis,[22] who used money from her late husband to found a lucrative business. Similarly, the tragedies that unfold throughout the episode can be linked to Lucinda's inability to understand a world in which people don't just give her things because of how well she plays the female role. These couple to create the crisis that draws Nick and his friends into the story: the murder of Lucinda's stepmother, with one stepsister soon to follow. As they unravel the crimes, they uncover Lucinda's secret Wesen identity and devise a plan to stop her before she can kill her remaining stepsister. However, this is not until after they have interrogated both Arthur and Spencer. The assumption shared by all of the men is that both money and murder are a masculine affair.

"Happily Ever Aftermath" looks into the consequences of Lucinda's carefree material existence, the display of gendered virtue that accompanies it, and the problematic entangling of virtue and dependency. Lucinda, after all, is all the things a fairy-tale princess should be—beautiful, sweet, fashionable, social, and unchallenging—and embodies Western hegemonic gender ideals—young, white, blonde, married, bound to the private sphere. She does not work but uses her beauty to charm for the benefit of charities, the perfect female counterpart to her prince. Lucinda lives in a fantasy world in which desires are immediately met, everything is beautiful, and life is a dream; she, in turn, embodies the dream of the dependent, devoted, soft feminine ideal. Hers is life beyond good and evil because there is never any complication to fulfilling the desires or the adoration she receives from her prince, until of course, there is.

The dream-life masks two horrifying realities that give two explanations for the dramatic events of the episode, one fantastical, one socio-critical. The ostensible reason given for her sweetness-or-rage binary is that Lucinda is a *Murciélago* like her godfather[23]: a bat-like dualistic being that originated in South America. According to Grimmlore, the *Murciélago* embodies two opposite, absolute states in one. In Lucinda, these align with traditional notions of gendered behavior. One state yields the beautiful fairy-tale princess Arthur and the audience see; the other is a violent humanoid bat that kills through supersonic sounds that it emits in a rage. However, her evil alter-ego emerges not only in woge but also in a wardrobe change that emphasizes the gender transgression of independence over dependency. Following a binary gendered representation, the princess in her human-self is coded feminine. She has a squeaky voice, sweet laughter, and an innocent look. In her evil side as *Murciélago*, she transgresses the attributes traditionally associated with femininity, manifesting not just as the monster but also in a more masculine wardrobe before she woges. How she dresses gives a comical critique of the importance of clothing in the original tale: Cinderella only appears as princess material when she wears her magical dress. It also communicates her "good" and "bad" sides visually. In her role as a fairy-tale wife, she wears dresses and the color pink—traditionally associated with femininity. When en route to a confrontation that ends in murder, she wears trousers and clothes in shades of blue—traditionally associated with masculinity. Her woged representation, however, exploits physical identity to communicate good and bad gendered behavior visually. Lucinda is fair and blonde; when she woges into a *Murciélago*, her hair turns black, and her skin turns brown. This perhaps alludes to the Wesen's South American origin or is simply an adaptation of bat in hybrid form. However, the visual dynamics reproduce a racialized Western designation of good and evil through light and dark skin in which the dark Other is the villain. Thus, there are two sides to Lucinda: the beauty and the beast. She is the virtuous feminine domestic ideal and the uninvited bat that lurks in the darkness.

What triggers these changes is the degree to which her desires are satisfied or her dream life propped up by money from male sources: her father, her godfather, and her husband. Arthur fails to supply money and cannot attain it from her stepmother (to whose important role I shall turn shortly) or Spencer, who denies having sufficient funds to amend their debt. Because of his inability to fulfill his side of the bargain, her dream world is threatened, and she pursues it in the most logical ways in her fairy-tale idiom, asking for and receiving it because she is beautiful and good. Her step-family, all being female, does not see her through the male gaze as a being to be rewarded: asking does not work. This leaves inheritance, which requires the death of her Stepsisters and Stepmother, who already fear her. Though they do not know that she is a *Murciélago*, they know that she flips from sweet to terrifying when unappeased. In those states, she terrorized her step-siblings, whom she understands as having been mean to her by denying her wants, whatever they may be.

It is important to note that Lucinda does not set out to kill her step-family; instead, she believes that they will give her money if she asks. Everyone has always given what she wanted either in exchange for her embodiment of good gendered behavior or out of terror when she snaps, revealing her other, suppressed "evil" nature, of which she seems unaware. The violent murders of her stepmother and stepsister, therefore, unfold more like amplified tantrums in which she has lost self-control rather than cold-blooded killings. The obverse of the child-like fairy-tale princess who needs protection is thus the spoiled child of desire and rage without empathy, boundaries, or conscience. When her stepmother and sister each deny her what she desires, she woges in a fury, emitting a perilous, silent cry. Curiously, this dangerous, uncontainable duality is not apparent in her godfather, who manages to control himself without incident. When he does finally woge, it is intentional and coded as male heroics that save the day by ending Lucinda's murderous violence. Not insignificantly, when fighting for her life, her right to exist, she remains a *Murciélago*: presumably, a princess would die when told to. In this final battle, Spencer also dies.

Spencer's death is cast as the apogee of masculinity in his mind: he dies killing a monster to "help" the princess while the other female deaths align with gender transgressions and carry a punitive weight. In contrast to Lucinda, the other women killed in this episode defy the female expectation of marriage as the ultimate goal for happiness. Aligned with traditional fairy-tale paradigms, Mavis is presented as a cold, wealthy widow who dislikes her stepdaughter while privileging her daughters. Situated within the series' heteronormative construction, she has been involved in at least two heterosexual relationships during her life. However, as a successful, single businesswoman, she challenges the traditional notion of women seeking a male provider—in counterpoint to her stepdaughter's housewife role—and exceeds it by making and managing her own money.

Mavis blurs the line between unconditional maternal love and the expectation of emotional reciprocity, complicating the traditional image of the self-sacrificing caregiver. While a busy professional woman in the public sphere, she is also an engaged mother to her biological children. Moving beyond the assumption that, as a stepmother, she has no intention of aiding Lucinda, her motives may be read as a moralizing discourse consistent with parenting. It is revealed that she refuses to share her money and save her son-in-law from financial crisis because they only reach out to her when they are in need. She feels they ought to make an effort to build a relationship with her that exceeds demands for money. She states that they are adults who should accept the consequences and "get a sense of the real world." This creates ambiguity about her villainy—while she does not appear to inhabit the role of self-sacrificing mother, she also does not appear irrationally evil. This ambiguity further exposes Arthur's false narrative about marriage and hegemonic masculinity. Moreover, by refusing to give him what he wants and taking the position of advising on what he should do, she infantilizes him and impedes his ability to act as Lucinda's prince.

The Prince in Distress and the Godfather to the "Rescue"?

While women are punished for deviating too far from "fairy-tale" gender norms, this episode also reveals the limited roles of their male counterparts. The prince's masculine downfall is linked to the princess's transgression of femininity. This section will look at the male characters in this episode to further explore this claim. It is important to recall that Mavis is not the cause of the married couple's misery. Her only "evil" act was not giving money to her step-son-in-law. Arthur triggers this series of crimes when he fails to enact his masculine role of provider. In short, it is the discovery that her husband isn't a "prince" that leads to the murders.

Arthur becomes aware of his fragile masculinity when he first loses his money. That he does not share his economic burden with his wife may be read as a struggle to maintain his hegemonic masculine façade. Enacting "protective" masculinity, Arthur constantly undermines his wife:

excluding her from their financial crisis, seeking help from others, and eventually dictating that they will have to cut back on their expenses. He repeatedly states that he intends to protect her, but this discourse proves problematic. Though refuted many times, Arthur also shares his perspective that jealousy is an inherently female trait, emphasizing his fragile masculinity. Mavis does not seem interested in having either of her daughters married to him: as a successful woman herself, she likely does not share his vision of himself as a charming prince. Moreover, the stepsisters clarify that disliking their sister is unrelated to Arthur, which further dissolves his false masculine narrative.

Lucinda fractures Arthur's masculinity after his standing up to her is met with violence and her leaving him. Thus, Arthur is left without wealth or his female counterpart. While Lucinda hurts Arthur both physically and emotionally in her attempt to fulfill her desires, her initial intentions toward him are unclear. Nevertheless, she does not kill Arthur in pursuit of money, because he has none to give. Her fatal transgression comes at the cost of men, reprising the portrayal of witch and stepmother figures as single. Arthur, however, remains, demonstrating a failure to live up to the provider role, affirming the social network that infantilizes women by making them dependent and dictating what they are allowed to want, need, and feel.

Spencer counterbalances Arthur's inability to control his wife. A single, black businessman in his late fifties or early sixties, Spencer perceives himself as honorable, telling the detectives that he made a vow to Lucinda's father that he would always protect her. This is perceived negatively by the stepmother, who encourages him (mockingly) to get a life of his own. While Spencer's self-image is one of honor, this perception is problematic in relation to the female characters. During Spencer's interrogation as a possible suspect for murder, the detectives ask him why Lucinda's father had not made a will. He implies that his deceased friend and business partner was a poor judge of women. Spencer himself seems to adopt a role of patriarchal authority and misogyny—which is reinforced with the way he "controls" Lucinda first with money, then with violence. Spencer has a prominent, self-serving narrative about his intent to protect his goddaughter that requires she remain a beautiful, harmless little girl. Therefore, when Lucinda takes independent actions exceeding male control, Spencer feels both entitled and enjoined to murder her. For she must forever remain a dependent child, if only in memory, if he is to continue in the fantasy role of her "fairy" godfather.

Both the prince and the fairy godfather reinforce patriarchal dynamics in their attempt to control females. Spencer views marriage as a transaction in which Lucinda becomes Arthur's responsibility and not his.

However, the prince fails to fulfill this obligation by not providing for and failing to limit or control his wife—reinforcing the importance of patriarchal gender relation through his failures. The narrative complicates the fairy-tale figure of the prince by examining the masculinity it proposes while also interrogating the necessary gendering of the godmother in creating a godfather who controls rather than enables, though both reinforce patriarchal dynamics, one through reward alone, the other through reward and punishment. Arthur's masculinity is dependent on Lucinda's submissive femininity, which he attempts to control and surveil. Under this gender policing, she cannot be her entire self, her dual being. With Arthur, she is only half a person (or Wesen). Spencer knows her true nature and distorts it, perhaps creating the unintegrated rage that explodes in her inaudible, murderous screams. Mavis was murdered for refusing to share her wealth and Tiffany was subsequently killed after she tried to run away from her stepsister. Lucinda's crimes are not premeditated; they are impulsive responses to not getting what she wants. While it is unclear whether this *Murciélago* creature is aware of her own uncontrollable and irrational behavior, Spencer ensures she grows up with only the approved desire of becoming a dependent, passive, naïve child-bride. She never has the chance to consciously explore any different part of who she might be.

And They Did Not Live Happily Ever After

"Organ Grinder" and "Happily Ever Aftermath" conclude with the violent death of their female villains, with the latter dispensing with gender-role non-conforming women along the way. Dr. Levine accidentally falls into a fire pit while fighting Nick—who attempts to save her from the fall. Lucinda's godfather murders her before Nick manages to arrest her. The deaths of these antagonists are hardly a surprise since, in most patriarchal stories, the goddess/monster is killed off.[24] In the Brothers Grimm's fairy tales, acceptable norms are constituted by the protagonist whose happy ending adheres to a resolution according to the codes framed by a benevolent patriarchal rule.[25] Following this claim, the tragic ending of these female deviants may be read as a reestablishment of the patriarchal social order.

While progressive in many aspects, *Grimm* reflects an inherent link between male domination and the notion of justice. In most of Grimm's fairy tales, male domination is rationalized as long as the ruler is benevolent and just.[26] In these episodes, however, male dominion perseveres, but the justness of its justice is blurred. In the final scene of "Happily Ever Aftermath," Spencer's character may be read as a metaphor for patriarchal society and institutions that police female deviance to contain women within desired norms. In this light, Lucinda's murder of Spencer can be read as a final act of defiance before a patriarchal system that aims to silence her.

"I'm sorry; I did the best I could" are Spencer's final words before he dies. Without ignoring her crimes, the question of his entitlement to decide her life or death stands. Their mutual murder underlines a relation between Lucinda's transgression and Spencer's failure to contain her. Because his role embodies patriarchal institutions, the princess's murder in this episode may be read as the death of the "deviant" woman at the hands of society. Lucinda moved away from her submissive and naïve role as a housewife and dared to scream higher as a *Murciélago*. Voicing her desires not only resulted in the murder of family, who might otherwise have been allies: they too posed a threat to patriarchal society's aim to keep women at bay. In short, male domination plays a crucial role in punishing female deviance, and thus the social order is restored. Spencer may die but the gendered ideology he championed lives on. Similarly, though the wicked witch may die at the end of "Organ Grinder," there is no intimation that appetites for her trade have diminished or homeless children will be valued as people rather than ignored or dismissed as unpleasant, tragic things.

Exploring the witch, the stepmother, and the princess figures as portrayed in NBC's *Grimm* provides insight into acceptable and deviant codes of gendered behavior. First, notions of good and evil are deeply embedded in traditional paradigms of femininity and masculinity, wherein adherence to expected gender roles is praised, and deviance is punished. Second, while the female villains had different criminal motives, their acts are rooted in ambition, independence, and money. They lose their social ties to men and the home in becoming villains—breaking loose from the infantilization of the private, domestic sphere, transgressing into the public realm. Ultimately, these female villains transgress the established social order, stepping out of mother or princess roles. As a result, their double deviance is punished, not to serve justice, but to restore the patriarchal social order.

Notes

1. Santos 35–52.
2. See Caputi.
3. Zipes, "Spells of Enchantment" 5–6.
4. Briggs 1.
5. See Lindenauer. The link between witches and evil stepmothers can be traced back to the eighteenth century. At this moment, Leslie Lindenauer argues that the "stepmother assumed the witch's place, the epitome of female evil intent on undermining the stability of family and community. The evil stepmother stepped out of the fairytale [sic] and into popular sources that reflected the period in which they were produced" (xxiv).

6. *Ibid.* Also see Davis.
7. Caputi 19.
8. Zipes, *Fairy Tales and the Art of Subversion* 70.
9. *Ibid.*
10. See Caputi.
11. See Zipes *Complete Fairy Tales.*
12. It is worth noting that earlier editions of the Grimm's fairy tales portrayed biological mothers instead of stepmothers. These changes were made in later editions. See Tatar; Warner.
13. Actor, Valerie Cruz.
14. For purposes of emphasis, this character will also be referred to as the witch or *Geier* throughout the essay.
15. See Munford and Waters.
16. Actor, James Maxey.
17. Actor, Daryl Sabara.
18. Actor, Amanda Schull.
19. Actor, Tom Wright.
20. Actor, David Clayton Rogers.
21. See Munford and Waters.
22. Actor, Patricia Hunter.
23. *Murciélago* is a Spanish word, which translates to bat. This word reinforces an association between female evilness and vampirism.
24. Caputi 19.
25. Zipes 71.
26. *Ibid.*, 72.

Works Cited

Briggs, Robin. "Introduction." *Witches and Neighbours: The Social and Cultural Context of European Witchcraft.* 2nd ed., Blackwell, 2002, pp. 1–11.
Caputi, Jane. *Goddesses and Monsters. Women, Myth, Power, and Popular Culture.* U Wisconsin P, 2004.
Davis, Amy M. "Film as a Cultural Mirror." *Good Girls & Wicked Witches: Women in Disney's Feature Animation.* E-book, Indiana UP, 2007.
Lindenauer, Leslie. *I Could Not Call Her Mother. The Stepmother in American Popular Culture, 1750–1960.* Lexington Books, 2014.
Munford, Rebecca, and Melanie Waters. *Feminism and Popular Culture.* I.B Tauris, 2014.
Santos, Cristina. "Vampires and Witches and Werewolves…Oh My!" *Defiant Deviance: The Irreality of Reality in the Cultural Imaginary,* edited by Cristina Santos and Adriana Spahr, Peter Lang, 2006, pp. 35–52.
Tatar, Maria. *The Hard Facts of the Grimm's Fairy Tales: Expanded Edition,* Princeton Classics, 2019.
Warner, Marina. *From the Beast to the Blonde,* Vintage: 1994.
Zipes, Jack. "Breaking the Magic Spell: Politics and Fairy Tales." *Literature Criticism from 1400 to 1800,* edited by Thomas J. Schoenberg and Lawrence J. Trudeau, vol. 171, Gale, 2010. *Literature Resource Center,* https://link.gale.com/apps/doc/H1420094280/LitRC?u=uvictoria&sid=LitRC. Accessed 13 Sept. 2019. Originally published in *New German Critique,* vol. 6, 1975, pp. 116–135.
_____ "Spells of Enchantment." *When Dreams Come True.* Routledge, 1999, pp. 1–29.
_____ "Who's Afraid of the Brothers Grimm? Socialization and Politicization through Fairy Tales." *Fairy Tales and the Art of Subversion.* 2nd ed., Routledge, 2006, pp. 59–79.
_____, Translator. *The Complete Fairy Tales of the Brothers Grimm.* 3rd ed. By Jacob Grimm and Wilhelm Grimm, Bantam Books, 2002.

Pro-Animal Ideology and the Philosophy of Coexistence

An Ecocritical Perspective on Grimm

Tatiana Konrad

The TV show *Grimm* (2011–2017) combines natural and supernatural elements to explore the relationship between humans and nonhumans. In the fictional world of *Grimm,* inspired by the plots of the Brothers Grimm fairy tales, humans unknowingly co-exist with supernatural creatures, Wesen. Wesen naturally exhibit the attributes and characteristics of animals but can appear as humans in public. Throughout this essay, I refer to the creatures in the show that look and behave like animals as *animals*. They are not animals in the traditional sense; instead, they are beings that combine human and animal identities. This essay emphasizes the animal over the human to demonstrate the positive significance of the animal side in *Grimm* and the series' overall articulation of a pro-environment stance. While *Grimm* is a fantasy series, it separates and naturalizes particular supernatural areas through characters that resemble real-world animals, forming a distinction between the supernatural and the natural-supernatural. Insofar as it functions diegetically in the show, the supernatural is the purview of creatures without animal affiliations, such as witches (*Hexenbiests*) or spirit-beings. The audience is not meant to think of these animals or Wesen as supernatural in this enchanted sense. Instead, they are presented as natural in a way that extends general human understanding of the natural world, creating a natural supernaturalism. It is through its presentation and development of these animals that *Grimm* argues for a pro-environmental relationship with our natural world.

Grimm explores the human-nature relationship or, to be more specific, the human-animal relationship primarily through the character of Nick Burkhardt. Nick is one of few humans who can see the actual animal nature of Wesen that appear human to most. He is a police detective, but he is better known as a descendent of Grimms and presumed to be hunter of Wesen in the world of supernatural beings. While his role as a Grimm designates him as the assassin of these creatures for the betterment of humanity, in learning more about them, Nick comes to understand that majority live peaceful lives, pose no danger to humans, and are essentially good. He befriends many while hunting only the aggressive, violent, and dangerous ones. Although some of the supernatural creatures of the series are not animals (for example, *Hexenbiests*, spirits like *La Llorona*, elemental forces like *Volcanalis*), the majority have an animal nature. These characters, their human relationships, and the consequences of those relationships are the primary focus of this essay.

The hybridity of Wesen—animals by nature that can "pass" as humans in appearance—allows for their participation in a larger (human) social world. This hybridity creates complex and, at times, ambiguous considerations of what constitutes animals and their social status. On the one hand, they are socially, culturally, and morally equal to humans. Yet, on the other hand, as a species, they may directly pose a threat to humanity (especially the animals who are violent criminals, robbers, murderers, etc.). Further complexities and ambiguities exist because their hybrid nature goes unseen by humans while the nature and motives of their social contributions and relationships, or alternately any crimes they commit, often parallel those of their human counterparts. Importantly, this essay does not view these hybrids as humans who turn into animals when committing various crimes. On the contrary, it argues that these are *animals* who can adjust and function as members of human society. Through its portrayal of the hybrid, emphasizing the animal in this way, a bold aspect of this series comes to light—one that is always present in the background highlighting the conflicts of this fantasy world—that *Grimm* advocates a philosophy of coexistence. It promotes a range of stances from pro-environmentalism and animal rights to veganism, urging a reconsideration of the human-animal relationship amid the urgency of environmental degradation and climate change.

Grimm *and Animal Ethics*

Grimm interrogates the human-animal relationship in two ways. The first is through Nick's direct interaction with these animals as one of the few humans who can see their otherwise hidden animal nature. One can speculate that the series imagines the potential for social awareness of a natural world wherein humans and animals are equally essential inhabitants of the planet. The second is through people's reactions when learning that the "human" in front of them is really an animal. Their reactions range from surprise to fear and illustrate both humans' reluctance to accept animals (and other nonhumans) as equal inhabitants of the planet and to resist accepting multi-speciesism as a legitimate approach to life on Earth.

The inherent conflicts of a multi-species reality within a presumed single-species social context frames the challenges of *Grimm*'s monster-of-the-week episodes. Kristiana Willsey defines a "'monster of the week'" format as one in which "each episode features some new species of fairy-tale creature and the fallout of those creatures' interactions with an unsuspecting human world."[1] While larger plotlines extend through the series, these new, episodic natural-supernatural agents deconstruct and reimagine the human relationship with a *diverse* (super)natural world. These are complex and nuanced portrayals of animals that exceed the mere category of "monsters." While the transformations of humans into animals and vice-versa help create an atmosphere of horror and mysticism that is central to the series' aesthetic, the metamorphoses which occur to adjust to particular environments or environmental changes raise profound questions of animal ethics and the human-animal relationship of the present.

The natural-supernatural beings, or Wesen, combine their two natures—human and animal—skillfully drawing from each to adapt to either of two environments, the human world and the animal world. The ability to pass as human helps keep them safe in the human world. Such an ability, however, performs another vital function. René Descartes once claimed that animals are unable to speak,[2] intending that they are incapable of communicating in the language that humans use. By contrast, *Grimm*'s animals can communicate in both species-specific and human languages. Their secondary, human communication, is beneficial to both the animals who can directly speak to humans and the humans spoken-to because it presents an opportunity to communicate what animals want, how they think, what their problems are, and what makes them happy. By moving animals closer to humans, the series creates a compelling exploration of humanity's ecological role on the planet.

The series encourages consideration of Wesen as animals that can turn into humans (rather than the reverse) by emphasizing and valorizing animalistic habits and abilities and the environments in which they live. For example, Nick repeatedly relies upon his close friend and mentor

Monroe's status as a wolf, or *Blutbad*, to make advantageous use of his acute sense of smell, as illustrated in the Pilot when seeking out a lost child in the woods. Similarly, "The Three Bad Wolves" (S1, E6) draws direct attention to Monroe's animal nature through an extended sequence conspicuously displaying his adventures in a forest where he runs free, howls, mates with the she-wolf Angelina, and hunts for rabbits. Another vivid example is Nick's friend Bud,[3] an *Eisbiber*—a Wesen broadly based on beavers.[4] As a non-predatory animal, he is often portrayed as scared of other creatures, timid; he also lives in a relatively small house with his wife and three children and works as an appliance repairman. He also socializes with other *Eisbibers* in a Beaver "Lodge." These attributes broadly parallel the activities of beavers in their natural environment, as they build dams and lodges and repair their "homes." In this fashion, animal characters in *Grimm* mimic the habits and activities of the real animals that they personify, adapting them to the human world. This emulation bolsters the claim of the animal over the human as their primary nature. Their human appearance functions only as a mask that allows them to live among humans without being identified as intruders, rendering them as the Other.

Some scholars have participated in the Othering identification and distinction that *Grimm* challenges by presenting animality as a purely negative or pejorative characteristic. In this regard, Willsey writes that the series "move[s] from savagery to civilization," strictly identifying the animal within the human as a savage and the human within the animal as a civilized being.[5] The colonialist vocabulary used to designate the human from the animal emphasizes animal oppression and subjugation. Here, animality is characterized as a deficiency or liability that should be kept out of sight. The series wants us "to sympathize" with these creatures, for they cannot show their true self but "must hide the animalistic urges."[6] Yet, by showing themselves as animals, they, in the words of Willsey, exhibit "their fundamental inhumanity."[7]

While the distinction between human and animal nature in an analysis of these creatures is plausible (after all, the human and the animal are believed to be "traditionally explosive binaries"[8]), approaching the animal as uncivilized, savage, inhuman, and essentially monstrous entails several problems and overlooks the eco-cultural dimensions of the series. Instead of focusing on the differences between humans and animals that would identify the two as antagonist species, *Grimm* explores the possibility of peaceful coexistence. It is not the series' primary goal to portray animals as stronger, faster, or smarter than humans and thus dangerous, nor weaker and inferior, and therefore subject to human superiority. In either case, the animal is constructed as the Other. *Grimm* takes a different approach, inviting the audience to consider the potential equality of humans and animals in a world where animals live among people without distinction, have the same legal rights, and have a voice. In so doing, the series communicates a powerful pro-animal ideology to its audience.

Jacques Derrida's vision of the animal provides a valuable framework for deconstructing the images of the animals in *Grimm* and understanding its human-animal relationship. While recognizing various qualities that make humans different from animals, Derrida explicitly says "the animal that I am,"[9] thus also acknowledging similarities between the two. But even more importantly, the philosopher questions the very term "the animal," unveiling its oppressive nature. He rejects "homogeneity or biological continuity without difference."[10] Derrida vehemently foregrounds the diversity of the animal world, and this is also the position that *Grimm* communicates to its audience. Through the different images of animals and multiple transformations into humans and vice versa, the series illustrates "humanity's primal, animalistic nature waiting to be discovered."[11] But even more importantly, the series emphasizes diversity in the animal world while promoting the potential of animal-human coexistence. Animals transcend the three human-relation categories they have been thrust as Others: domestic pets, wild and dangerous creatures, and, simply put, food. *Grimm*'s portrayals of animals reflect a variety of species that construct complex eco-systems arguing an important eco-philosophy: today, in the age of climate change, it is urgently necessary to reimagine the role of humanity on the planet beyond the binary status of human and non-human or, as Heather Houser calls them, "more-than-human"[12] beings. The challenge emerges: "can we continue to argue for a superiority over other animals that justifies dominating and exploiting them?"[13] or is it the moment to understand that "we are deeply, instinctively connected to all living beings." It is this later ideology, termed "biophilia,"[14] that *Grimm* persuasively conveys.

The Vegetarian Diet in Grimm

The presentation of animals existing equally with humans reinforces a pro-animal stance and inevitably requires reimagining their very meaning. One way in which *Grimm* does this explicitly is by challenging the status of animals as food, actively promoting vegetarianism and veganism. The portrayal of animals that are part human makes it clear that they are not for human consumption. Their humanity protects them from human consumption, essentially rendering it cannibalism. Indeed, while some Wesen in the series might be traditionally regarded as fit for human

160 Part Two: Justice and Social Spaces

consumption because of their animal cognates—pigs (*Bauerschwein*), bulls (*Taureus-Armenta*), sheep (*Seelengut*), and fish (*Cracher-Mortel, Hasenfussige Schnecke*)—none are portrayed as potential food. They are too human-like to be categorized in such a manner. In offering these equivocal images of animals, *Grimm* implicitly intensifies its pro-animal ideology, presenting human consumption of animals as an illegitimate practice. When the audience witnesses one animal creature hunting or consuming another, the scenes are either largely naturalized or criminalized, suggesting that this is what animals do in their natural habitat. When criminalized, however, it is usually only because humans cannot see the animal in these creatures and perceive their predation or consumption as aggressive, dangerous behavior, or even cannibalism.

Crucially, one of the series' main characters—Monroe—is a vegetarian.[15] As a *Blutbad* or wolf-hybrid, carnivorous by nature, the significance of this vegetarian diet is paramount. Monroe consciously suppresses his animal nature by choosing to avoid animal eating and rejecting wolf culture and violence. He believes that he can stop being a predator through diet and behavioral discipline. The choice to be a vegetarian is not significant to his animality alone. It is also a suppression of his (presumably omnivorous) human nature. His vegetarianism makes a holistic statement of coexistence, one that is mirrored by his interspecies marriage and friendship with a Grimm. It is also worth noting that Grimms, as defined by the fictional pre-history of the show, are indiscriminate killers of Wesen or animals. Nick repudiates this behavior and focuses on the moral/legal actions of Wesen (as he would with humans) rather than the animality which marks them solely as prey.

By not eating meat, Monroe suppresses the predator within. The peaceful nature of his profession, the patient hours spent repairing delicate watches and clocks, further reinforces this commitment. Through this character, a vegetarian diet is represented as not only pro-animal but also generally pro-life. Monroe himself is not aggressive or dangerous for human society or other animal creatures who could become his meal. Moreover, in one instance, his vegetarianism even saves his life. In "A Dish Best Served Cold" (S3, E3) the pigs (*Bauerschwein*) plot revenge on wolves for the atrocities committed in their long predatory history, reflected in the story "The Three Little Pigs" from which the episode draws. The episode focuses on a group of pigs working in a restaurant who add a special ingredient—a rare mushroom—to a complimentary delicacy served to every patron. The mushroom is harmless to everyone but wolves, causing their bellies to explode. The pigs use the mushroom to murder several wolves, presenting an alternate, vengeful reality of prey hunting the predator. Yet Monroe avoids an explosive end, defying the violent logic of hunt or be hunted. At the beginning of the episode, he avoids eating the fatal tartlet appetizer because it contains meat. Whether the source is a traditional animal or a supernatural animal, eating meat correlates in this episode with a savage, criminal, and murderous activity that deserves punishment. Notably, neither Nick nor any wolves murder the chef of the restaurant. While it seems logical to do so (after all, wolves hunt and consume pigs, and Grimms hunt and kill Wesen), Nick chooses legal repercussions. In so doing, he paves the way to begin a civilized relationship between Grimms and the animal world and within the animal world itself between wolves and pigs. Instead of being consumed, the *Bauerschwein* are eventually arrested for murdering wolves. The episode's arc thereby argues against eating animals in any form by directly linking meat consumption with murder and further indicating that the righteous, civilized, or transcendent choice is to abstain from meat consumption and its implicit violence altogether.

Thirty years ago, the feminist and animal rights advocate Carol J. Adams claimed: "Through butchering, animals become absent referents. Animals in name and body are made absent *as animals* for meat to exist."[16] Adams specifies:

> There are actually three ways by which animals become absent referents. One is literal: ... through meat eating they are literally absent because they are dead. Another is definitional: when we eat animals we change the way we talk about them, for instance, we no longer talk about baby animals but about veal or lamb.... The third way is metaphorical. Animals become metaphors for describing people's experiences. In this metaphorical sense, the meaning of the absent referent derives from its application or reference to something else.[17]

In each instance, one can spot "the rendering of animals as consumable bodies."[18] More recently, Guy Cook has underscored the continuous devaluing of the meaning of animals:

> In contemporary urban society, animals have been erased in many people's lives. They are generally encountered only as meat, pets, pests or vicariously in fiction and documentaries; yet the relation of humans to other animals is a matter of pressing environmental, social, economic and philosophical concern.[19]

Scholars thus accentuate the significant yet degrading and oppressive meanings that humans have given animals in Western culture. Similarly, "A Dish Best Served Cold" (S3, E3) foregrounds animal consumption as a social concern (murdering Wesen is a crime), an economic problem (restaurants serving meat), and a philosophical issue (killing for food alone is wrong when there are other choices).

Rejecting animal consumption is a powerful way to acknowledge their equivalent status, decolonizing nature in general and animals in particular. Vegetarianism, and especially veganism, are thus an effective solution to the problem of animal subjugation. Yet both diets are often regarded with skepticism and, sometimes, even aggression. Such opposition is unsurprising because various holidays and cultural celebrations have strong associations with specific animal food products. As Karen S. Emmerman explains,

> Many familial and cultural traditions rely on animals for their fulfillment—think of Christmas ham, Rosh Hashannah [sic] chicken soup, Fourth of July barbeques, and so forth. Though philosophers writing in animal ethics often dismiss interests in certain foods as trivial, these food-based traditions pose a significant moral problem for those who take animals' lives and interests seriously. One must either turn one's back on one's community or the animals.[20]

Thus, not eating animals can be interpreted as tantamount to a socio-cultural crime, implying a rejection of centuries-old traditions and ancestral practices. *Grimm* explores this kind of conflict in other contexts such as the secretive *Roh-hatz*, a coming-of-age ceremony[21] in which masculinity is achieved through the cruel hunt and slaughter of a human by bear-hybrids (*Jägerbar*) (S1, E2: "Bears Will Be Bears"). In this inversion of the traditional hunting relation, however, the human death would be socially construed as murder. The contextual irony poignantly points the finger at hunting and ritualistic practices involving animal cruelty and death, explicitly valuing life (animal or human) over heritage or cultural practice.

With a more political orientation for group identity, critiques of animal-free diets emerged in the United States shortly after the terrorist attacks by Islamic extremists on September 11, 2001. The vegan studies scholar Laura Wright identifies 9/11 as "a moment during which veganism became both visible and highly suspect in a period just after both vegetarianism and veganism had gained some cultural prominence and cachet."[22] According to Wright, that was the time when, in the U.S., "a new national narrative that constituted an overt and explicit politics of fear, of profound bifurcation, and of xenophobic intolerance" emerged.[23] The extensive reinforcement of this Othering philosophy made diet one of an individual's or group's defining characteristics. Wright claims: "Nation, religion, and diet all functioned as the criteria by which we posited our difference—our very humanity—from the animality of our attackers."[24] Diet played a profound role in constructing a perverse and essentialist nationalist ideology based on explicit religious discrimination:

> We were American, and they were "Al-Qaeda." We were good, and they were evil. We were Christian, and they were Muslim. We ate like Americans, and they ate according to the dictates of Islam, which expressly forbids the ingestion of pork and requires strict adherence to halal standards of animal slaughter. We are humans. They are animals.[25]

In this xenophobic logic, uninhibited and unrestricted animal consumption constitutes a person's humanity, morality, and righteousness.

The practice of meat-eating also plays a critical role in chauvinist constructions of "correct" bodies and masculinities. Eating meat has been viewed by gender-essentialist attitudes as an inherently and necessarily male activity. As Adams argues,

> Meat's recognizable message includes association with the male role; its meaning recurs within a fixed gender system; the coherence it achieves as a meaningful item of food arises from patriarchal attitudes including the idea that the end justifies the means, that the objectification of other beings is a necessary part of life, and that violence can and should be masked[26]

Through the vegetarian character Monroe, *Grimm* successfully shatters this stereotype, revealing how vegetarianism does not harm a man's body or masculinity. Monroe is portrayed as a heterosexual man, partnered with a woman with whom he can conceive children, affirming his virility. Although Monroe has chosen to be less aggressive and violent by consuming a meat-free diet, this in no way undermines his maleness or masculinity. He continues to be able to fight alongside and defend friends and family as needed.

The series critiques the association of animal consumption and extreme masculinity through the relationship of a specific form of meat-eating, frogs, and violence against women. Across two episodes, *Ziegevolk* men eat frogs to heighten their ability to perform mind control through pheromones. In "Lonelyhearts" (S1, E4), frog consumption is used explicitly as a way of sexually assaulting women. Notably, the assailant not only assaults women by removing their ability to consent, but also keeps them in kennels in his basement, treating them like animals. He even murders one who tries to escape. More complexly, "One Angry Fuchsbau" (S2, E17) shows a defense attorney consuming frogs to seduce a jury into acquitting a predatory abuser with a seemingly long history of domestic violence who murdered his wife. In both cases, the consumption of frogs is used to dominate women and protect and amplify toxic masculinity. The consumption of frogs is explicitly linked with a symbolic consumption of women that renders them disposable objects within a perverse extreme of masculine aggression.

Choosing to become vegetarian or vegan is often falsely and discriminatorily understood as deviant. However, the discussed episodes force us to question: a deviation from what? Are these diets challenges to the imposed patriarchal norms regarding one's body and masculinity that establishes a hierarchy of men over women, and of special interest here, men over animals, shaping perceptions of the role animals play in our lives? Scholars claim that vegans view their diet as "an aspect of anti-speciesist practice"[27] rejecting anthropocentric views and celebrating the lives of animals. Motivations towards veganism are varied, but "the impetus that drives most people to eschew all animal products is a profound belief that animals can and do suffer and that to inflict suffering on them in order to render them into food and clothing (items that are necessary to humans but that do not necessarily need to come from animals) is inherently and unequivocally wrong."[28]

Grimm promotes vegetarianism and veganism by presenting images of enhanced, human-like animals (both visually and in terms of their behavior, habits, hobbies, likes and dislikes, etc.) and by drawing explicit connections between the victimization of animals and the victimization of humans. The series equates meat-eating to something between murder and cannibalism—a practice that most of the world's population considers revolting and morally wrong. The literal equating of cannibalism with the monstrous is seen with *Wendigo*[29] in "To Protect and Serve Man" (S2, E11).

However, choosing to abstain from animal products, particularly in the U.S., can be a discouraged and challenging practice. As Wright explains,

[T]o live one's life without consuming or wearing animal products, particularly in the United States, is such a major shift [away from dominating animals] that to choose such a lifestyle essentially is to place oneself perpetually on the extreme margins of society. It is to invite questions, criticism, alienation, suspicion, and misunderstanding. And at various points in history, it has been to be persecuted both implicitly and explicitly in the popular press, in literature, and mainstream academic, and scientific media as unnatural, unhealthy, and decidedly un–American.[30]

Grimm thus becomes a particularly effective platform for normalizing vegetarian and vegan practices and philosophy. It reinforces the positive nature of these diets, inviting the audience to reconsider animals as independent subjects rather than oppressed objects. The portrayal of a Wesen-predator as capable of abstaining from meat is particularly significant to the show's pro-animal stance. Via Monroe, the series emphasizes the barbarism of consuming animals and the ethical responsibility of making a different choice.

Grimm broadens considerations of the human-animal relationship with a more extensive examination of environmentalism and environmental impact that foregrounds the human as a villain. In "Tree People" (S6, E9), the audience sees Nature fighting to protect itself from human aggression. The episode opens with two men shooting a deer and a woman illegally dumping toxic waste in a forest. These actions elicit punishment from a *Kinoshimobe* (an elemental being that serves trees) which kills them, putatively in self-defense. The episode dramatizes a struggle between the environment and human malfeasance to communicate the criminality of human actions toward the planet and nature's vulnerability. Significantly, the defender of nature in this context is not the aggressor, rather is responding to defend itself from harm. Nick and his friends decide to kill the *Kinoshimobe*—the mission is accomplished with some ambiguity as the creature's body is seen drawn by roots at the end of the episode. Importantly, Monroe is the only character to question this course of action. His reasoning is logical and empathic: Why is it wrong to kill someone/thing to defend your habitat from destruction, yourself from death, and your species from extinction? If someone posed a vital danger to a human and their loved ones, wouldn't they respond in the same way? Human deaths resulting from the *Kinoshimobe*'s retaliation allow the human characters in this instance to dismiss the potential for peaceful coexistence with nature. Still, Monroe insists upon the possibility, suggesting that humanity, not nature is the problem. His pro-environmental stance and desire to teach humans how to be more careful to the environment do not cease.

Grimm's choice to speak about animals that exist among humans in a post–9/11 paradigm can be interpreted as a reaction to a world that has become wilder, more aggressive, and dangerous. There are instances in the series that support this claim: for example, many criminals in the series are shown to be supernatural animals, many of whom are animal predators, especially among the incarcerated.[31] This aligns with dehumanizing tendencies to diminish the Other, the marginalized, and the vulnerable by equating them with animals.[32] By choosing to portray Wesen as animals rather than humans, mainly when these characters are criminals, the series refrains from presenting a wholly positive or superior view of the animal. Yet *Grimm*'s portrayals of animals are generally not anti-animal. On the contrary, through the variety of animal characters—some are strong and aggressive, some weak and timid, some kind and helpful—the show stresses animal diversity. It thereby suggestively reflects Derrida's argument that "the animal" is not a distinct species but includes various beings and natures—necessitating a call for recognition of that diversity.

Co-existing with animals, according to *Grimm*, is possible and desirable. The series reimagines animals as not subordinate beings used to make the human happy, give them food, clothing, and so on, but rather as equals in a shared space. The feminist Donna Haraway confesses:

> I love the fact that human genomes can be found in only about 10 percent of all the cells that occupy the mundane space that I call my body; the other 90 percent of the cells are filled with genomes of bacteria, fungi, protists, and such.... I am vastly outnumbered by my tiny companions. ... To be one is always to become with many.[33]

Introducing animals as members of human society profoundly challenges the very idea of humanity, provoking the re-imagination of various cultural, political, and social constructs, including gender, class, race, disability, and the environment. *Grimm* invites the audience to engage in the complex task of recreating a world changed by ecological decline and environmental degradation—one that we are all now living in.

Conclusion

Humanity has been using and abusing animals for centuries. On that basis, the idea of "human dominance over nonhuman animals" has been widely recognized as a "normative practice."[34] Yet, in an era of significant environmental change, many are starting to reconsider the role and status of the other inhabitants on this planet, realizing the criminal, ethical, and untenable politics of exploitation and domination exercised toward nonhuman animal beings. Mark Jackson asks, "Is it even possible to identify some thing [sic] or some process that renders humanity unique? What does the search for such an essence or locus reveal about a politics of identity and those making the designation: This is 'human'; that is 'not human'?"[35] History records many instances of colonization, domination, and abuse; the story of humanity's oppression of nature is but one powerful example. Living in an era of global environmental transformations and climate change, we must rethink our roles and responsibilities as humans, acknowledging other nonhuman agents. *Grimm* effectively does so by introducing animals as practically indistinguishable members of society. In so doing, it promotes a pro-animal ideology, finding multiple ways to say that animals are not inferior beings and they should not be diminished to mere objects of consumption. Perhaps even more importantly, it adumbrates coexistence as the only legitimate option available to living beings today. *Grimm* promotes environmentalism through its unique approach to the human-animal relationship. It presents negotiations of such complex issues as exploitation, consumption, vegetarianism and veganism, and animal ethics as sites of reflection where we can reconceptualize human relationships not with the supernatural world of fairy tales but with the natural world of which we are a part.

Notes

1. Willsey 211.
2. Derrida 53.
3. Actor, Danny Bruno.
4. The *Eisbibers* are introduced and explored in "Leave it to Beavers" (S1, E19).

5. Willsey 223.
6. *Ibid.*
7. *Ibid.*
8. Lavery 127.
9. Derrida 2.
10. Still 2.
11. Willsey 223.
12. Houser 3.
13. Bump 57.
14. *Ibid.* 58.
15. The status is compromised only once in the series when Angelina triggers his wolf nature.
16. Adams 20, italics in original.
17. *Ibid.* 21.
18. *Ibid.* xxxv.
19. Cook 587.
20. Emmerman 77.
21. S1, E2: "Bears Will Be Bears."
22. Wright, *Vegan Studies Project* 30.
23. *Ibid.*
24. *Ibid.* 37.
25. *Ibid.*
26. Adams xxxv.
27. Cole and Morgan quoted. in Wright 32.
28. Wright 32.
29. *Wendigo*, while animal-like, are not readily identified to a specific animal. They engage in cannibalistic consumption of humans and are exemplified by serial killer cannibals, such as Jeffrey Dahmer.
30. Wright 32.
31. S2, E11: "Protect and Serve Man."
32. Examples of this kind of dehumanizing discourse are as pernicious as they are common. They can be seen at work diminishing the horror of unthinkable deaths, such as in the tragedy of immigrants discovered suffocated to death in a stuffy truck in the U.S., described by the driver as "'lying on the floor like *meat*,'" as well as amplifying disdain such as in Donald Trump's references to immigrants as "'animals'" meant to underscore their aggression and violence. Anonymous driver qtd. in Wright, "Doing Vegan Studies" xii, my italics; Donald Trump, quoted in Wright xi.
33. Donna Haraway quoted in Wright, "Introducing Vegan Studies" 731.
34. McDonald 1.
35. Jackson 20.

Works Cited

Adams, Carol J. *The Sexual Politics of Meat: A Feminist-Vegetarian Critical Theory.* Bloomsbury, 1999.

Bump, Jerome. "Biophilia and Emotive Ethics: Derrida, Alice, and Animals." *Ethics & the Environment,* vol. 19, no. 2, 2014, pp. 57–89. https://muse.jhu.edu/article/564625

Cook, Guy. "'A Pig Is a Person' or 'You Can Love a Fox and Hunt It': Innovation and Tradition in the Discursive Representation of Animals." *Discourse & Society,* vol. 26, no. 5, 2015, pp. 587–607.

Derrida, Jacques. *The Animal That Therefore I Am.* edited by Marie-Louise Mallet, translated by David Wills, Fordham UP, 2008.

Emmerman, Karen S. "What's Love Got to Do with It? An Ecofeminist Approach to Inter-Animal and Intra-Cultural Conflicts of Interest." *Ethical Theory and Moral Practice,* vol. 22, no. 1, 2019, pp. 77–91.

Grimm, Seasons 1–6. Created by Jim Kouf, David Greenwalt and Stephen Carpenter. TV Series. Netflix, 2011–2017.

Houser, Heather. *Ecosickness in Contemporary U.S. Fiction: Environment and Affect.* Columbia UP, 2014.

Jackson, Mark. "For New Ecologies of Thought: Towards Decolonising Critique." *Coloniality, Ontology, and the Question of the Posthuman.* Edited by Mark Jackson, Routledge, 2018, pp. 19–62.

Lavery, Joseph. "Deconstruction and Petting: Untamed Animots in Derrida and Kafka." *Demenageries: Thinking (of) Animals After Derrida*, edited by Anne Emmanuelle Berger and Marta Segarra, Rodopi, 2014, pp. 125–143.

McDonald, Barbara. "'Once You Know Something, You Can't Not Know It': An Empirical Look at Becoming Vegan." *Society & Animals*, vol. 8, no. 1, 2000, pp. 1–23.

Still, Judith. *Derrida and Other Animals: The Boundaries of the Human.* Edinburgh UP, 2015.

Willsey, Kristiana. "*Grimm* and the Brothers Grimm." *Channeling Wonder: Fairy Tales on Television*, edited by Pauline Greenhill and Jill Terry Rudy, Wayne State UP, 2014, pp. 210–228.

Wright, Laura. "Doing Vegan Studies: An Introduction." *Through a Vegan Studies Lens: Textual Ethics and Lived Activism*, edited by Laura Wright, U of Nevada P, 2019, pp. vii–xxiv.

———. "Introducing Vegan Studies." *ISLE: Interdisciplinary Studies in Literature and Environment*, vol. 24, no. 4, 2017, pp. 727–736.

———. *The Vegan Studies Project: Food, Animals, and Gender in the Age of Terror.* U Georgia P, 2015.

PART THREE

Media and Genre

Who's Still Afraid of the Wolf?
Fairy-Tale Characters as a Medium of Cultural Change

Sara Casoli

In the landscape of television series of the early 21st century, *Grimm* (David Greenwalt and Jim Kouf, 2011–2017) represents an illustrative and enduring example of a hybrid genre that blends procedural drama and supernatural atmospheres and plots. In constructing its own *Grimmverse*, the series builds a fictional world at once new and old, fantasy and reality, invention and inheritance. While many television shows have featured elements of the fantastic or supernatural in their series arcs, *Grimm* draws from fairy tales to explore contemporary issues through adaptations of fairy-tale characters. Every fairy tale exists amid a dense network of adaptations, revisions, and retellings. This has left Cristina Bacchilega to posit the metaphor of a "fairy-tale web."[1] This network comprises an intermedia system created by written, audio-visual, and oral and figurative practices connected with a fairy-tale that acts as the center that irradiates outwards for the creation of other texts. Throughout this sprawling web, the tale ensures its continuity, resilience, and cultural significance during different times and societies. By continually being remediated and reinvested with new significance and mantling old stories, themes, tropes, and characters with a new guise, fairy tales can converse with us and our present time.

This essay aims to consider the status of *Grimm* within the fairy-tale web, exploring how it draws from and adapts fairy tales to explore contemporary concerns. Taking advantage of narratological and textual analysis, we will investigate how fairy-tale characters, as part of this "web," proliferate over time and space by adapting their pre-existent narrative and figurative material to new aesthetics and cultural requirements, thereby creating systemic links with present social and cultural issues. In this respect, fairy-tale characters have found in television seriality a fertile ground in which to grow.

Fairy-tale characters operate as serial and iconic characters and can therefore register, respond to, and mediate cultural changes. *Grimm* builds upon the intrinsic mutability of fairy-tale characters—their ability to adapt to different media and, at the same time, to personify cultural anxieties throughout their careers. Because of their peculiar identity structure, which combines strong and resilient traits with varied ones, fairy-tale characters are durable figures of our cultural imagination. This capacity allows them to change cultural currency and perform different social and cultural functions according to the necessities of the context in which they are embedded. At the same time, they maintain a sense of familiarity, thus facilitating the representation of controversial social and cultural themes. The character of Monroe in *Grimm* illustrates this process through his connection to the prototypical fairy-tale figure of the Big Bad Wolf. Through the framework of historically enduring abstractions of fairy-tale characters, he exemplifies fairy-tale figures' capacity in modern contexts to highlight, explore and problematize some of the ideological and cultural concerns.

The "Magical" Bond Between Fairy Tales and TV Series

Grimm builds upon the success of previous television shows to embed elements of fantasy in a modern setting in its pursuit of representation of contemporary issues. As Greenhill and Rudy and Donald Haase have shown,[2] TV series and fairy-tale narratives have frequently entangled their paths in the last decades, and television's contribution to the dissemination and consolidation of fairy tales along the twentieth and twenty-first centuries is relevant and undeniable. TV specials (for example, Jim Hanson's *Tales from Muppetland*), cartoons (like Jay Ward's *Fractured Fairy Tales*), TV shows (like Jim Henson's *The Storyteller*), and live-action TV series (from Shelley Duvall's *Faerie Tales Theatre* to the various versions of *Beauty and the Beast, Once Upon a Time,* and *Grimm*)[3] have flourished since the 1960s and increased in volume and variety. These productions have taken advantage of the rich and multifaceted material coming from fairy tales, fables, and folkloric traditions to exploit their ready and well-known plots and characters and the popularity and fascination of these stories among different audience targets.

Over the last decades, this bond has progressively consolidated: both television and fairy tales have undergone changes and adjustments that have occurred in the socio-historical background and the technological and cultural ones, and all have benefited from a fruitful association. In particular, television has contributed to disseminating innovative narrative and aesthetic adaptations, socio-cultural revisions, and domestication of parts of fairy tales or fairy tales in their entirety. More than printing press and graphic illustration, contemporary television's pervasive distribution of fairy tales, as Donald Haase highlights, "has made the genre an enduring part of late 20th-century popular culture,"[4] assuring its circulation and transmission. For its part, television has exploited the fairy-tale imaginary with the (quite frequent) purpose to commodify[5] it and to sell goods and entertainment by producing predictable adaptations. Many reasons explain the tight bond between TV seriality and fairy tales: both aim to address a broad, middle-class audience; TV series frequently retrieve some oral and visual qualities of traditional fairy tales while exploiting, at the same time, the figurativeness of the print tradition.

More significantly, the narrative structure of fairy tales displays an affinity with the form of televisual seriality. For instance, the fragmentation of TV serial narratives in cadenced installments is well suited to a genre historically based on brief stories gathered in anthologies and collections. The case of Jim Henson's *The Storyteller* is here quite significant: the series highlights the self-containment and independence of the episodes—each one dedicated to a different fairy tale—by using the narrative frame of a storyteller who presents every tale. Even when fairy-tale TV series do not adopt an anthological approach, opting instead for narrative continuity, there are "anthology plots" focused on particular fairy-tale motifs and characters that interrupt the narrative continuity of the "running plot,"[6] as illustrated by *Once Upon a Time* (Edward Kitsis and Adam Horowitz, 2011–2018), *Galavant* (Dan Fogelman, 2015–2016), and *Grimm*. *Grimm* is exemplary in its usage of this latter strategy, pairing the series arc with an anthology of "cases of the week" that, in keeping with the show's intersection with police procedurals, most often *actual cases* of the week in a legal sense. The series runs plots that extend over several episodes focused on the private/sentimental relations among the main characters, and anthology plots are dedicated to different secondary characters. Almost every case of the week's plotline focuses on the cases Nick has to resolve as a police detective while portraying or adapting an individual fairy tale or folkloric creature. Mimicking the anthology function, *Grimm* provides a collection of motifs and figures that merges the narrative structures both of police procedural and fairy tale.

Examining their narrative configuration, both television seriality and fairy tales share the same (serial) mode of storytelling. As many theorists have underlined,[7] every serial narration comes into existence by balancing the perpetuation of repeated materials recognized by the audience as the narrative and aesthetic marks of the series and the novelty brought by the varied traits that ensure the series' continuity, cognitive, and emotional connection with viewers. In other words, behind the content architecture, formal configuration, and long duration of serial narrative, there is a dialectic mechanism based on difference and repetition that balances the repetitiveness of some characters, situations, settings, and events, and the variations of others. In this way, every episode of the series is always "offered as original and different."[8] With repetition, indeed, we must not intend replication and sameness but, as Gilles Deleuze has suggested, a reappearance that includes difference and possibilities for variation.[9] In TV series, especially those belonging to the contemporary "Complex Television"[10] paradigm, the continuity of the repeated elements, which ensure the series' identity and readability, is balanced by a momentum toward the metamorphosis of other elements through their differentiation[11] from previous appearances.

Unsurprisingly, fairy tales demonstrate the dialectical movement at the core of any serial narration. The distinctive "storytelling momentum" of serial narratives finds an echo in the mechanism adopted by fairy tales in order to adjust themselves and proliferate across time and space. "As a genre characterized by endless variation and adaptability," Haase explains, "the fairy tale lends itself especially well to reinvention"[12] starting from a well-established narrative and figurative material that is somehow repeated. In that respect, as Max Lüthi highlights,

> repetitions and variations occur in many forms in the fairy tale, and on several levels. Within the individual fairy tale, [...] patterns of behaviour and plot sequences (episodes) are repeated, either exactly or with slight variation, and along with them. Naturally, the same or similar figures also turn up. [...] And finally, in various stories of the same or some other type, well-known themes, motif, and individual features familiar from other fairy tales keep turning up.[13]

Snow White provides an efficient and straightforward example of this phenomenon: a familiar character calling for a pale, dark-haired princess persecuted by an evil queen and poisoned by an apple. To be recognized as Snow White, every character must possess these iconic and narrative traits. Nonetheless, it is quite hard to flatten the complexity and variety of her occurrences, different versions, and intermedia translations on such commonalities. Variation is as fundamental as repetition for assuring the perpetuation of fairy tales in mutated textual, medial, and cultural contexts. Neither fairy-tale adaptations nor serial narrations (including and especially in TV series) demonstrate the simple recurrence of the same elements. Instead, they feature what Gilles Deleuze calls *repetition*, which preserves the form of its particularity and cannot be reduced to the perpetuation of the same: there is something *in addition* to the same.

Alongside repeated elements such as narrative patterns, characters, motifs, and representational modalities, we should also consider the different ones and how they impact adaptation. For example, how the conditions of production and reception have changed, the specificity of each medium, the adjustment of the narrative format, and the context's different social and cultural conditions. Through the process of repetition and adaptation operating on numerous levels (e.g., narrative and aesthetic formats, media and cultural settings), every fairy tale features labyrinthine intertextuality, an openness and perpetual transformation that Omar Calabrese saw at the center of the serial logic of storytelling. Indeed, fairy tales and serial narrative share the same structural functioning, composed by "a low number of structural invariants, called a 'base model,' a high number of figurative invariants, a very high number of regulated variables, and, finally, a large number of the so called 'optionals.'"[14] Both television seriality and fairy tales possess a similar malleability that allows for narrative and figurative content to change without renouncing immediate accessibility and familiarity. It is, therefore, no wonder that, precisely because of these relations, television has always taken advantage of fairy-tale narratives, images, situations, and characters.

With an increasing frequency in recent years, television has capitalized on the "marvellous geometry"[15] of fairy tales, the familiar material repetition, alongside a wide range of potential variations they entail. The result is a host of fairy-tale-based TV series offering experimentation and innovative reworking of traditional tales and motifs, especially significant and aware if we consider those series belonging to the "complex" narrational mode typical of contemporary television. With their puzzling and intricate, and interrelated storylines interlocking running plots with several anthology plots, complex TV series' narrative structure and aesthetics create more opportunities for the dialectic of repetition and variation to express its potentialities. In this regard, *Grimm* is a remarkable example of television using traditional fairy tales and folklore representations and motifs in a creative and contemporary way. The dialectics of repetition and variation are evident at the beginning of each episode in the epitaphs taken from famous literary sources (in particular, Brothers Grimm's *Kinder-und Hausmärchen*),[16] and function the most fruitfully in the retelling and reimagining of fairy-tale characters. Drawing figures from their original fairy tales, the TV series twists the narrative and figurative tropes associated with them, charging these characters with new socio-cultural meanings. A significant example of this mechanism is offered by the iconic Big Bad Wolf, whom the series transforms into a gentle and friendly creature who helps Nick Burchard catch the real murderer of a red-riding-hood-like figure in the series pilot. Because of this identitary construction, as we will try to demonstrate through the analysis of how and why the Big Bad Wolf has been reshaped into Monroe, fairy-tale characters can also be considered as free-floating signifiers that assume different social and cultural values "in the signifying functions attributable to the individual"[17] adaptation, and thus are a "medium" of cultural anxieties and changes.

"I'm a reformed Blutbad.*" Fairy-Tale Characters as Serial Figures*

In the pilot, Monroe explains to a very confused Nick that he is a *Blutbad* or, as he clarifies, that which Nick's ancestors would have called "the Big Bad Wolf." Nick reacts fearfully to this revelation, likely recalling in his mind the image of the classic Wolf appearing in *Red Riding Hood* and other fairy tales. In response, Monroe hurries with the explanation that he is a "reformed *Blutbad*," a modern Wolf that is not "that big" and is "done with the bad thing" (S1, E1: "Pilot"). In this brief dialogue, Monroe exemplifies the duplicity at the very base of any fairy-tale character: on one side, the iconicity of the figure and its abstraction ensure the preservation of its identity and recognizability (e.g., the prototype of the Big Bad Wolf); on the other side, the capacity to adapt and inscribe itself in a specific diegetic world and assume unique and more tangible forms (e.g., the specific Wolf named Monroe).

Among all characters colonizing our collective imagination and cultural background, few have the resilience, the long-lasting presence, and the survival strength associated with iconic fairy-tale characters. As part of the contemporary cultural DNA of Western culture, these figures pervade and saturate experience beginning with childhood: from books to film adaptations, from television to advertising, from games (more recently videogames) to merchandising, fairy-tale characters are everywhere, displaying in plain sight their *iconicity*. Broadly speaking, icons are those elements, people, images, and figures that are highly representative of a culture and deeply entangled within a matrix of meanings that become familiar objects despite their transnational and transmedia propagation. Iconic characters can be defined as "ready-made, flat, ahistorical"[18] figures iterating themselves in many versions and impersonations. As part of this cohort, fairy-tale characters acquire their iconicity and extraordinary adaptive capacity because of their fundamental duplicity: they are, as summarized by Klaus Rieser, "concrete, manifest, materialized [...] but also abstractions, condensations, images in our minds."[19] In other terms, when we think about fairy-tale characters, we always imagine two overlapping versions: the *type-like* figure, modeling and idealized version, and some *individual-like* figures, corresponding to the many specific incarnations of the type. At the base of this two-faced identity, there is what Rieser defines as "the concurrent presence of *soft* and *hard* schematizing,"[20] namely an intersection between a codification of traits that is open to diversified readings, thus retaining a certain openness to variation, and condensation of meanings and denotations that constitute the core of a character's identity and it is responsible for its recognizability and resilience.

In *Grimm,* Monroe embodies the Big Bad Wolf in a way that makes evident how fairy-tale characters are capable of long-lasting existence and extraordinary adaptability because of the co-presence of hard and soft schematizing in the architecture of identity. From the first episode, the narrative structure of *Grimm* and its emotional and cognitive impact on the audience relies on resemblance to classical tales, such as *Red Riding Hood.*[21] The pilot's plot initiates with a young woman with a red hood found dead in the woods surrounding Portland and develops with the chasing of the "Wolf" who killed her. The episode's major twist leans precisely on finding out that, despite his suspicious, solitary way of life and his scary appearance when he "woges," the Wolf (Monroe) is actually innocent. This plot twist gains its power from the iconicity of the Big Bad Wolf and the subversion of narrative and iconic traits traditionally associated with this figure. The spectators presume that Monroe is the "bad guy" because, like Nick, they are misled by their acquaintance with the fairy tale, according to which if a young woman or a girl is attacked in the woods, the (supposedly) ferocious and devilish Wolf is to blame.

The Big Bad Wolf (and other fairy-tale characters like him) lacks a strong identity. It is impossible to track down the original source and compare the previous characterizations, their narrative and figurative attributes, given the many iterations it undergoes in the process of adaptation. In this way, the identity of the Big Bad Wolf takes advantage of a *soft* schematizing because we do not have an original with which the audience can judge an adaptation's accuracy and respectfulness. The absence of a concrete definition in the "source-code" of identity is what makes these types of characters so portable. It allows their openness to migration, interpretation, reworking, and variation, each an essential requirement for their survival and dissemination in different times, spaces, cultures, and media environments. However, these figures can assume many forms because their identity as fictional characters also benefits from a process of *hard* schematizing. The resilience, adaptability, and recognizability of these characters rely on a few, distinguishing traits repeated in the many instantiations, producing a resilient and resistant identity kernel. We can easily identify Monroe as the Wolf of *Red Riding Hood* by some iconic figurative and narrative traits. Indeed, part of the pleasure we feel in watching *Grimm* arises from the ease by which we detect well-known fairy-tale characters and narratives and then observe how specific alterations disappoint or elude our expectations for them. This cluster of repeated traits constitutes the condensed identity of the character, namely a sort of narrative and figurative backup it manifests every time it reappears in a new textual or medial makeover to ensure its consistency.

These iconic narratives and figurative traits result from accumulation and stratification occurring over time rather than an inheritance from an "original." After many adaptations, remediations, and recontextualizations, the hard-schematized traits of the character accumulate and crystalize to constitute a character's identity. However, along with this accumulation, there is another process in motion, selection, which implies that, as time goes on, some traits disappear and others stay; some versions become iconic while others simply vanish. Take, for instance, Sleeping Beauty and her appearance in *Grimm*: the identity kernel of this fairy-tale character is so hard-schematized that, despite the countless transformations and adaptations she has undergone, it is reduced to two fundamental traits—to fall into a deep sleep and to be woken by a prince. These elements are so strong that they are sufficient in themselves to recall this figure and her tradition, as demonstrated in "The Kiss" (S2, E2). Here, the setting is not a castle but a Portland hospital room. No Prince is scaling a wall of brambles, and just a mild reference to the original plot when the enchanted cat of the vengeful and wicked Adalind picks Juliette, recalling the scene of the spinning wheel. Nevertheless, when Juliette falls into a deep sleep and is reawakened by the prince's kiss, embodied by the local police captain (and secret royal prince) Sean Renard, we see her as an occurrence of Sleeping Beauty.

Operating in between soft and hard is the same dialectic logic of difference and repetition that is at the base of every serial narrative. As Ruth Mayer states,

> seriality relies on iconicity, on emblematic constellations, and on recognizable images, figures, plots, phrases, and accessories. Once established, these can be rearranged, reinterpreted, recombined, and invested with new significance and thus constitute major parts of the serial memory that upholds complex serial narrative and representational networks.[22]

The iconicity of fairy-tale characters allows us to qualify them as what Shane Denson and Ruth Mayer call "serial figures."[23] A serial figure is "a type of stock character populating the popular-cultural imagination of modernity—a 'flat' and recurring figure, subject to one or more media changes over the course of its career."[24] As the authors explain, "aspects of repetition and recognizability, which are central to serial figures, are thus set in relation to the explicit variations or subtle revisions inherent in the figures' various stagings."[25] Because they are stable, iconic, and highly recognizable, these "hardly schematized" traits accompany fairy-tale characters in their multiple incarnations and medial peregrinations, ensuring their persistence. Nevertheless, these traces leave room to maneuver for changes and alterations in such figures' medial, visual, and narrative textures. Therein, repetition and recognizability are as much fundamental as are variation and transformation for serial figures in order to perpetuate their essence and, at the same time, to adapt themselves accordingly to medial, textual, and cultural changes.

Fairy-tale protagonists represent significant examples of serial figures, as *Grimm* demonstrates. By citing many varied fairy tales and their characters, this series relates the repetition of the iconic traces of these figures with the variation of other salient elements like the setting, the narrative arcs of the characters and their interactions, and the overall narrative genre of the story. Creating a sort of semantic short-circuit, *Grimm* exploits the iconicity of fairy-tale characters to propose significant variations, not only on a purely narrative and textual level but even on a cultural and social one. When a serial figure reappears in a new incarnation, it engages a struggle with its other, previous manifestations that also concern the cultural meanings associated with the figure, that is to say, the socio-cultural issues the figure has embodied along its career. Powerful serial figures like the Big Bad Wolf, through their iconicity, are indeed transmutable figures that assume different cultural meanings and semantic connotations, redefining and renegotiating themselves in relation to cultural, ideological, social, and aesthetic shifts. Insofar as they are constantly disseminated without being entirely situated in one particular text and diegetic world, as Susanne Hamscha writes, "they function as cultural types that can be reproduced, transformed, translated into new contexts."[26]

Fairy-Tale Characters as Cultural Shapeshifters

By a morphology based in a dialectic of repetition and variation, fairy-tale characters can adapt to changes in media and aesthetics and socio-cultural shifts in the context of production and reception. Thanks to the ability to migrate and readjust accordingly to the specific narrative, aesthetic or medial necessities, serial figures can go through the changes of the cultural context in which they are placed, helping us perceive and reflect upon these fluctuations more effectively. Fairy-tale characters are resilient figures that have colonized our cultural imaginary and its narratives for a long time, and regardless of the medial form. Along this path, they have represented, embodied, or exemplified many different cultural meanings and represented different symbolic and value systems. Indeed, it is precisely the construction of their identities, which balance openness to differentiation with flatness and iconicity, that makes them "disposable in an ideological sense."[27] This propensity implies they are too meaningful and rich in connotation to allow for definitive readings and interpretations. At the same time, they can represent and personify different—or even contradictory—cultural meanings.

While many scholars have considered the connection between fairy-tale adaptations and their conditions of production and reception, less attention has been paid to specific characters.[28] Nevertheless, these figures are valuable and useful elements for analyzing and understanding the variations that occurred not only in texts but also in contexts. In order to do that, however, we have to pay attention to elements of continuity as much as to those of discontinuity and differentiation. Indeed, both Shane Denson and Ruth Mayer insist on the necessity to consider the variability of serial figures close to their iconicity and think about how these characters absorb and reflect socio-cultural issues differently.[29] While some occurrences of the same fairy-tale character reinforce a certain ideology, others may contest it. In this sense, in the course of their long existence, fairy-tale characters have performed and still perform different cultural and ideological works according to context modifications. In this respect, they operate as what Tony Bennett calls "free-floating signifiers," since they are ideologically flexible and able to "coordinate and condense a series of overlapping ideological concerns."[30]

Fairy-tale characters appear in various forms and have frequently become spokespeople for divergent cultural and ideological views, alternately perpetuating and discrediting different positions and belief systems.. As "focal points of cultural reference, [these characters, *ndr.*] condense and connect, serve as shorthand expression for a number of deeply implanted cultural and ideological concerns."[31] Because they are well-known, iconic, and resilient figures existing in various versions, fairy-tale characters, in other words, create a "semiosphere" where some occurrences, which support a certain ideology, coexist with others that defy it. Hence, by analyzing what these figures' specific incarnations have changed and what cultural work they perform, we can glimpse how society has transformed.

Because fairy-tale characters are "cultural shapeshifters," they are potentially helpful tools for inquiring into reflection upon our society and its transformations, as is demonstrated by the various changes to "Big Bad

Wolf" in the course of his fairy-tale character career. At least since his Perrault and Brothers Grimm *canonizations, the Red-Riding-Hood* Wolf has been associated with voracious appetites and frequently portrayed as a villainous figure that swallows young women, thereby becoming an emblem of a lusty and rapacious seduction. However, as Jack Zipes notes, over the 20th century, we have seen many versions "that rehabilitate the Wolf" and "undermine the assumptions of the traditional cultural patterns"[32] associated with him. As Zipes explains, the image of the Wolf as a tempting seducer who encourages the girls to diverge from the path has lost a great part of its fascinating power in a culture where far darker images exacerbate sexualization. Furthermore, the empowerment of Red Riding Hood as a strong-willed and self-confident woman operated by feminist revisions of this fairy-tale—beginning with Angela Carter's *In the Company of Wolves* (1979)—has weakened the traditional vision of the Wolf as an aggressive representation of sexuality. In an era dominated by the awakening of a new feminist wave (crowned by the resonance of a movement like the #MeToo), the image of the Wolf as a sexual predator has declined little by little in concomitance with a representation of Red Riding Hood as a more assertive, seductive, and active woman. *Grimm*'s Monroe, in this perspective, is none other than the latest link in a chain of transformations that led the Wolf from being a totally negative figure to being a more morally complex and nuanced character. Indeed, Monroe exalts this metamorphosis through an overturning of the characteristics typically associated with this fictional being. While maintaining some iconic traits that assure his identity (like his beastly appearance when he "woges"), Monroe emerges as the antithesis of the threatening Wolf to which we have become accustomed: he appears as a good-natured and easy-going man, passionate about clocks and a little awkward with ladies—his shyness in direct opposition to the seductive audacity of the prototypical Wolf. When he is the main suspect for a young woman's murder, he becomes the victim of "Big Bad Wolf's prejudice," according to which he should have "devoured" the girl. Yet, the dissonance between reality and expectations is immediately apparent because of the dissonance between the "hard-schematized" characterization of the fairy-tale Wolf and Monroe's effective, specific characterization. Additionally, even the popular readings of the Wolf as a rebel and outcast of human society are disrupted by the Monroe version of the Wolf. In fact, even if Monroe maintains traces of a rebellious past, this is performed with respect to the Wesen community through his disregard for *Blutbad*'s traditional way of life. Moreover, as he moves away from the Wesen community, he becomes more and more involved and integrated within human society and its social rules.

Since the beginning of the series, Monroe yearns for a normal (even boring) human life and tries to keep himself away from everything connected with the other Wesen. The disdain toward the traditionally associated moral connotations of the Wolf and the unorthodox behavior of Monroe as an incarnation of the Big (now not so) Bad Wolf prototype make him a captivating figure. Indeed, through his rejection of the role commonly assigned to the Wolf by fairy-tale tradition (on a general level) and by the Wesen society (on a particular one), Monroe contests the clear-cut division of social roles in fairy tales. He also exposes the injustices and inadequacies of a social structure based on superimposed and assigned roles.

Within the fictional world of the series, the *Grimmverse,* the Wesen community is represented as a strongly classist, organized hierarchy of prey and predators, echoing the clear-cut social positioning we perceive in fairy tales (with, for example, royals and commoners, magic creatures and humans, rich and poor, etc.) and the explicit separation between good and evil characters or between innocent protagonists and wicked antagonists. The Monroe version of the Wolf unhinges this social and moral taxonomy on more than one occasion: by having a fraternal friendship with a Grimm[33] while they are intended to be sworn enemies, by challenging his own family and the traditions of his lineage for the sake of Rosalee,[34] by refusing to kill a *Bauerschwein*, a pig-type Wesen (S1, E6: "The Three Bad Wolves"), thus subverting the supposed social order and, from a transtextual point of view, rejecting his conventional role as the devilish figure that appears in *Three Little Pigs'* fairy tale.

The peculiar incarnation of the Wolf offered by Monroe undermines the traditional cultural connotations associated with this typical fairy-tale character. This subversion has narrative implications, associated with a simple contemporary retelling and reimagining of a long-established figure and consequences for the social and cultural function the figure performs. Monroe is beyond any doubt a reincarnation of the Big Bad Wolf prototype, but one that had to adapt itself to changed contextual, social, and cultural conditions compared to those that were in force in the past. The gap between the traditional characterization of the Big Bad Wolf and the one of Monroe can be understood by taking into account the transformed cultural and social context in which Monroe is situated in comparison with that of the conventional figure. The Wolf in Perrault's and Brothers Grimm's versions works as the emblem of sexual threat, moral misguidance, and female defilement. As Perrault wrote, the Wolf "would have very much liked to eat" the girl, who did not know "it was dangerous to stop and listen to a wolf" and was not afraid of him. The "wicked creature" and "old sinner," as Brothers Grimm refer to the Wolf, with his big ears, big eyes, large hand, and a terrible big mouth, as well as his atrocious devouring the grandmother and the child, functioned to deliver a message to the readers of such stories: do not deviate from the right path when someone (the Mother) has forbidden to do so, and beware of the Wolf and his temptations. The societies of the Perrault's and Brothers Grimm's were dominated by male fears of female sexuality animated in the wolf as a deterrent to discipline female behavior.[35] With the passage of time and the gradual change of women's social role and its representations—since women are no more pictured as powerless and fragile figures to protect—Perrault's and Grimms' vision and function of the Wolf have become unsustainable, necessitating a metamorphosis.

The version of the Wolf incarnated by Monroe stresses the fact that he is a "reformed" Big Bad Wolf: he enjoys Christmas, follows a vegan diet, and practices Pilates. These qualities emphasize the cultural distance between this specific reconfiguration of the type and those proposed by Perrault or by the Grimms, that is to say, a ferocious, merciless, and devilish figure. Because he is so different from the canonized version of the Wolf, Monroe serves the cultural function of representing the extent to which Western cultural norms have changed. It would currently be inadequate and outrageous for the Wolf (as a vehicle of tacit ideology) to continue looking at women as weak, naïve, and defenseless prey of male appetites. Considering the Big Bad Wolf as a serial figure allows us to focus on those narrative, figurative, and cultural elements that have changed from one version to another. It also enables speculation upon what modifications in the textual/medial and contextual framework have caused such character transformation. As serial figures, fairy-tale characters can adjust their aesthetic and narrative traits every time they perform a new textual or contextual appearance. In the process of recalibration of their own identity, however, they can also modify their "ideological currency."[36] This currency's value constantly fluctuates, redefining itself in dialogue with the cultural necessities and social backgrounds in which the figure (re)appears. From this standpoint, we can say that, as serial figures, fairy-tale characters "act as calibrating instruments for cultural anxieties and nervous crisis of the period."[37]

Fairy-tale characters act as figures of mediation and self-reflexivity, operating between the inside and the outside of a text. Because of their ability to enter and exit from any text, narrative, and media universe, alongside the iconicity that made them an integral part of Western cultural heritage, fairy-tale characters are able to "change skin" and adapt themselves to the needs imposed by specific aesthetic turns, but also by socio-cultural conjunctions. Because they may convey different themes and ideologies (or, at least, they convey them differently), fairy-tale characters unmask cultural meanings and contradictions. As Mayer continues, they "register such deviations and try to put them into relation with standards of normality," using their familiar images and narrative paths to *mediate* these changes. This mediating quality gives a strong indication of why fairy-tale characters appear so frequently in moments of social fracture and cultural redefinition. In the case of *Red Riding Hood*'s and Big Bad Wolf's retellings, we see such cultural change in the feminist waves that upset the traditionally gendered power structures. In this way, according to Denson and Mayer, serial figures are "heroic" characters insofar as they (re-)appear in specific moments of medial, aesthetic, cultural, and even social modification in order to facilitate the transition. This is due to the familiarity of fairy-tale characters, which renders them particularly adept "at performing or contesting novelty against the backdrop of (...) familiarity."[38] Fairy-tale characters "both exorcize and familiarize the foreign or unknown by foregrounding it"[39] through their negotiation between iconic/recurring and new/varied traits. Every time they resurface in a new incarnation or fresh adaptation, these figures mediate between the different perspectives and concerns animating a society's cultural and social debate.

Concentrating attention on discontinuous elements rather than transhistorical continuity demonstrates that fairy-tale characters are cultural as well as aesthetic *shapeshifters*. They are figures that balance iconicity and variability and become self-reflexive agents that help us to negotiate socio-cultural issues along with aesthetic and medial concerns. Thus, the significance and appeal of *Grimm* may rely in its use of fairy-tale characters, by which the series allows the audience and scholars to explore and better understand the society in which they live and its contradictions and its own shapeshifting potential.

Notes

1. Bacchilega 203.
2. See Greenhill and Rudy; Haase.
3. *Tales from Muppetland* is a series of fairy-tale-themed Muppets' TV specials, aired on CBS in the early Seventies. The series comprehends the show *Hey, Cinderella* (1969), *The Frog Prince* (1971), and *The Muppets Musicians of Bremen* (1972). Jay Ward's *Fractured Fairy Tales* is a series of cartoons aired from 1959 to 1964. Shelley Duvall's *Faerie Tales Theatre* is a live-action anthological TV series aired on Showtime from 1982 to 1987, while *Beauty and the Beast* is the title of a CBS TV series aired from 1987 to 1990 and of its reboot, created by The CW and broadcasted from 2012 to 2016. *Once Upon a Time* is a very successful live-action tv series produced by and aired on ABC from 2011 to 2018, whose favorable outcome has generated a spin-off, *Once Upon a Time in Wonderland* (ABC, 2013–2014).
4. Haase 609.
5. See Zipes. For a more recent analysis, see Greenhill and Rudy.
6. With the term the "running plot," I mean a continuing plot that develops over several

episodes or seasons. In contrast, the term "anthology plot" indicates a plot that starts, develops, and concludes within a single episode.

7. See Calabrese; Cardini; Eco "Tipologia"; Kelletersee.
8. Eco 167 (author translation).
9. Similarly, Jeffrey Sconce wrote: "television must produce 'parts' that each week embody the whole while also finding, within such repetition, possibilities for novel and diverting variations" (101).
10. As stated by Jason Mittell, the term "narrative complexity" defines the aesthetic paradigm of contemporary televisual seriality. At its basics, it "is a redefinition of episodic forms under the influence of serial narration—not necessarily a complete merger of episodic and serial forms but a shifting balance. Rejecting the need for plot closure within every episode that typifies conventional episodic form, narrative complexity foregrounds ongoing stories across a range of genres" ("Narrative Complexity" 32). On the same topic, see also Mittell *Complex TV*.
11. In particular, it constitutes the grounds of what Omar Calabrese and Angela Ndalianis have called Neo-Baroque seriality, a type of serial aesthetics that "is concerned with variation, rather than unoriginality and invariability" (Ndalianis 33).
12. Haase 951.
13. Lüthi 78–79.
14. Calabrese 59.
15. See Tiffin.
16. On the use of epigraphs in *Grimm* see Willsey.
17. Bennett, "Bond Phenomenon" 195.
18. Mayer 79.
19. Rieser 5.
20. Reiser 8.
21. Since the series is a crime drama, the choice made by the showrunners to open the show with *Red Riding Hood*, a traditional fairy tale strictly connected with crime, criminal, murders, and justice, appears to be a good one. For the collection of adaptations and remediations of "Red Riding Hood" see Zipes; Calabrese and Feltracco; Orenstein.
22. Mayer 10–11.
23. We should be careful not to confuse "serial figure" and "series character." The latter term identifies all those characters "in the more or less closed fictional universe of a serially-ongoing narrative (such as a soap opera or serialized novel). In the course of their narrative development, series characters tend to acquire psychological depth, they are given complex biographies and branching genealogies, and they are primarily of interest because of their prehistories and potential future development" (Denson and Mayer, "Border Crossings" 67).
24. Denson and Mayer "Spectral Seriality" 108.
25. Denson and Mayer "Border Crossings" 65.
26. Hamscha 121.
27. Mayer 113.
28. See Tatar; Weber.
29. Denson and Mayer "Spectral Seriality" 108.
30. Bennett 202.
31. Bennett and Woollacott 14.
32. Zipes 63.
33. Monroe goes so far as to choose Nick as his best man, recognizing the role of the Grimm in his love story with Rosalee (as we can deduce from "The Show Must Go On" [S3, E16]).
34. When Monroe decided to marry the *Fuchsbau* Rosalee, he deliberately contravenes the rules imposed by his family of not mixing his blood with other "races" of Wesen. It is apparent in "The Wild Hunt" (S3, E12) when during a family dinner, Monroe's parents find out about Rosalee's real nature and openly disapprove of their sons' choice. Moreover, Monroe's disregard for the social order of the Wesen community causes him the indignation of the Wesenrein, the conservative secret society (also called "*Secundum Naturae*

Ordinem") devoted to maintaining stability and to observing traditions in the Wesen society. Monroe challenges this powerful and respected order by crossbreeding with someone considered inferior, even undergoing a sort of cultural backlash due to their inter-Wesen marriage (on that regard, see S4, E4: "Dyin' on a Prayer").

    35. See Beckett 12–41; Zipes 63, *passim*.
    36. Mayer 113, 122.
    37. Indeed, Monroe is almost overwhelmed by Rosalee's passion when she kisses him on their first date (S2, E4: "Quill").
    38. Denson and Mayer, "Spectral Seriality" 108, 111.
    39. *Ibid.*

Works Cited

Bacchilega, Cristina. *Fairy-Tales Transformed? Twenty-First-Century Adaptations and the Politics of Wonder*. Wayne State UP, 2013.

Beckett, Sandra L. *Red Riding Hood for All Ages: A Fairy-Tale Icon in Cross-Cultural Contexts*. Wayne State UP, 2008.

Bennett, Tony. "The Bond Phenomenon: Theorizing a Popular Hero." *Southern Review*, vol. 16, no. 2, 1983, pp. 195–225.

———, and Janet Woollacott. *Bond and Beyond. The Political Career of a Popular Hero*. Macmillan Education, 1987.

Calabrese, Omar. *The Neo-Baroque. Between Modern and Post-Modern Aesthetics*. Princeton UP, 1992.

Calabrese, Stefano, and Daniela Feltracco, editors. *Cappuccetto Rosso: una Fiaba Vera*. Meltemi, 1998

Cardini, Daniela. *Long TV: Le Serie Televisive Viste da Vicino*. Edizioni Unicopli, 2017.

Deleuze, Gilles. *Difference and Repetition*. Columbia UP, 1994.

Denson, Shane, and Ruth Mayer. "Border Crossings: Serial Figures and the Evolution of Media." *NECSUS. European Journal of Media Studies*, vol. 7, no. 2, 2018, pp. 65–84.

———. "Spectral Seriality: The Sights and Sounds of Count Dracula." *Media of Serial Narrative*, edited by Frank Kelleter, Ohio UP, 2017, pp.108–124.

Eco, Umberto. "Innovation and Repetition: Between Modern and Post-Modern Aesthetics," *Daedalus*, Vol. 114, No. 4, pp. 161–184, 1985.

———. "Tipologia Della Ripetizione." *L'immagine al Plurale. Serialità e Ripetizione nel Cinema e Nella Televisione*, edited by Francesco Casetti, Marsilio, 1984, pp. 19–36.

Greenhill, Pauline, and Jill Terry Rudy. "Channeling Wonder: Fairy Tales, Television, and Intermediality." *Channeling Wonder. Fairy Tales on Television*, edited by Pauline Greenhill and Jill Terry Rudy, Wayne State UP, 2014, pp.1–24.

Haase, Donald. "Television." *The Greenwood Encyclopedia of Folktales and Fairy Tales*, edited by Donald Haase, Greenwood Press, 2008, pp. 947–51.

Hamscha, Susanne. "Thirty are Better Than One: Marilyn Monroe and the Performance of the Americaness." *Configuring America: Iconic Figures, Visuality, and the American Identity*, edited by Klaus Rieser, Michael Fuchs, and Michael Phillips, Intellect Books, 2013, pp. 115–132.

Kelleter, Frank. "Five Ways of Looking at Popular Seriality." *Media of Serial Narratives*, edited by Frank Kelleter, Ohio UP, 2017, pp. 7–36.

Lüthi, Max. *The Fairytale as Art Form and Portrait of Man*. Indiana UP, 1987.

Mayer, Ruth. *Serial Fu Manchu: The Chinese Supervillain and the Spread of Yellow Peril Ideology*. Temple UP, 2014.

Mittell, Jason. *Complex TV. The Poetics of Contemporary Television Storytelling*. NYU Press, 2015.

———. "Narrative Complexity in Contemporary American Television." *The Velvet Light Trap*, no. 58, 2006, pp. 30–40.

Ndalianis, Angela. *Neo-Baroque Aesthetics and Contemporary Entertainment*. MIT Press, 2004.

Orenstein, Catherine. *Little Red Riding Hood Uncloaked. Sex, Morality and the Evolution of a Fairy Tale.* Basic Books, 2002.
Rieser, Klaus. "Theorizing Iconic Figures." *Configuring America: Iconic Figures, Visuality, and the American Identity,* edited by Klaus Rieser, Michael Fuchs, and Michael Phillips, Intellect Books, 2013, pp. 3–22.
Sconce, Jeffrey. "What If? Charting Television's New Textual Boundaries." *Television After TV: Essays on a Medium in Transition,* edited by Lynn Spiegel and Jan Olsson, Duke UP, 2004, pp. 93–112.
Tatar, Maria. *The Hard Facts of the Grimms' Fairy Tales.* 2nd ed., Princeton UP, 2003.
Tiffin, Jessica. *Marvelous Geometry: Narrative and Metafiction in Modern Fairy Tale.* Wayne State UP, 2009.
Weber, Eugen. "Fairies and Hard Facts: The Reality of Folktales." *Journal of the History of Ideas,* vol. 42, no. 1, 1981, pp. 93–113.
Willsey, Kristiana. "New Fairy Tales are Old Again. *Grimm* and the Brothers Grimm." *Channeling Wonder: Fairy Tales on Television,* edited by Pauline Greenhill and Jill Terry Rudy, Wayne State UP, 2014, pp. 210–28.
Zipes, Jack, editor. *The Trials & Tribulations of Little Red Riding Hood.* Routledge, 1993.

It Is Up to the "One" ... Or Is It?

The Significance of Others in 21st-Century TV Hero Tales

Kathleen McDonald

> As children, we all hear fairy tales and read our lives into them. But we also want to see and realize our lives as virtual fairy tales even as we grow older. We never abandon fairy tales. So it is not by chance that the fairy-tale film has become the most popular cultural commodity in America.[1]

What does it mean to be a hero? Western culture has inherited a construction of heroism that is focused on the single, exceptional actor. In 1949 Joseph Campbell traced this version of "the hero" across various times, places, and cultures through mythology and folklore. This research culminated in the proposition of a universal hero's journey in the seminal theoretical work, *The Hero with a Thousand Faces*. This text remains the go-to for an academic understanding of what it means to be a hero and what society wants and needs from that hero. This essay focuses on the kstatus of the hero in NBC's television series *Grimm* through Campbell's critical work and his successors, paying particular mind to the theorization of supporting characters in the resulting paradigm. This analysis is paired with a comparison of *Grimm*'s heroic constructions with similarly constituted television series from the turn of the millennium (1997–2017) to show that it proposes a type of heroism distinct from its television predecessors. *Grimm* theorizes supporting characters as part of a larger heroic grouping which this essay will term "camaraderie heroism." Here all the characters work together to perform heroic tasks, diverging from the model of a support system serving a singular hero. Comradery heroism does not argue against Campbell's definition of the hero. Instead, it extends its potential across characters in a way that reflects *Grimm*'s social-cultural moment.

In his work, Campbell delineates the characteristics of the Western hero's exceptionalism: the hero has unique gifts and succeeds at a small, localized challenge before encountering a more significant, "world-saving" event. The element of the definition that is particularly notable is that "hero" is *singular*: The hero is Moses, not Moses and his ten tribes; Jesus, not Jesus and his Apostles. Of course, those other characters exist in the stories, but the hero stands out as a lone, singular entity.

Campbell's extrapolation of the hero's journey—the process that confirms a character's heroic nature—identifies three stages. The first stage, "separation or departure," begins the heroic odyssey: the hero goes from receiving the "call," to "refusing" it, to receiving "supernatural aid" that ultimately persuades the hero to take up the challenge and enter into the fray. Step two, "Trials and Victories of Initiation," consists of six sub-steps by which the hero navigates the crisis itself. Finally, step three, "return to society," also has six sub-steps in which the hero faces further challenges as s/he returns to the world left behind. In the end, the hero has changed as an individual, possessing new gifts and new responsibilities.[2] These stages characterize the trajectory of *Grimm*'s Nick Burkhardt, the focus of the show. However, and crucially, they also inform the narratives of the surrounding characters. The following paragraphs trace these paths to demonstrate that it is not Nick alone who saves the world.

While the hero's journey may be fixed, there need not be only one journey for one character in a narrative. Tutta Kesti has argued for this multiplicity in *The Lord of the Rings Trilogy*, arguing that "there are *many* heroes"[3] even if the figure around whom most of the narrative action centers is Frodo, whose journey mirrors Campbell's process. Kesti explores the "heroic" journeys of many characters in the trilogy to propose that the minor or supporting characters also have their own journeys to heroism. However, they are less explored and emphasized.[4] From this perspective, *The Lord of the Rings* offers a heroic group theory preceding *Grimm* and serving as a model.

While Testi focuses on a given character's narrative development, Eranda Jayawickreme and Paul Di Stefano inquire into individual qualities by reviewing social-science inquiries into ascribed heroism characteristics in human action. Their findings are summarized in the following composite heroic trait: "an individual's commitment to a noble purpose, usually aimed at furthering the welfare of others, and involving the willingness to accept the consequences of achieving that purpose, regardless of whether they are positive or negative."[5] As a coda, however, they clarify that "little is known about what distinguishes such heroes from bystanders."[6] Their research ultimately identifies "bravery and integrity" as the two most commonly found characteristics of those perceived as heroic.

Central to this investigation is the presupposition that heroism is the isolated function of an individual, thus rendering other individuals collectively as "bystanders." While this aligns with the dominant representation of heroism from classical literature, it intentionally discounts the contributions of others. Moreover, it dismisses mere "bystanders" and thereby forecloses on possible alternative constructions of heroism in life and texts.

The 21st-century television show *Grimm* reconstructs heroism as collective action across the arc of the series. *Grimm* begins by declaring that its protagonist, Detective Nick Burkhardt, is the "one." However, the heroic conceit expands to camaraderie heroism that dismantles the monomyth of the singular hero. In this way, *Grimm* demonstrates a complexity that exceeds the formula of closely preceding series that share the creative influence of David Greenwalt, such as *Buffy the Vampire Slayer* (*BtVS*)[7] and *Angel*.[8] These shows similarly begin with a chosen one and throughout illustrate the dependence of the hero on a team of supporters, but are never able to abandon mono-mythology in the course of the series.[9] *Grimm* can be understood as a successor to these series while also recognized as exceeding their conceptual limitations by moving from the lone, central hero to fully-fledged camaraderie heroism.

Substantial Sidekicks, or Exceptional Heroes: Buffy, the Vampire Slayer, *and* Angel

Greenawalt's previous series *BtVS* and *Angel* focus on their titular heroic figures that are aided in their quests by a supporting cast. Across the *BtVS* literature, Buffy has been compared to many mythical singular heroes: Orpheus,[10] Minerva,[11] and Beowulf,[12] among others. Nevertheless, Buffy,[13] a high-school-age hero, ends up with a "Scooby gang"[14] of helpers drawn from her high school peer group. Buffy's friends become involved in her quest after encountering monsters who dwell in and surface from the Hellmouth upon which their high school is located. Additionally, the high school library supplies Buffy with a "watcher," the librarian Giles,[15] who educates her about the history of the slayers, the evil creatures they encounter, and how to fight them. All of these characters provide social stability and support in her fight against evil. While these supporting characters perform specific functions, they do not emerge as heroes equivalent to the protagonist in the respective series. Instead, they remain technically subordinate to the "one" until the complex end of the series. In the very final episode of *BtVS*, all potential slayers are called up and participate along with Buffy's friends in defeating the last evil uprising of the series: while this distributes heroism, it does so only through a multiplying effect rather than yielding group heroic dynamic.

In addition to the multiple chosen one version of heroic dispersion, scholars have argued that two members of the Scooby gang, Xander[16] and Willow,[17] may be considered heroic contributors. In her exploration of the character Xander, Katrina O'Dette employs Zeno Franco's heroic taxonomy of military and civil. The military hero has duties and becomes heroic by exceeding them. In contrast, the civil hero has no obligations and puts themselves at risk voluntarily.[18] Xander, she argues, is the latter: without obligation to fight evil and often active discouragement, he runs toward danger and, on occasion, provides the crucial element to save the day.[19] In a similar sidekick analysis, Matthew Pateman explores how Willow's empathy and identification with marginal people "provides a muted moral compass which stands both alongside but sometimes in opposition to the dominant morality of the show, which is not Christianity but is Buffy herself."[20] Despite Pateman's claim of central importance for Willow's soft skills, he leaves Buffy as *the* hero with Willow as a contributor. Sarah Zettel's work on *BtVS* clarifies these arguments with her claim that the show is about "friendship, independence, and self-acceptance."[21] While Buffy has been told that in the end, she is "always alone ... that's never been true. There's always been help,"[22] which is to say, help to achieve her heroism. Thus, instead of enabling Buffy-heroism among the Scooby gang, the series suggests an inverse and crucial dynamic: the Scooby gang allows for Buffy's identity to expand. Rather than showing more than one hero, *BtVS* cultivates Buffy to be more than just a hero.[23]

As a spin-off from *BtVS*, *Angel* more closely mirrors Campbell's expectations singular hero. As one character describes him, he is a vampire who is here to "fight evil and atone for his crimes; he is a shadow, a faceless champion of the hapless human race."[24] Like Buffy, Angel[25] assembles a crew of "helpers" (many of whom are employees) who illustrate heroic impulses but subordinate them to the larger project of helping Angel in his mission. In a gritty echo of *BtVS*, Angel finds support and companionship among his subordinates that draws him out of his heroic isolation. He remains the central heroic figure but gains a trust in others that renders his atonement less perdition and more of a calling.

Grimm, *from the Beginning*

Grimm shares with *BtVS* and *Angel* the figure of the warrior-hero chosen by outside forces to save the world: they are told that they are unique and must undertake their duties alone. In all cases, it is made clear that involving others may lessen the efficacy of the quest and will likely put the others in mortal peril. Similarly, the protagonist is surrounded by friends who participate in their mission. Nevertheless, the premise of *Grimm* departs from *BtVS* and *Angel* in both its structure and its context. The protagonist, Nick Burkhardt, is a police detective: he has a fully established, mature identity and relationships independent of his future superheroism. The pilots for *BtVS* and *Angel* begin more or less in media res with the titular characters already aware that they are the "hero" of the story. By contrast, *Grimm* portrays Nick's discovery of his familial inheritance and his extraordinary destiny. In the pilot, his Aunt Marie comes to town and explains his calling and special abilities, then dies, leaving him alone with a trailer filled with books and weapons to fight the Wesen. Nick's newfound ability to see and fight Wesen bewilders him, and the books are initially of little help in his dealings with this newly discovered, secret world.

The first signal of the interdependence of heroism in *Grimm* emerges in the pilot episode with Monroe, a Wesen, and the part he plays in Nick's first Grimm adventure. Nick stumbles across an individual whom he suspects may be involved with a missing child. The man lives across the street from the park where the child disappeared, and Nick sees him transform into a wolf-like creature. Nick assumes that he took the girl and launches a police search of his house. Taking on the case introduces Nick to Monroe, a vegetarian *Blutbad* (werewolf). Monroe is not looking to become part of Nick's "destiny" or involved with his fight with Wesen; however, once Nick realizes that Monroe can explain all things Wesen to him, he relies heavily upon him for help. Monroe becomes an invaluable resource because he can answer many of Nick's questions about this newly discovered world of Wesen and Grimm. So far, *Grimm* stays true to the concept of the lone hero and sidekicks, but this will soon morph into something much more.

When Nick and Monroe are first acquainted, Monroe notes that Nick seems new at the Grimm thing because he appears surprisingly ignorant of the hidden world of Wesen and Grimms. He asks Nick if someone in his family had just died (implying that is how the mantle is passed, echoing the call of a new slayer in *BtVS*). He also tells Nick that his family "used to tell me stories about you guys; scared the hell out of me when I was a kid."[26] Complicating the inherent evil of vampires and other dark entities in *BtVS* and, to a lesser degree in *Angel*, the Wesen of *Grimm* are not summarily antagonistic. Moreover, they see the Grimm as the "monster" and parlay him in a "bogey-man" for Wesen children. Because Nick feels enjoined to secrecy and his human friends cannot see Wesen for what they are, Monroe becomes his "partner" in supernatural work. He provides guidance, information, and, with increasing frequency, physical assistance in Nick's Wesen encounters. For example, in the first episode, Nick would never have rescued the young girl without Monroe's assistance regarding information about Wesen and his *Blutbad* sense of smell, which locates the cottage in the woods where she was being held. Although Monroe flees once he has led Nick to the cottage, without his help, this particular Wesen would never have been identified, and the girl would have been lost.

The kidnaper turns out to be a postman coded as mild and effeminate: he crochets and cooks, and his presentation appears to deceive all but the Grimm who knows (because of Monroe) it is a facade. Having only Nick see the postman as a potential danger would be an obvious way for this story to evolve: the humans only see what appearances show them. However, *Grimm* provides a twist. When Nick and his police partner, Hank, confront the postman, Hank rather than Nick makes the crucial connection that breaks the case. Hank realizes that the mailman was humming the same song that had been on their first victim's iPod (*Sweet Dreams*), thus prodding them to return to the postman's house, ultimately locating and saving the young girl. In this scenario, Nick is not receiving assistance as a neophyte Grimm but working in partnership with a veteran detective who notices things like this. Nick's Grimm role overlaps with his police detective job. In his human existence, Nick is used to the interdependence of fellow police officers in completing a case. Thus, it makes sense that this skill set continues, and continues successfully, into his Grimm duties. Although our society does not enthusiastically mythologize "teamwork," we do enact it. *Grimm*, however, incorporates the team into its mythology. Nick may be "the hero" in a Campbell sense, but in terms of resolving the crisis at hand, the involvement of all three individuals was crucial.

Most Wesen are terrified when they realize that Nick is a Grimm. He usually does so when they woge into their alternate forms, as they often do when they become angry or scared. Nick had never seen this before, as it is not apparent to humans unless the Wesen wants it to be. However, now that Nick has the power of the Grimm, he sees them all the time. When the Wesen woge, they can immediately recognize Nick for the Grimm that he is, and the most common response is a plea not to be killed. Historically, it has been the Grimms' primary objective to decapitate Wesen upon sight. Thus, Nick would seem well-positioned to exemplify the iconic hero. He is an individual who is willing to risk his own life and happiness to rid the world of a hidden danger for the betterment of all (humans). However, Nick does not handle even a single case as the Grimm before it becomes clear that others must participate in order for the quest to succeed.

In the very next episode, Monroe begins his evolution from being a one-off source of information for Nick into a fellow heroic character, as he provides knowledge and skills required to undertake the fight with the Wesen going forward. In "Bears Will Be Bears" (S1, E2), Nick, as a police detective, is called upon to investigate a home-invasion case in the home of a family of bear-like creatures (*Jägerbar*). He is confused about what they are and how to handle them, especially when he suspects they are involved in the disappearance of one of the home invaders. When he finds a bear claw hidden in Aunt Marie's trailer (just like the one Hank pointed out in the *Jägerbar* home), he returns to Monroe for help.

In this second meeting, the audience realizes that Monroe works hard not to resist his animalistic desires for violence: he does Pilates and is a vegetarian; he likes bagels and fancy coffee. Thus, for Nick and the audience, he exemplifies how appearances can be misleading and should not be trusted. As Nick peppers Monroe with questions about Jägerbar wesen, it is explained that what Nick is regarding as a cultural rite of passage is far more. For these boys and for all Wesen there is a significant and meaningful physical aspect to their animal-like dualities. To the "physical beast in all of us," Monroe explains, "And, believe me, I do mean ALL of us."[27] The line being said with a pointed look at Nick as he makes coffee. This moment does the double duty of encouraging the audience to think of Nick (a human) also as one of the beasts of the world while illustrating the (rather dull) everyday behaviors of the *Blutbad* beast. Of course, humans are as likely to give in to their bestial tendencies as any other species. However, this particular exchange also provokes the audience to consider which of them appears to be the more refined and civilized character, which has the more heroic character.

Although they provide a template for him to distribute heroic authority, Nick's years on the police force have not trained him to handle supernatural creatures. He needs help, and he is prepared to ask for it because he has a partner as a police detective. Detective Hank Griffith is his immediate partner, and they together work in partnership with officers, centrally Sergeant Wu, who adds his talents and abilities to the resolution of cases. Once Nick has the information from Monroe, he literally puts his coffee cup down, turns, and leaves abruptly without thanks for the coffee or advice. The abruptness allows Monroe a moment of humor as he (sarcastically) remarks, "Oh, well, thanks for stopping by." Suppose we were looking for polite behavior as a mark of the elect. In that case, Monroe demonstrates it (as he is making breakfast for an uninvited guest) rather than Nick (who gets the information he wants from Monroe and abruptly departs). It is a not-so-subtle way to show viewers that they must look beyond the surface of things, as well as narratives. It also demonstrates Nick's style when he is questioning people in his professional capacity. As a police officer, once he got the information he needed through questioning, he would not remain for social niceties. This is how he initially treats Monroe as a source before he becomes a partner.

The presence of the others in these storylines encourages comprehensive examinations of character well beyond the "chosen one" and provides a foil or point of comparison. In classical didactic tales, exemplary heroes were understood as superior to the average listener/reader, so much so that the average listener could only imitate, absorb, or reject a limited amount or degree of a hero's character traits, good or bad. Allowing characters into "the know" on the television shows multiplies exponentially the ability to explore the lines between good and evil, heroism and villainy, through various characters with whom the audience can more variously relate. Additionally, character multiplicity enables a broad field for the reconsideration of traditional tropes adjacent to the monomyth. In *Grimm*, these tend to play out in inversions: For example, there are *Blutbads* with exercise regimens that suppress their violent tendencies (an innovation of the vampire cursed with a soul); the stereotypical bad character becomes part of the collective needed for camaraderie heroism. Police captains and principals are working for the dark side: stereotypical good characters working against the hero and society. There are good characters and bad ones, but they are not easy to tell apart, primarily based on mere group identification. This destabilization intimates a move away from externally and internally imposed group, status, or class designations, allowing for a move from tribalism to the much more complicated melting pot of individuals to which modern society aspires.

Expanding the story's focus to characters beyond the putative hero in *Grimm* through friendship also expands from the questions of good and evil to consider the social interactions between the human world and the Wesen one. As Kristiana Willsey notes, "Traditionally Grimms have been their [Wesen] enemies, but through his friendship with the vegetarian reformed werewolf-turned-sidekick Monroe, Nick comes to occupy a more ambiguous place between the human and supernatural worlds."[28] Nick's friendship with Monroe gives him greater access to information, enabling him to execute his heroic duties as a Grimm with more precision, confidence, and clarity. Monroe's intercession on Nick's behalf also allows the other Wesen to (re)consider that Nick might be more than just the scary villain of childhood fears. Finally, Nick's friendship with Monroe permits him to have empathy for the world of Wesen. As a result, he ends protecting parts of that world and acting as a liaison between it and the human world. Liaising often becomes advocacy and translation, especially with his human friends who do not understand what they see when encountering Wesen.

While Hank is Nick's police partner, and Monroe quickly mirrors that position as his Grimm partner: these are two other characters who span the series and are instrumental in their roles as co-actors in the

196 Part Three: Media and Genre

camaraderie heroism. These are the two romantic partners of Monroe and Nick: Rosalee and Juliette, respectfully. Rosalee is a Wesen who first appears in the episode "Island of Dreams" (S1, E15). She arrives in town to claim the body of her murdered brother and ends up staying to run his herbalist shop. In this capacity, she gets involved with Nick as both a cop and a Grimm. As Nick and Hank try to find the Wesen who killed her brother for the illicit drugs he was selling, Rosalee brings her skill-set and experience as a former addict to their assistance. Later in the series, Monroe recalls that it was among these series of events that he fell for her and she saved his life during an altercation.

Juliette's heroic status is more complex than others: she begins the series as a normal human woman with no supernatural abilities, even inhabiting the position of damsel in distress for Nick to save in the first season. However, after a *Hexenbiest* targets her, he reveals the hidden Wesen world to her to save her life. With this knowledge, she willingly participates in a ritual that allows Nick to reclaim the Grimm powers he had lost. In Nick's least effective moment as a hero, Juliette drinks a potion Rosalee and Monroe create to bring his powers back. Thus, the three of them literally re-Grimm Nick. They make him back into a hero, acting as heroes each in their own right.

For the Benefit of Others

There is a division at the core of *Grimm*'s adventures between those aware of the Wesen world and history and those that are not. This configuration echoes earlier TV shows like *BtVS* and *Angel,* which posit a hidden world of vampires, devils, ghosts, and monsters. However, unlike in *BtVS,* where Buffy's friends came "into the know" of her Slayer world because they were experiencing the events that Buffy needed to control, human characters are exposed to the Grimm "truth" in order to protect them both physically and psychologically. It is from this protective introduction that they emerge as comrades in arms rather than helpers or dependents. They are brought "into the know" for their own physical and, more often, psychological protection. Nick's partner, Hank, having begun to notice Wesen and supernatural events, begins to question if he is going crazy. In "Bad Moon Rising" (S2, E3), Hank confesses that he doesn't think he can continue to do this job, admitting that he has lost himself and is seriously struggling. Nick realizes that he has to explain to Hank about the Wesen and Grimms to protect his sanity. However, before Nick can do so, Hank's best friend from childhood, Jarold,[29] comes to the station looking for help because his daughter, Carly,[30] has disappeared. Nick discovers that she was

It Is Up to the "One" … Or Is It? (McDonald) 197

taken by a group of *Coyotls* (a species of pack Wesen like coyotes). The *Coyotls* have a ritual that they perform on their females once they turn seventeen, as Carly just had: a gang rape inducts the females into the pack. It turns out that Carly and her parents had run away from their pack when she was a little girl to protect her from this "ritual." The men who have come for her are relatives of her mother's family who want to kill her father and take her back with them, signaling the force of male dominance over women and desire for control motivating the ritual.

When Nick, Hank, and Jarod get to the deserted ranch where Carly is being held, she recognizes Nick as a Grimm and becomes terrified and woges. This in turn terrifies Hank, and he pulls out his gun to shoot her. Nick jumps in between the two: and assures Hank that he is not crazy, that he also saw her turn into something else, but that she is still "just Carly." Nick stands aside, and Carly, no longer woged steps forward. Hank looks stunned but lowers his gun.

This exemplifies how Nick straddles the line between the human and supernatural worlds. He is involved with Carly's abduction because he is a police officer (human world), but when Nick and Hank get to the ranch where she is being held, they are drastically outnumbered by gun toting men. They do not recognize Nick as a Grimm until they have woged. Having counted on scaring the human cops with their Wesen visages to aid in their disarming of the police, they are themselves surprised by a Grimm (supernatural world). They all just put down their guns, and Nick and Hank easily arrest them. By the end of the episode, they have rescued Carly and saved Jarold. Nick tries to talk to Hank about what he had learned over the course of the episode, but Hank notes: "this was one of the better days of my life … because I might be crazy, but now I know I am not alone."[31]

Two seasons later, Sgt. Wu, another police officer who regularly works with Hank and Nick, is starting to feel as if he is losing his mind because he has seen too many things that he cannot explain. In "Chupacabra" (S4, E8), Wu shows up outside a house where Nick and Hank are interviewing a woman. As they exit the house, Wu rushes up to them and tells them he is quitting the force because he believes is going insane. Nick and Hank (eventually) take Wu to see the Grimm trailer, giving him access to the secret world of Grimms and Wesen and its lore. Hank confides to Wu that he had a similar experience, thinking he was going crazy before learning the truth.[32] Revealing this world to Wu closes the circle so that all of Nick's partners, humans and Wesen, share access to the hidden truths.

In the beginning, Nick had been the student, and Monroe had initially become part of Nick's inner circle because he had knowledge that no one else could provide when Nick first took on his role as a Grimm. By contrast, Hank and Wu were pulled in for their mental health. Because they worked close to Nick—and therefore the Wesen with whom he engages—they saw too many things they could not explain. Hank and Wu were essential in Nick's human workspace. Giving them information translates these partnerships into the hidden world. Thus, they are both his touchstones to the non-magical world and allies in the magical. Nick breaks the code of secrecy and silence for the double purpose of protecting his human partners and his own reciprocal need for their heroic abilities.

The need for collective heroism is clarified just after Wu learns of Nick's secret. He is pulled into the Captain's office, and Nick, Hank, and the Captain (who is part *Zauberbiest*, a Wesen-like magical entity) inform him that Monroe has been kidnapped by the *Wesenrein*, a Wesen hate group. Nick informs Wu that they will likely have to go outside of standard police procedures to get Monroe back in this mission. He asks Wu if he is willing. Demonstrating his bravery and commitment, Wu says yes, instantly. Nevertheless, he notes that after they are done, he expects that they will sit down to have a serious discussion.

On the one hand, his willingness to proceed with this order of events highlights that he trusts in and believes in his friends despite the highly unusual things he has learned. Therefore, he will follow them into dangerous and perhaps even illegal behavior, if needed. The series never indicates that Wu has ever acted beyond the boundaries of proper, legal behavior or even that he has ever been tempted. Instead, he is a model officer fluent in the protocols and procedures of the precinct. Thus, the unhesitating agreement demonstrates a high degree of fraternal respect.

On the other hand, noting that he desires a serious discussion afterward indicates that he does not follow Nick, the Captain, or anyone else blindly and demands equal inclusion in the group's knowledge of Wesen and the world most people can never see. It is worth highlighting that in this exchange, the presumption of an after bespeaks his unreflecting, heroic confidence that he and the others will together accomplish whatever they intend, monsters or no monsters. At the end of the next episode, the final scene finds Wu alone in the Grimm trailer reviewing the books: now that he has accepted that the Wesen exist, he wants to know everything he can about them and how to fight them. He wants to be a contributing rather than dependent member of the group. Going forward he does just that as part of a heroic collective.

In a later episode, after Monroe is saved from the *Wesenrein*,[33] and all of its members are either dead or under arrest, Monroe and Rosalee offer a toast of thanks for the best friends people could ask for: friends who put their own lives on the line to save each other. While this scene is not coded as feminine, it is also not the traditionally accepted post-battle male bravado and pushing down of emotions to appear stoic in the face of danger and its aftermath.[34] The group in Monroe and Rosalee's house toasting the end of the *Wesenrein* threat are a "band of brothers" that has been through battle together and emerged as a stronger unit on the other side. This is despite the fact that two of these "brothers" are women and that there are two romantic couples within the larger group. The fraternal bonds shared among them are so strong that everything else is made ancillary. These "brothers" have been through the wars together and have developed a camaraderie that allowed them to succeed where would otherwise have failed, and have done so while modeling a diverse collectivity of race and gender.

In the first case that Nick worked on after learning he was a Grimm, he engaged Monroe for his knowledge and supernatural sense of smell. He helps Nick know what he is looking for and locating it: alone, he would have been able to do determine neither, regardless of his Grimm abilities. Hank had always been part of Nick's human world of camaraderie heroism, as his police partner, and he is allowed to continue in this role once he is oriented to the existence of the Wesen, as is Wu. Time and again, the audience realizes that Nick cannot do this job alone. Fortunately, he does not have to. America in the 21st century enacts camaraderie heroism that is equitable and reciprocal, whether it discusses it this way or not.

Campbell's theory of the hero stated that "The composite hero of the monomyth is a person of exceptional gifts."[35] *Grimm* does not dispute that claim. Instead, it enlarges it: *Grimm* does not have *a* hero, but heroes who work as an ensemble, joined together not just by talent but also by strong emotional bonds. They are not colleagues working together for a cause but comrades whose heroic journeys intertwine. Previous shows such as *BtVS* and *Angel* laid the groundwork for *Grimm's* innovation by positing a supportive group of talented "scoobies," whose all too human inferiority to the hero has the effect of expanding the heroic identity to include more than the mission. They humanize the hero and draw them into a social network. Although Nick's is the story that is followed most closely in the series, *Grimm* implies that each of the characters who join him has their own stories of becoming that mirror Campbell's observations. In this way, the show echoes the "*many* heroes" Tutti identifies in Tolkien's *Lord of the Rings*. However, *Grimm* expands from this model by demonstrating the equality and mutual necessity of its many heroes. More to the point, the characters in the show recognize this as well. The chosen one would never have succeeded without the others. The same may be said for any of the others involved. In the world of *Grimm,* which lives so close to our own, heroes fail without comrades, while together, they thrive. They are all risking their lives for and saving one another while saving the world and depicting a new, modern mode of heroism for the audiences who watch them.

Notes

1. Zipes 1.
2. Campbell 37, 38.
3. Kesite 35. Emphasis added.
4. See Kesti.
5. Jayawickreme and Di Stefano 165.
6. Jayacwickreme and Di Stefano 165, 166.
7. *The WB* 1999–2004.
8. *The WB* 1999–2004.
9. *BtVS* does end with all potential slayers being called upon to help rid the world of the First Evil.
10. See Halfyard.
11. See Krzywinska.
12. See Fritts.
13. Actor, Sarah Michelle Gellar.
14. The "Scooby gang" is the name adopted by central characters in the show to denote their group. The prominent members are Willow, Xander, and Giles. Other supporting characters come and go over the seasons.
15. Actor, Anthony Head.
16. Actor, Nicholas Brendon.
17. Actor, Alyson Hannigan.
18. O'Dette 5.
19. O'Dette 8.
20. Pateman 12.
21. Zettel 115.
22. Zettel 114.
23. The core document of Slayer-lore, the *Slayer Manual*, states a slayer's identity must be kept a secret, but Buffy (with the support of Giles) cultivates a sphere of informed support in the Scooby gang. An encounter with a complexly generated second slayer, Kendra, illustrates the measure of Buffy's social exceptionalism. Kendra exudes incredulity at Buffy's seemingly wanton failure of secrecy and her watcher's laxity: "You allow this sir? But the slayer must work in secret, for security" (*BtVS* S2, E10: "What's My Line, Part Two"). In the slayer ethos, secrecy and security go hand and hand: anything else is criminally reckless.
24. Episode 1.1 "The City of Angels" *Angel*.
25. Actor, David Boreanaz.
26. S1, E1: "Pilot."
27. S1, E2: "Bears Will Be Bears."
28. Willsley 211.
29. Actor, Mark Pellegrino.
30. Actor, Maddie Hasson.
31. E2, S3: "Bad Moon Rising."
32. Episode 4.8 *Grimm*.
33. A Wesen power group.
34. MacKenzie 1.
35. Campbell 37.

Works Cited

Campbell, Joseph. *A Hero with a Thousand Faces*. Bollingen Books, 1949.
Fritts, David. "Warrior Heroes: *Buffy the Vampire Slayer* and *Beowulf*." *Slayage*, vol. 5, no.1, 2005, n.p. https://www.whedonstudies.tv/uploads/2/6/2/8/26288593/fritts_slayage_5.1.pdf.

Halfyard, Janet K. "Hero's Journey, Heroine's Return?: *Buffy*, Eurydice and the Orpheus Myth." *Reading Joss Whedon*, edited by Rhonda V. Wilcox, Tanya R. Cochran, Cynthea Masson, and David Lavery, Syracuse UP, 2014, pp. 40–52.

Jayawickreme, Eranda, and Paul Di Stefano. "How Can We Study Heroism? Integrating Persons, Situations and Communities." *Political Psychology,* vol. 33, no. 1, 2012, pp. 165–78. https://www.jstor.org/stable/41407026.

Kesti, Tutti. *Heroes of Middle-Earth: J. Campbell's Monomyth in J.R.R. Tolkien's* The Lord of the Rings *(1954–1955)*, 2007. University of Jyväskylä, Pro Gradu Thesis. https://jyx.jyu.fi/bitstream/handle/123456789/7305/URN_NBN_fi_jyu-2007550.pdf.

Krzywinska, Tanya. "Arachne challenges Minerva: The Spinning Out of Long Narrative in *World of Warcraft* and *Buffy the Vampire Slayer.*" 2007. https://bura.brunel.ac.uk/bitstream/2438/1058/1/Arachne%20challenges%20Minerva.pdf.

MacKenzie, Megan. *Beyond the Band of Brothers: The US Military and the Myth that Women Can't Fight.* Cambridge UP, 2015.

O'Dette, Katarina. "Heroic Mediocrity: Xander Harris and the Civil Heroism of the Ordinary." *Slayage*, vol. 16, no. 1, 2018, n.p. https://www.whedonstudies.tv/uploads/2/6/2/8/26288593/odette_-_slayage_16.1.pdf.

Pateman, Matthew. "'That was nifty: Willow Rosenberg Saves the World in *Buffy, the Vampire Slayer.*" *Shofar,* vol. 25, no. 4, 2007, pp. 64–77.

Willsey, Kristiana. "Old Fairy Tales are New Again: *Grimm* and the Brothers Grimm." *Channeling Wonder: Fairy Tales on Television*, edited by Pauline Greenhill and Jill Terry Rudy Wayne State UP, 2014, pp. 210–29.

Zettel, Sarah. "When did the Scoobies become Insiders?" *Seven Seasons of Buffy: Science Fiction and Fantasy Writers Discuss their Favorite Television Show*, edited by Glenn Yeffeth, BenBella Books, 2003, pp. 109–15.

Zipes, Jack. *Happily Ever After: Fairy Tales, Children, and the Culture Industry.* Routledge, 1997.

Grimm Afterlives
The Show Lives On in the Media Tie-In Novels
Rachel Noorda

Media tie-in novels allow TV shows to "live on" between seasons and after the series conclude. Fans eager to continue their love for TV shows like *Grimm* often do so by reading novels that have the official endorsement of the series-franchise to expand its fictional world. These novels explore additional plot arcs and narrative possibilities drawn from the series. Technically, they are called "media tie-in novels," and they differ from fan-fiction, which is unsanctioned and unregulated. Media-tie in novels, nevertheless, have a complex relationship with the series they extend; they exist in a contested space between the extraneous and the essential on the border of a franchise "cannon," the body of essential artifacts that establish a fundamental being or identity. Focusing on the three *Grimm* media tie-in novels from Titan Books (henceforth, the *Grimm* novels), this essay will explore the complicated relationship between the novels and the TV show episodes and their production, as well as the interconnectedness the genre creates across different, though related TV shows like *Buffy the Vampire Slayer* and *Supernatural*. These novels generate a space for fans to further participate in *Grimm*'s storyworld. The nature of this participation, however, is unclear, because it is uncertain whether the novels are part of what could be called the *Grimm* "cannon" alongside the episodes of the TV series. Is *Grimm* tied to a specific medium, or is it a fictional world that has many possible expressions?

In the year between *Grimm*'s first and second seasons (2013–2014), Titan Books released three official media tie-in novels about the *Grimm* universe. Occupying the empty temporal space in which there were no new TV episodes, each book features narratives that follow Detective Nick Burkhardt and his partner Hank Griffin investigating Wesen-related crime in Portland, Oregon. In the first novel, *The Icy Touch*, the two detectives attempt to dismantle an international crime cartel. The second novel, *The Chopping Block*, features the duo investigating missing-person cases connected to a strange Wesen culinary ritual. And lastly, the third novel, *The Killing Time*, describes their investigation of murders carried out by an obscure shapeshifting creature.

For this type of media, the *Grimm* novels were inarguably popular. According to NPD BookScan, the primary quantitative sales tool for the book publishing industry, they have sold well, particularly considering that most published novels sell fewer than 500 copies[1] and that the *Grimm* novels are from an independent publisher (Titan Books). As of November 10, 2020, the first book, *The Icy Touch*, had sold the most of the three books, followed by the second, *The Chopping Block*, and then the third, *The Killing Time*, but all three sold over 4,000 copies each. The strong sales record indicates that fans are interested in consuming this content. However, because of the different medium, it is unclear how to understand these narratives in relationship to the arcs of the TV series and its story world.

These novels are among the many alternate and afterlives of *Grimm*'s characters across media forms. Specifically, they participate in the print-based afterlife[2] of *Grimm*. While book-to-film or book-to-TV is a familiar and respected intermedial exchange, print-based afterlives from film-to-book or TV-to-book have received little critical and academic attention.[3] There are three main categories of TV-to-book (and film-to-book) print-based afterlives: guides, novelizations, and media tie-in novels. Guidebooks—encyclopedic reference materials that provide the details of the fictional world—often have no attributed author, just the publisher.[4] Novelizations are novels based on a film or a TV series. They are usually released around the same time as the film or TV series.[5] These are primarily based on the screenplay. In contrast, media tie-in novels portray characters and events from the TV series in new narratives.[6] In the case of the three *Grimm* novels, the narratives are original stories that are set within the parameters of the *Grimm* universe and characters. Therefore, they are media tie-in novels, utilizing characters and building on events from the series while also providing an independent narrative within those parameters.

Johannes Mahlknecht argues that novelizations are rarely examined as literary works in their own right but that they should be. Often novelizations and media-tie novels—print-based adaptations of TV series and films—are perceived as simply tools for film advertising and dismissed as "worthless by-products."[7] Usually, the direction of intermedial exchange or adaptation is governed by two principles: (1) it goes from a medium with the most cultural prestige to a medium of lesser prestige, and (2) it moves from "old" to "new" media.[8] Thus, it is more common to see intermedial exchanges from book to TV/film than from TV/film to book: the codex is an older medium than TV/film, and is often perceived as more prestigious. Media tie-in novels subvert these expectations by moving from newer and less prestigious to older and more prestigious media forms. While they may be esteemed as lesser story forms in academic debates, for industry professionals (and some audiences), these print afterlives are also part of the storyworld. In the case of *Grimm*, the media tie-in novels and the reviews of them from fans offer a window into thoughts and perspectives on the TV series itself as well.

Context: Production and Consumption of Grimm-*Novels*

Simone Murray argues that any examination of adaptation, which includes media tie-in novels for a TV series, must examine the social, economic, and legal frameworks that shape production and consumption.[9] The business frameworks for how the media tie-in novel industry operates and how franchises are owned and managed give meaningful context to *Grimm's* connectedness and its novel adaptations. Production for these novels includes many of the same agents one finds in other fields of book publishing: authors, literary agents, publishers, wholesalers, retailers, and readers. Nevertheless, there are additional agents in media tie-ins that dramatically change the nature and power structure of the field. Licensors are chiefly influence among these because they ultimately decide what content goes into the book: they wield creative power over the author and publisher.[10] Licensors maintain the intellectual capital embodied in the legal value of the copyright they hold. Without the established fictional universe belonging to the licensor, book's claim to authenticity, its value, and it potential body of fan-readership would be compromised. Publishers pay licensors for a specific number of media tie-in novels that they subsequently publish across a period of time, with possibilities for renegotiation.[11] In contrast to many areas of publishing, media tie-in novels also may involve multiple authors. While all publishers deal with multiple authors, a fictional book series is usually authored by the same individual throughout. By contrast, a media tie-in novel series often has a different author for each book in the series, as is the case for the *Grimm* novels. Therefore the "ownership" of the content—the characters and the story—lives primarily with the licensor and franchise managers, not with the authors.

As with their agents, many of the processes for the production of media tie-in novels mirror those of other fields of publishing. However, there are a few key aspects that differ. The specific processes involved in media tie-in novels include accelerated writing and production timelines, specific product guidelines, experienced and well-known authors, and legal copyright constraints. While publishers of traditional novels typically have timelines of twelve to eighteen months, these authors are usually asked to produce complete manuscripts for media tie-in novels in as little as eight weeks upon commission.[12] Not only is this a rapid turnaround, but with a traditional fiction novel, an author would come to a publisher with a draft in. hand. Media tie-in novel writers, however, start from scratch once commissioned. Additionally, the marketing outlets for media tie-in publishing vary, which can also affect timelines. For example, traditional review venues like *Kirkus, School Library Journal, The New York Times*, and *The Washington Post* are not pursued by media tie-in publishers, in part because of the nature of the audience. Additionally, specific product guidelines are more heavily curated and policed in media tie-in publishing than in other publishing fields. Media tie-in novels are not only overseen by publishing house editors, but most importantly, by the licensor of the content of the TV or film universe. In the case of *Grimm*, NBCUniversal owns and licenses content. While Cath Trechman was the editor at Titan Books overseeing the *Grimm* series and served as a liaison with the NBCUniversal team, it is ultimately NBCUniversal who had the final word on editorial matters. According to the acknowledgment pages in the three *Grimm*-novels, the authors worked with three particular liaisons at NBCUniversal, including the Director of Global Licensing and Senior Manager of Licensing and Merchandising.

Media tie-in writers are generally experienced and well-known authors within their niche. This is partly because accelerated timelines prompt focus on a writer's demonstrated success. Because licensors hand over tightly guarded franchises to writers for media tie-in novels, the licensors (and publishers) are unlikely to risk maintaining that franchise brand with debut authors.

Another distinguishing feature of media tie-in publishing regards the copyright. Media tie-in publishing distributes copyright differently from traditional publishing. This is primarily because authors work in a writer-for-hire capacity and do not have control over the world about which they write or own the copyright. As media tie-in writer Max Allan Collins said, "Perhaps the biggest pitfall for the writer of tie-in novels—whether original work or script adaptation—is developing too much of a proprietary sense."[13] Because these works are new stories, it is understandable that the writer could begin to feel ownership of the storyworld. Nevertheless, in reality, they are temporary stewards of another's characters and creations.[14]

The ownership levels, capital, and economic exchange of media tie-in publishing are therefore separate from those commonly seen in a typical author-publisher scenario. Various agents accumulate and exchange capital at many different moments in the media tie-in production process. Economic capital, which is financial value, is essential to all agents involved who want to gain financially from their investment and relationships in the field. Media tie-in publishing complicates these investments and relationships. For one thing, publishers have the added economic burden of paying an additional entity: the licensor. Because the licensor requires additional economic capital needed from the publisher, less economic capital is transferred to the author from the publisher. Thus, author compensation for media tie-in novels is characterized by small royalties. Whereas a 6 percent to 8 percent royalty range is typical for paperback royalty rates in trade/consumer publishing,[15] authors of media tie-in novels receive royalties in the range of 1 percent to 3 percent.[16] Because it is challenging for debut writers to break into the media tie-in publishing business, an author must possess and accumulate social and symbolic capital of sufficient quantities to attract the eye of a publisher looking for a media tie-in writer. Finally, the unique legal structures and constraints that characterize media tie-in publishing affect how intellectual capital is accumulated and exchanged within this publishing field. Authors produce less intellectual capital in media tie-in publishing than in other publishing areas because they are not working with original material. Ultimately, the licensor maintains the powerful intellectual capital position in the relationships and exchanges.

Goodreads Reviews: Why Fans Read Media Tie-In Novels

The media tie-in novel industry provides the conditions of possibility for the relationship between *Grimm* TV show fans and the *Grimm* novels. Reader reviews on Goodreads, however, give insight in the relationship itself. Goodreads is "the world's dominant book-centric social networking and cataloguing platform," with 65 million users and 68 million reviewers (Murray, 2019, 10), owned by Amazon since 2016.[17] Readers can rate the book from 1 to 5 stars and leave a review for other Goodreads readers to see. The first *Grimm* novel, *The Icy Touch*, by John Shirley, had 457 ratings and 83 reviews, with an average of 3.61. The second novel, *The Chopping Block*, by John Passarella, had 364 ratings and 55 reviews, with an average rating of 3.99. The last *Grimm* novel, *The Killing Time*, by Tim Waggoner, had 253 ratings and 36 reviews with an average rating of 3.98. The average star rating given to books on Goodreads is 3.88[18]: The second and third novels, *The Chopping Block* and *The Killing Time*, received a rating score above the overall Goodreads average while the average rating for the first novel, *The Icy Touch*, was below average. The qualitative reviews give insight into the quantitative disparities amid the books as well as information on reader relationships.

For this essay, Goodreads reviews of the *Grimm* novels were assessed through close reading. Readers who post reviews on Goodreads do not expect their reviews to be researched and analyzed even though they are publicly available. Therefore, this essay takes the ethical position of Driscoll and Rehberg Sedo in their analysis of Goodreads reviews of protecting reviewer privacy by not citing usernames with review quotes.[19] Based on the close reading of the Goodreads reviews for the *Grim*m-novels, there are three main reasons that fans engage with the novels: (1) to explore additional plot arcs, (2) to connect *Grimm* to other beloved fandoms and franchises, (3) and to establish the *Grimm* "canon."

Exploring Additional Plot Arcs

One of the main benefits of the *Grim*m novels is their ability to explore new plot arcs in the *Grimm* universe when the TV show had ended or was between seasons. Nevertheless, the intermedial relationship between *Grimm* and the *Grimm* novels demonstrates that this exchange is more-or-less one-directional: from TV series to novel. Fans and the licensors expect character developments and plot points featured in the TV series to continue into the novel's narratives and characters with seamless continuity. However, there is no reciprocal expectation though the possibility was not out of the question since the *Grimm* novels were released between seasons and a few years before the TV series ended. Therefore, they could have contributed (at the time they were released) to the ongoing storylines. Thus, the media tie-in novel is "a book functioning similar to a new episode of an ongoing series,"[20] but this does not translate into integration into the TV series.

Despite the one-sidedness of the intermedial exchange, the Goodreads reviews show that fans are interested in seeing elements from the novels featured in *Grimm* TV series episodes. One reader complimented the novel by saying, "it could easily be a two-part episode of the TV show it is based on" and thus felt innovative rather than derivative. Another reader compared the novel to a script of the actual show: "The whole time I was reading it I was thinking what episode this was but found it was all John's creativity creating this book." Yet another reader longed to see the book turned into an episode on the show, saying, "I would have liked to have seen this story as an episode." This praise is typical of the favorable reception of the novels on Goodreads, which raises the question: Why didn't *Grimm* integrate the original material from the novels into the TV show? In other words, why is the intermedial relationship between TV shows and media tie-in novels so one-directional, especially when licensors maintain legal and editorial control over the franchise, including the media tie-in novels?

Licensors (in this case, NBCUniversal) have complete legal and copyright control over the content of the media tie-in novels, which means that these licensors could integrate or replicate media if they wanted to join plots and characters from the novels with the TV series. However, there are transitional logistics to consider, and these are complicated by the differences between books and television, and the particular kinds of storytelling each facilitates. While it would be legally unproblematic to adapt the novels for television, features of the novels would prove challenging to replicate another medium. One Goodreads reviewer noted the difficulties that logistics posed by saying that while the book would have been the "best hour of the show ever aired" due to the "excellent plot" and "intriguing villain," there were logistics to consider. "To film this novel as written would be budget-busting to say the least." Since, as this reviewer notes, the *Grimm* TV series is known for its hallmark of minimum creature display for presumably budgetary reasons, the particular Wesen in *The Killing Time* would have been too complicated and expensive to visually reproduce.

Thus, despite the reviewer's interest in seeing *The Killing Time* become an episode of the *Grimm* TV series, the reviewer acknowledges the logistical difficulties that such a project would pose. However, the authors of media tie-in novels have the freedom and creativity to be unfettered by a special effects budget, which provides added value and different kinds of storytelling than is available through the TV show. Of his own media tie-in writing experience, Anderson says, "I try to do an 'episode' that they could never afford to do on the actual show. After all, as a writer, you have an unlimited special effects budget."[21] Likewise, speaking from his own experience writing media tie-in novels, Cox argues that, "unlike a film, which is limited by time and budget restraints, you can flesh out characters and concepts that might have been dealt with quickly in the movie."[22] Of course, media tie-in novels are still subject to constraints, such as tight editorial control and accelerated deadlines. However, these constraints are different from those TV production faces. As a result, the novel can fulfill a storytelling role and offer narrative possibilities out of television's reach.

In addition to the logistical challenges that make converting media tie-in novels in TV episodes difficult, the publishing industry, and perhaps even the franchises themselves, perceive media tie-in novels as supplemental to the core content of the TV series. Henry Jenkins has argued that current licensing systems create redundant, watered-down works or riddled with sloppy contradictions.[23] However, Jenkins's perspective ignores the creativity that authors of media tie-in novels employ when operating within franchise worlds. Tim Waggoner, the author of the third *Grimm* novel (*The Killing Time*), challenges the notion that media tie-in works are redundant, calling this work "innovation rather than invention," and proposing that an author does not have to invent the fictional world to innovate within it. A further contributor to the stigma surrounding novel adaptations of this kind concerns the prestige of the platform. The movement from TV to codex is a movement from newer to older media forms and from forms of lesser to greater perceived prestige, influencing the perception of this movement as a less respectable one than its counterpart: book to TV (or book to film).

Interfandom/Interfranchise Exchanges

Accelerated timelines induce publishers and licensors to invest in well-known writers who have proven track records of writing excellence and timeliness, especially if they write in genres relevant to the franchise. Consequently, the pool of media tie-in writers in this space tends to be a small one, with the same set of authors writing novels across fandoms. This is the case for the three authors of the *Grimm*-novels: John Shirley has written novels of franchises such as *Alien, Predator, Constantine, Bioshock*, and *Halo*; John Passarella has written novels of franchises such as *Supernatural, Buffy the Vampire Slayer*, and *Angel*; and Tim Waggoner has written novels and novelizations of franchises such as *Supernatural, Kingsmen*, and *Stargate*.

While these authors have not produced any official interfranchise media tie-ins, these various franchises influence each other. Franchises like *Buffy the Vampire Slayer, X-files*, and *Supernatural* exemplify this relationship because they operate within the same fictional genres and share many aspects of character narratives, such as protagonists chosen to fight monsters that are unknown to the rest of humanity. These connections are usually subtle but meaningful. For example, in *The Killing Time*, the antagonist is a shapeshifting Wesen called a Wechselbalg. The creation of this character for the media tie-in novel respects the Grimmverse protocols of Germanic naming and a fairy-tale or folklore connection (in this case, the changeling folklore). In addition, there are connections between the Wechselbalg and *Supernatural*'s shapeshifting creature, which also sheds its skin into a liquidy goo. Author Tim Waggoner, who wrote *The Killing Time*, also wrote books within the *Supernatural* franchise. Like examples abound in media tie-in novels because of the interconnectedness of these franchises.

These franchises also share interconnected fandoms. Sometimes these fandoms are explicitly interconnected, such as in SuperWhoLock: the fan-instigated mashup of *Supernatural, Doctor Who,* and *Sherlock*.[24] Hills uses trans-fandom to describe such a phenomenon: "wherein multiple fan audiences interact with today's cult media products (and with each other) in ways that span texts and boundaries."[25] This is evident in the Goodreads reviews for the *Grimm* novels, in which reviewers display awareness and interest in these other franchises/fandoms. For example, one reviewer mentions *Dark Angel, Burn Notice,* and *Supernatural* among some of the other TV shows and related novels they consume that eventually led them to the *Grimm* novels. Another reviewer was impressed by the author of *Grimm: The Chopping Block* because this author had written for other successful franchises such as *Buffy the Vampire Slayer, Angel,* and *Supernatural*. Yet another reviewer even picked up two books (from different franchises) by the same author at the same time:

> I picked up two books this last week, this one and a *Supernatural* one—they were coincidentally written by the same author. They both manage to touch on subjects that tend to creep me out in written horror—in this case dining on human flesh—not just dining but preparing. This is an excellent *Grimm* story, the author has a good grasp of the characters.

When *Grimm* fans further immerse themselves in the Grimmverse through media tie-in novels, they enlarge their understanding of character backstories and worldbuilding. They can also connect that content to other worlds and franchise universes in which they are interested. Connecting through other forms to the fandom of *Grimm* also connects fans to other fandoms, other forms, and other storyworlds.

Consistency and the Area of the "Semi-Canon"

Media tie-in novels, because they offer original content within the parameters of an established universe, are members of what Jason Mittell calls the "awkward realm of semi-canon" because "they are endorsed by the show's creative team but not fully integrated into the show's complex serial arcs."[26] Both licensors and fans expect consistency across *Grimm*'s forms (like the novels), but they also expect something new and expansive. While the *Grimm* novels operate with the main characters and within the same fictional world as the TV series, there is still room for invention and divergence, which raises considerations of the degree of fidelity required. What is the right balance between consistency and creativity? It is a complicated question. And while fans may not agree on where the line of fidelity is to be drawn, they recognize when it has been crossed. In comparing the reviews for the three *Grimm* novels, we see that the first novel, *The Icy Touch*, received the most criticism for inconsistency with the TV series. The inconsistencies pointed out by readers on Goodreads were centered mainly around consistency in characterization. Representations of Monroe and Burkhardt, arguably the two most loved and prominent characters in both the TV series and, subsequently, the *Grimm* novels, are especially criticized for being inconsistent in their characterizations. One Goodreads reader said, "The characters are so unlike themselves." Another talked about the characterization of the main characters as "uneven." The reviews also discussed the characters as not matching the perspective of those characters represented in the "canon." One reader said that the author "over-exaggerated the characters" and "did not have the voice of the characters."

Beyond general statements identifying and critiquing inconsistencies between characters in the TV series and the first *Grimm* novel, there were some specific complaints that readers voiced as well. For example, the characterizations of the women in the book, particularly Juliette and Rosalee, were criticized as weakening characters who were strong in the show. One of the specific criticisms against the characters of Hank and Nick concerns a rape joke that Hank makes toward the end of the novel. After been beaten during interrogation, Hank tells Nick, "Gave me a good thumping. Then they dosed me with something. Like, blew it in my mouth with a tube. I don't remember much after that. Hope they didn't rape me."[27] In response to Hank's joke, Nick laughs. Readers, however, were not amused. Not only did readers note the inappropriateness of the joke, but they also argued that Hank and Nick would never engage in such humor in the Grimmverse. As Mittell notes, "The problems with tie-in characters often stem from a lack of depth and a fidelity to the original."[28] Readers reviews had much to say in response to the perceived inauthenticity of Nick and Hank's exchange in the first of the *Grimm* novels:

> The last straw was when Hank and Nick made a rape joke. Hank, maybe I can buy, but probably not since his best friend is dating Juliette, who would never let either of them make a rape joke and not get chewed out for being insensitive ass nuggets.
>
> Then there's the rape joke towards the end that Hank and Nick share. Haha. Y'all so funny. Not.

There is also a rape joke which is totally inappropriate for any book.

> Also, what the EFF was with the random rape joke?! how did this become an official book?

Because the media tie-in novels occupy the intermediate territory of the semi-canon, readers expect to see consistency, particularly when it comes to character actions, and will passionately police mischaracterization. However, the line for where consistency ends and originality begins is a blurry one. While fans want consistency within the universe, they also want the new and original content that a media tie-in novel offers. On the one hand, the *Grimm* novels are arguably not canonized because they were not integrated back into the TV series, perceived as supplementary rather than a core feature of the franchise. On the other hand, the *Grimm* novels are authorized by the prestige and authority that comes from the licensor. Anyone can write fan fiction within the *Grimm* universe and post it online; indeed, many fans have. Titan Books' *Grimm* novels, however, come with the authorization and figurative stamp of approval and authenticity from the licensor of the franchise: NBCUniversal. The official nature of these books carries a certain weight. David Spencer asserts that readers of media tie-in novels are more willing to accept the novels as "representing a kind of alternate reality, a canon running parallel to the TV series without necessarily interweaving with it"[29] in part because of their perceived vetting and authentication through the traditional publishing process.

The media tie-in publishing field has logistical realities such as accelerated timelines that can compromise the canonization and authority of the novels. Accelerated timelines compress the editing schedule of the novels. When readers find what they see as errors in the text, they begin to question how the book fits within the canon and if it has the authority to represent the universe that fans love. For all three of the books, Goodreads reviewers not only noticed but were particularly fixated on poor editing. When readers find editing "mistakes" in a text, this undermines the credibility and trust between the author and the reader. Readers are unaware of the practicalities of this publishing field, such as accelerated timelines which limit time for copyediting, and see only a punctuation error signaling sloppiness, carelessness, or unresearched material regarding a franchise in which these fans are invested.

> Where in the hell was this "author's" editor? Asleep at the printing press, or the computer screen.
>
> The Kindle edition has missing punctuation and it's glaringly obvious that the punctuation is missing. Does no one proofread their work anymore?
>
> As an aspiring writer myself I could not get past the lazy/sloppy editing that I encountered in the paperback edition. I always carefully re-read my work but it seems that this wasn't the case here. There are glaring errors with unnecessary words that interrupt the flow of sentences as well as some words that are missing entirely. This should have been picked up during editing by the author and if not definitely by the editorial team.

This book was poorly edited. The editor should have caught things like Renard closing and locking the Spice Shop front door yet a short time later, Nick and Hank open and walk through the locked door. The editor should also have caught missing words in prepositional phrases and repetitive text from one page to the next.

The only things holding this book back are ... some editing errors that should have been caught by a publication that is backed by a major studio.

Because lapses in consistency and irregularity in editing between the TV show and the *Grimm* novels undermine the authority of the novels, while they are nevertheless authorized by the franchise, they inhabit a semi-canon: a space in which both fans and franchise brilliantly build, struggle to uphold, or unintentionally undermine the canonization of the novels and their relationship to the *Grimm* TV series and franchise.

Conclusion

The terrain of *Grimm* novels and their intermediality with the TV series is a complicated one. On the one hand, these novels suffer from occasional infidelities to the original TV series and tight timelines that influence the editorial quality. Yet, on the other hand, they allow for the creation of new "episodes" that are not limited by the logistics of television production and create new possibilities for an enhanced understanding of characters and the Grimmverse and facilitate a connection to other fandoms of different franchises. The *Grimm* universe is thus a storyworld that exists beyond the original TV series, manifest in other forms, such as novels and other print material.

The intermedial relationship between the *Grimm* TV series and the *Grimm* novels is one in which the TV series produces a canonized or authorized storyworld, with franchise management that oversees how the Grimmverse translates from TV to book. The books, in turn, can draw from the source expand the Grimmverse beyond the limits of the televised form while drawing from it as the source material for its innovation. The connected nature of the TV series and books, which share their licensed umbrella, provides an undercurrent of consistency overlaid with original content that builds on the characters and plotlines from the TV series. Thus, while the TV series has come to a close, the franchise, the characters, and the fandom live on in *Grimm*'s afterlives: *Grimm* novels included.

Notes

1. See Anderson, Chris.

2. The term "print-based afterlife" comes from Murray 2008 in "Materializing Adaptation Theory."
3. Mahlknecht; Murray "Materializing Adaptation Theory."
4. Examples of guidebooks in the *Grimm* universe include *Grimm Below the Surface: The Insider's Guide to the Show* and *Grimm: Aunt Marie's Book of Lore*, which are both published and "authored" by Titan Books. *Aunt Marie's Book of Lore* is meant to represent the actual book of lore that Nick references and in the TV show itself, while the *Insider's Guide* is a behind-the-scenes guidebook for fans of the ins and outs of the show itself.
5. Mahlknecht 141.
6. Hills 409.
7. Mahlknecht 139.
8. See Bolter and Grusin.
9. Murray, "Materializing Adaptation Theory" 5.
10. Tarvin 215.
11. Cox 30.
12. DeCandido 50.
13. Collins 19.
14. *Ibid*.
15. Thompson 149; DeCandido 29.
16. DeCandido 31; Cox 31.
17. See Deahl and Milliot.
18. Dimitrov et al. 3.
19. Driscoll and Rehberg Sedo 251.
20. Mittell 204.
21. Anderson, Kevin 45.
22. Cox 155.
23. Jenkins 105.
24. See Booth.
25. Hill 3.
26. Mittell 205.
27. Shirly 294.
28. Mittell 207.
29. Spencer 120.

Works Cited

Anderson, Chris. "A Bookselling Tail." *Publishers Weekly*. 14 Jul 2006, https://www.publishersweekly.com/pw/by-topic/columns-and-blogs/soapbox/article/6153-a-bookselling-tail.html. Accessed 07 Oct 2019.

Anderson, Kevin. "The Business and Craft of Tie-In Writing—A Roundtable Discussion." *Tied In: The Business, History and Craft of Media Tie-In Writing*, edited by Lee Goldberg, International Association of Media Tie-In Writers, 2010, pp. 27–58.

Bolter, Jay David and Richard A. Grusin. *Remediation: Understanding New Media*. MIT Press, 2000.

Booth, Paul. *Crossing Fandoms: SuperWhoLock and the Contemporary Fan Audience*. Springer, 2016.

Collins, Max Allan. "This Time It's Personal." *Tied In: The Business, History and Craft of Media Tie-In Writing*, edited by Lee Goldberg, International Association of Media Tie-In Writers, 2010, pp. 19–25.

Cox, Greg. "Not Quite Based on a Hit Film: Writing Movie Spin-Off Novels." *Tied In: The Business, History and Craft of Media Tie-In Writing*, edited by Lee Goldberg, International Association of Media Tie-In Writers, 2010, pp. 149–56.

Deahl, Rachel, and Jim Milliot. "Amazon Buys Goodreads." *Publishers Weekly*, 28 Mar

2013, https://www.publishersweekly.com/pw/by-topic/digital/retailing/article/56575-amazon-buys-goodreads.html. Accessed 07 Oct 2019.

DeCandido, Keith R.A. "The Business and Craft of Tie-In Writing—A Roundtable Discussion." *Tied In: The Business, History and Craft of Media Tie-In Writing,* edited by Lee Goldberg, International Association of Media Tie-In Writers, 2010, pp. 27–58.

Dimitrov, Stefan, Faiyaz Al Zamal, Andrew Piper, and D. Ruths. "Goodreads Versus Amazon: The Effect of Decoupling Book Reviewing and Book Selling." *Proceedings of the Ninth International AAAI Conference on Web and Social Media.* 2015.

Driscoll, Beth, and DeNel Rehberg Sedo. "Faraway, So Close: Seeing the Intimacy in Goodreads Reviews." *Qualitative Inquiry,* vol. 25, no. 3, 2019, pp. 248–59.

Hills, Matt. "*Torchwood's* Trans-Transmedia: Media Tie-Ins and Brand 'Fanagement.'" *Participations,* vol. 9, no. 2, 2012, pp.409–28.

Jenkins, Henry. *Convergence Culture: Where Old and New Media Collide.* NYU Press, 2006.

Mahlknecht, Johannes. "The Hollywood Novelization: Film as Literature or Literature as Film Promotion?" *Poetics Today,* vol. 33, no. 2, 2012, pp. 137–68.

Mittell, Jason. "Strategies of Storytelling on Transmedia Television." *Storyworlds Across Media: Toward a Media-Conscious Narratology,* edited by Marie-Laure Ryan, Jan-Noël Thon, Jesse E. Matz, and David Herman, U Nebraska P, 2014, pp. 253–277.

Murray, Simone. *The Adaptation Industry: The Cultural Economy of Contemporary Literary Adaptation.* Routledge, 2012.

———. "Materializing Adaptation Theory: The Adaptation Industry." *Literature/Film Quarterly; Salisbury,* vol. 36, no. 1, 2008, pp. 4–20.

———. "Secret Agents: Algorithmic Culture, Goodreads and Datafication of the Contemporary Book World." *European Journal of Cultural Studies,* 2019, pp. 1–20. DOI: 10.1177/1367549419886026.

Spencer, David. "American TV Tie-Ins from the 50s through the early 70s." *Tied In: The Business, History and Craft of Media Tie-In Writing,* edited by Lee Goldberg, International Association of Media Tie-In Writers, 2010, pp. 105–147.

Tarvin, Brandie. "How to Become a Tie-In Writer." *Tied In: The Business, History and Craft of Media Tie-In Writing,* edited by Lee Goldberg, International Association of Media Tie-In Writers, 2010, pp. 215–223.

Thompson, John B. *Merchants of Culture: The Publishing Business in the Twenty-first Century.* John Wiley & Sons, 2013.

Waggoner, Tim. "Building a Theme." International Association of Media Tie-In Writers, 23 Jun 2013, https://iamtw.org/building-a-theme/. Accessed 07 Oct 2019.

About the Contributors

Emiliano **Aguilar** received an MA from the Universidad de Buenos Aires, Facultad de Filosofia y Letras. He has published about science fiction in *Lindes*, *Letraceluloide*, *The Bible Onscreen in the New Millennium: New Heart and New Spirit* (2020), *Orphan Black and Philosophy* (2016), *The Man in the High Castle and Philosophy* (2017), and *American Horror Stories and Philosophy* (2017), among others.

Sara **Casoli** received a Ph.D. from the University of Bologna with a project titled "The Forms of Characters: Typoologies, Morphologies, and Relational Systems in Contemporary TV Serial Narrations." Her research interests include the analysis of televisual long-lasting and transmedia characters with a narratological approach, seriality studies, popular culture, popular fiction, and fairy-tale studies.

Daniel **Farr** holds a Ph.D. in sociology and an MA in women's studies from the University at Albany. He is a senior lecturer of sociology at Kennesaw State University. His research interests explore issues of masculinities, LGBTQ studies, fat studies, and medical sociology. He has edited special issues of *Fat Studies*, *Journal of Lesbian Studies*, *Men and Masculinities*, and *Women's Studies*.

Matthew **Grinder** teaches in the humanities department at Central Maine Community College. He is finishing his dissertation on early modern Native American novels. He presents and writes on various popular culture and literary topics, especially those that consider Native American issues, the problems created by privilege, marginalization, and the practice of mindful honesty.

Melanie D. **Holm** is an associate professor of English at Indiana University of Pennsylvania where she is also co-director of the Dessy-Roffman Myth Collaborative. She is a coeditor of the 18th-century studies journal, *The Scriblerian*, and an essay collection on poetics, *Mocking Bird Technologies* (2018). She publishes regularly on literary and pedagogical issues of the British 18th century and romanticism.

Anastasia Rose **Hyden** holds an MA in English from the University of North Florida and an MA in liberal studies from Hollins University. Her writing and research activities principally focus upon American television, 1970s American film, women's media, and 20th-century literature.

About the Contributors

Tatiana **Konrad** is a postdoctoral researcher in the Department of English and American Studies at the University of Vienna, Austria. She holds a Ph.D. in American studies from the University of Marburg, Germany. Her research interests include war studies, ecocriticism, gender studies, and race studies. She is the author of *Docu-Fictions of War* (2019) and coeditor of *Cultures of War in Graphic Novels* (2018).

Kathleen **McDonald** is a professor of English at Norwich University in Vermont. She earned a Ph.D. in American literature at the University of Albany, SUNY. She is the editor of *Teaching the Short Fiction of Henry James* (2022) and *Americanization of History: Conflation of Time and Culture in Film and Television* (2011).

Rachel **Noorda** is the director of book publishing and an assistant professor in English at Portland State University. She has a Ph.D. in publishing studies from the University of Stirling. Her research interests include 21st-century book culture, diaspora communities, Scottish publishing, small business and international marketing, and entrepreneurship. She has published in *National Identities*, *Studies in Book Culture*, and *Publishing Research Quarterly*, among others.

Fernando Gabriel **Pagnoni Berns** is a Ph.D. candidate teaching at the Universidad de Buenos Aires, Facultad de Filosofia y Letras. He teaches courses on international horror film and is director of the research group on horror cinema, "Grite." He has published chapters in *Divine Horror* (2017), *Dreamscapes in Italian Cinema* (2015), *Reading Richard Matheson: A Critical Survey* (2014), and *Gender and Environment in Science Fiction* (2020), among others.

Sarah **Revilla-Sanchez** is a Ph.D. student at Instituto de Liderazgo Simone de Beauvoir (Mexico), having earned an MA at Brock University (Canada). Her areas of research interest include gendered violence, sexualities, Latin American feminism, popular culture, and masculinities, among others.

Andrea **Yingling** is a graduate student at Indiana University of Pennsylvania pursuing a Ph.D. in the graduate program of literature and criticism in the Department of English with a research concentration in 19th-century gothics. She earned an MA from Edinboro University. She also teaches senior high special education English in Erie, Pennsylvania.

Index

Abrams, M.H. 104, 155
Adalind *see* Schade, Adalind
Adams, Carol J. 161, 163
Adichie, Chimamanda Ngozi 20
Angel (TV show) 87–91, 190–192, 209–10
Angelina 57, 129, 136, 158
Aryan 105–108
Aunt Marie 5, 8, 13, 22–25, 40, 47, 92–93, 106, 131, 192
Aunt Marie's Trailer 38, 65, 105, 194

Bacchilega, Cristina 7, 12, 171
"Bad Luck" (S4, E14) 31
"Bad Moon Rising" (S2, E3) 196
"Bad Teeth" (S2, E1) 114
Bauerschwein 27, 118, 136, 160–61, 182
"Bears Will Be Bears" (S1, E2) 47, 116, 162, 193
Beauty & the Beast (TV series) 69, 172
beaver *see* Eisbiber
"Beeware" (S1, E3) 19,
"The Beginning of the End" (part 1) (S5, E21) 42, 48
"The Believer" (S5, E16) 41, 65
"Big Feet" (S1, E21) 25, 46, 113
Black Claw 32, 59–63, 117
Black Forest 13
"Blond Ambition" (S3, E22) 39, 80, 99
"Blood Magic" (S6, E10) 55
Bluebeard 74–75
Blutbad 13, 22, 27, 36, 46–47, 53, 55, 57, 65, 73, 93–94, 106, 112–20, 125, 129, 132, 135–36, 145, 158, 160, 176–179, 181, 192–95,
"The Bottle Imp" (S2, E7) 22
bridges 38, 42, 49–50, 74, 118
Brinkerhoff, Konstantin (Dr.) 46
Brothers Grimm 2–3, 5, 7–8, 12, 72, 105–6, 141, 143, 152, 155, 175, 181–83
Bud 94, 114, 116, 126, 158
Buffy the Vampire Slayer (TV show) 87–91, 190–91, 202, 209–10

Burkhardt, Nick (detective) 1, 6–8, 10, 13, 19–33, 37–47, 50, 54, 57–58, 60–61, 64–65, 71, 80, 88–100, 105–10, 114–15, 118–20, 123–26, 131–37, 144–47, 152, 156–57, 160–61, 173, 175–77, 189–90, 192–99, 211
Burkhardt, Kelly (Nick's mother) 13, 27, 29, 32–33, 45, 95, 113–14
Burkhardt, Kelly (Nick's son) 45–46, 65, 120

Calvert, Rosalee 13, 29, 40–41, 47, 57, 63–65, 94–95, 112–116, 126, 135, 182, 196, 198–99, 211
Campbell, Joseph 89, 188, 191, 193, 199
cannibalism 52, 113, 140, 143, 145–146, 160, 164
Capra 74–76, 79; *see also* Ziegevolk
"Cat and Mouse" (S1, E18) 79
The Chopping Block (novel) 203, 206–7, 210
Christmas 27, 36, 123, 125, 162, 183
Chupacabra 111
"Chupacabra" (S4, E8) 29, 42, 111, 197
Cinderella 140, 142, 146–48
"Clear and Wesen Danger" (S5, E2) 34
"Cold Blooded" (S3, E7) 110
Coyotl 56, 60, 197
Crecher-Mortel 26, 108
"Cry Havoc" (S4, E22) 32, 42, 98
"Cry Luison" (S4, E5) 39, 119
El Cucuy 27, 133–34
"El Cucuy" (S3, E5) 27, 130, 133–34
Cuegle 132–33
"El Cuegle" (S6, E4) 132–135

"Danse Macabre" (S1, E5) 49
"Death Do Us Part" (S4, E11) 29
Derrida, Jacques 159, 165
Diana 29, 32–33, 44–46, 65, 120
Dietrich, Felix 58
"A Dish Best Served Cold" (S3, E3) 27, 115, 160–61

219

220 Index

Ditmarsch, Errol 73–76
DNA 25, 67, 119

Eisbiber 49, 57, 94–95, 114, 118, 126, 158
Emmerman, Karen S. 162
"The End" (S6, E13) 43
Eve 13, 19–33, 37, 41–43, 48, 65
"Eve of Destruction" (S5, E7) 32
"Eyes of the Beholder" (S3, E10) 27

Faerie Tale Theater (TV series) 69
fandom 207, 209–10, 213
Folterseele 77–78, 112
forests 5, 38–39, 47–51, 72, 141, 143, 158, 164
Foucault, Michel 21
Frank, Arthur W. 12
The Frog Prince (fairy tale) 77
Frye, Marilyn 25
Fuchsbau 40, 57, 65, 94, 106–7, 120, 126, 135

"Game Ogre" (S1, E8) 24
gay *see* LGBTQ
Gay, Roxanne 20
Geier 140–46
Gelumcaedus 110
Glühenvolk 57
"The Good Soldier" (S3, E11) 30
Grausen 27
Grimm Books 40, 57, 62, 64, 192, 198
Griffith, Hank (detective) 13, 20, 26, 32, 38, 54, 60–65, 79–80, 95, 107, 110, 113, 119, 123–125, 130–35, 144, 193–99, 202, 211–213
"The Grimm Identity" (S5, E1) 80
Grimm identity 23, 30, 38–41, 43, 47, 50, 80, 93, 98
"The Grimm Who Stole Christmas" (S4, E7) 119

Hadrian's Wall 21, 32, 41–42, 62, 117
Hale, Michael 21
Hank *see* Griffith, Hank
Hansel and Gretel (fairy-tale) 140–44
happily ever after 1, 6, 75, 87, 91–94, 99–100, 146–47, 152–53
"Happily Ever Aftermath" (S1, E20) 49, 140, 146, 148, 152
Haraway, Donna 165
Hasenfussige Schnecke 160
Hässlich 6, 22, 49–50
headache 29
"Headache" (S4, E21) 48
"Heartbreaker" (S4, E16) 77, 112
Hexenbiest 8, 19–24, 28–33, 39, 42–45, 48, 51, 57, 65, 79, 81, 94, 98–99, 107–8, 110, 115, 117, 120, 126, 155–56, 196,
"Highway of Tears" (S4, E6) 119
"The Hour of Death" (S2, E10) 119

The Icy Touch (novel) 202–3, 206–207, 211
Inugami 50, 134
"Inugami" (S5, E17) 50, 134
"Iron Hans" (S4, E19) 40
"Island of Dreams" (S1, E15) 112, 196

Jack the Ripper 48
Jägerbar 47, 49–50, 116, 162, 192

Kehrseite 37, 39, 59–60, 112–13
Kelly *see* Burkhardt, Kelly
Kertzer, David I. 37
Kessler, Marie *see* Aunt Marie
kidnap 23, 54–55, 60, 93, 112, 116, 123, 125, 132, 135, 143, 193, 198
The Killing Time (novel) 203, 206–9
Kinoshimobe 164–65
"The Kiss" (S2, E2) 38, 178
"Kiss of the Muse" (S2, E20) 25
Klaustreich 30, 118–120
Königschlange 56
Krampus 123–130, 133, 136; *see also* "Twelve Days of Krampus"
Ku Klux Klan 59, 119

"The Last Fight" (S4, E3) 108
Lausenschlange 118–119
Lebensauger 119
"Leave It to Beavers" (S1, E19) 49, 114
"Let Your Hair Down" (S1, E7) 36, 111
Let's Get It On (song) 65
Levine, Dr. 142–46, 152
LGBTQ 52–56, 58–60
Little Red Riding Hood 22, 54–55, 72–74, 125, 131, 175–78, 181, 184
La Llorona 156
"La Llorona" (S2, E9) 113
"Lonelyhearts" (S1, E4) 74–77, 79, 110, 163
"Lost Boys" (S5, E3) 40
"Love Sick" (S1, E17) 44, 48, 64, 81
Löwen 117, 119, 132
Lüthi, Max 174
"Lycanthropia" (S5, E14) 31

MacKinnon, Catharine 31, 71
"Maiden Quest" (S5, E4) 56
Manticore 30
"Map of the Seven Knights" (S5, E10) 19, 58
"Maréchaussée" (S4, E12) 30

marge 36–39, 43–44, 49–51
Mauzhertz 117
Mayer, Ruth 178, 180
Meisner 32, 48
mirror 2, 29, 42–45, 48, 65
Mishipeshu 96–97, 111
"Mishipeshu" (S4, E18) 111
"Mommy Dearest" (S3, E14) 27, 44, 113
Monroe 13, 19–20, 27, 29, 32, 36–37, 39–41, 46–47, 57–58, 64–65, 93–96, 99, 107–8, 113–16, 118–19, 123–126, 132–37, 145, 158, 160, 163–65, 176–77, 181–83, 192–99, 211
Murciélago 49, 140, 148–49, 152–53

Naiad 57
Nazi 59, 62, 106, 119
novels 202–213

Occultatum Libera 59, 117
"Oh Captain, My Captain" (S6, E3) 41
Ojibwe 95, 111
Once Upon a Time (TV series) 5, 69, 172–73
"Once We Were Gods" (S3, E15) 27, 113
"One Angry Fuchsbau" (S2, E17) 132, 163
Orenstein, Catherine 73–74
"Organ Grinder" (S1, E10) 25, 140, 142–143, 152–53
"The Other Side" (S2, E8) 119

"Pilot" (S1, E1) 6, 21–23, 40, 53–54, 57, 72–74, 92–93, 112, 125–26, 131–32, 135, 158, 175–77, 192
Portland, Oregon 109–112, 115, 142–43, 145, 177, 202
prince 25–26, 87, 108, 150–52
princess 5, 87, 140–41, 146–50, 153
prison 59, 95, 97, 115, 127–29
PTSD 113, 130–31
"PTZD" (S3, E2) 26

queer *see* LGBTQ

rape culture 10–11, 69–72, 77–82
Reinigen 49, 119
Renard, Sean (Captain) 13, 23, 26, 30–32, 41, 47–49, 64–65, 80–81, 107, 110, 114–15, 178
"A Reptile Dysfunction" (S5, E8) 112
"Revelation" (S3, E13) 114
Roh-hatz 50, 116, 162
Rosalee *see* Calvert, Rosalee
Rowe, Karen E. 23,
Royals 21, 26, 37, 45, 47–49, 93, 107, 110–11, 113, 115, 120, 142, 206
Rubel, Teresa *see* Trubel

Saint John's Bridge 38, 42
Schade, Adalind 13, 23, 26, 28–30, 37, 39–41, 43–46, 48, 64–65, 79, 95, 98–99, 110, 126, 178,
Schade, Diana *see Diana*
Schneetmacher 118
Seelengut 117–18, 160
"The Seven Year Itch" (S6, E5) 43
Siegbarste 24, 30, 57
Silverton, Juliette 6, 10, 13, 19–33, 37–43, 48, 60–61, 64–65, 76, 80, 88, 92, 97–99, 106, 111, 113, 146, 178, 196, 211; *see also* Eve
Skalengeck 118
Sleeping Beauty 178
"The Son Also Rises" (S6, E8) 43
Spice and Tea Shop 40–41, 47
"Stories We Tell Our Young" (S3, E6) 27, 136
supernatural 10, 21, 27, 53–54, 56, 73, 75, 77, 88–93, 104–5, 108, 123–24, 132–33, 155–57, 196–97
Supernatural (TV show) 202, 209–10
Sweet Dreams (Are Made of This) (song) 22–23, 72–73, 193,
"Synchronicity" (S3, E17) 33, 45

"Tarantella" (S1, E11) 25, 118
Taureus-Armenta 160
"The Thing with Feathers" (S1, E16) 25
"The Three Bad Wolves" (S1, E6) 118, 130, 135, 158, 182
"Three Coins in a Fuchsbau" (S1, E13) 106–7
Three Little Pigs 118, 160, 182
"To Protect and Serve Man" (S2, E11) 113, 115, 130, 132, 164
Trailer *see* Aunt Marie's Trailer
"Tree People" (S6, E9) 164
"Trial By Fire" (S4, E13) 99
"Tribunal" (S4, E10) 29
Trubel 13, 28, 32, 260–64, 95, 113
tunnels 41, 43
"Twelve Days of Krampus" (S3, E8) 27, 112, 123–24

übermensch 108

van Gennep, Arnold 36–37
vegetarian 135, 159–166, 192, 194–95
Verfluchte Zwillingsschwester 28, 65
Vienna 44
"Volcanalis" (S2, E18) 111, 156

Waddel, Terrie 48
Wældreór 111

"The Waking Dead" (S2, E21) 113
Wendigo 113, 164
Wesenrein 29, 59, 119–20, 198–99
"Wesenrein" (S4, E9) 29, 135
"Where the Wild Things Were" (S6, E11) 20
"The Wild Hunt" (S3, E12) 27
Wildermann 46–47
Willahara 57
witch see *Hexenbiest*
woge 30–31, 36, 42–43, 48, 50, 56, 60–61, 63–64, 112–13, 117, 119, 133, 135, 144, 148–49, 177, 181, 193, 197

Wright, Laura 162, 164
Wu, Drew (sergeant) 13, 20, 27, 29, 31–32, 56, 60, 64, 110, 113, 115, 145, 194, 197–99

"You Don't Know Jack" (S4, E20) 20, 45, 48

Zauberbiest 8, 37, 44, 47, 51, 57, 107, 198
Zerstörer 33, 120,
Ziegevolk 74, 132, 163
Zipes, Jack 5, 141, 181